GESTURE AND THOUGHT

Gesture and Thought

DAVID MCNEILL

University of Chicago Press CHICAGO AND LONDON

David McNeill is professor emeritus of linguistics and psychology at the University of Chicago. He is the author of four previous books, including *Hand and Mind*, also published by the University of Chicago Press.

The University of Chicago Press, Chicago 60637
The University of Chicago Press, Ltd., London
© 2005 by The University of Chicago
All rights reserved. Published 2005
Printed in the United States of America

14 13 12 11 10 09 08 07 06   05 1 2 3 4 5

ISBN: 0-226-51462-5 (cloth)

Library of Congress Cataloging-in-Publication Data

McNeill, David.
  Gesture and thought / David McNeill.
    p. cm.
  Includes bibliographical references and index.
  ISBN 0-226-51462-5 (hardcover : alk. paper)
  1. Gesture.   2. Psycholinguistics.   3. Thought and thinking.
4. Speech.   5. Sign language.   6. Language and languages.   I. Title.

P117.M359   2005
808.5—dc22

                                        2005000612

For my family—Nobuko, Cheryl, and Randall

CONTENTS

ACKNOWLEDGMENTS

I have many people to thank. First of all, my students and coworkers who have contributed much to the study of gesture and language and from whom I am drawing so much information and good sense; the students in my lab over the years who have contributed more than they know. I hope to mention everyone who has had some connection to this book: Desha Baker, Justine Cassell, Breckie Church, Chris Corcoran, Nancy Dray, Susan Duncan, Inge-Marie Eigsti, Amy Franklin, Nobuhiro Furuyama, Alexia Galati, Whitney Goodrich, KaLynne Harris, Rosa Hernandez, Hui-Fang Hong, Mika Ishino, Jana Iverson, Spencer Kelly, Irene Kimbara, Sotaro Kita, Elena Levy, Jia Li, Evelyn McClave, Karl-Erik McCullough, Lisa Miotto, Juan Pablo Mora, Cornelia Müller, Shuichi Nobe, Arika Okrent, Asli Özyürek, Mischa Park-Doob, Fey Parrill, Laura Pedelty, Gale Stam, Debra Stephens, Jürgen Streeck, Eve Sweetser, Kevin Tuite, Martha Tyrone, and Lily Wong—not all my students by any means, but all have touched my thinking and enlarged my understanding as I worked on this book.

My debt to Susan Duncan will be clear from my many references to her insights, discoveries, and creative ideas in the book itself. Sue has also developed the art of gesture coding in the style that we employ it to a degree that it can be taught to others in an organized course. The appendix is largely built around her work (in more ways than one).

Fey Parrill has edited the book and moved it irresistibly in the direction of readability and accuracy, and provided invaluable help during the final weeks of preparing the manuscript for publication. The drawings are also her work.

Drawings, created with intelligence and sensitivity, are I think superior to video stills. Understanding the purpose of the example, Fey prepared drawings that display, clearly and without distortion, the points being made, and this adds greatly to the intelligibility of the book.

I should like to acknowledge my colleagues with whom I have embarked on wholly new lines of approach that I could not have followed on my own: Jonathan Cole, Shaun Gallagher, and Ian Waterman, on the IW project; Francis Quek, Rashid Ansari, Mary Harper, and Melanie Brandabur, on the automated recording project; Bennett Bertenthal, on the Center for Learning and Multimodal Communication; Susan Goldin-Meadow, with whom I have cotaught courses and collaborated on publications.

I want to single out my collaborator over the past decade, Francis Quek, computer engineer, whose intellectual breadth, flexibility, energy, and ingenuity have found ways to bridge the world of engineering and those of linguistics, psycholinguistics, and gesture research. I describe some of our joint work in the text of the book and give extensive coverage of it in the appendix.

My gesture research has been financially supported at different times by the National Science Foundation and the Spencer Foundation. Some of the data presented in chapter 7 were collected with support from the NIH.

I also wish to take this opportunity to give public thanks, however inadequate, to everyone who worked so hard to stage a wonderful Fest for me in June 2003—Justine Cassell, Sue Duncan, Amy Franklin, Susan Goldin-Meadow, Mika Ishino, Irene Kimbara, Elena Levy, Karl-Erik McCullough, Cornelia Müller, Arika Okrent, Fey Parrill, Laura Pedelty, and Gale Stam—plus many dear friends and colleagues who came to the Fest and joined me in enjoying this marvelous occasion, and many others who could not make it but sent lovely remarks and good wishes that were gathered into a remembrance book (along with a very surprising gift). To all, I am immensely grateful and shall never forget the kindness and affection of the Great Fest of 2003.

Finally, most important of all, I wish to thank Nobuko B. McNeill and my children, Cheryl McNeill Schwab and Randall L. B. McNeill, for their wonderful support and affection, and for their achievements in life, which gratify me so much. I am proud to dedicate the book to them, my family. I also want to say how much Nobuko is for me the very epitome of elegance, intelligence, humor, and engagement with the world—polygifts that I so greatly admire and cherish. I also thank her belatedly for the title of my earlier book on gesture,

Hand and Mind (she refused then and refuses now to let me acknowledge this crucial contribution, but I am just disregarding her scruples).

PERSONAL INVOLVEMENT WITH THE GESTURE TOPIC

While I do not think my personal history of interest in gesture is of any great importance, I am often asked how I became involved with the topic, and a brief sketch might be interesting. It also gives me a chance to mention two formative influences. Direct involvement began for me more than twenty years ago, when Elena Levy and I devised a systematic method for eliciting natural gestures from subjects in a semicontrolled setting (McNeill & Levy 1982); this method is described in the body of the book itself. But my fascination goes back much farther. I recounted some of this history in *Hand and Mind*— stories about colleagues, one tall and slender, one massive and muscular, who had such conspicuously opposite and yet equally operatic gesture styles; and my son, who suddenly began to produce gestures at a certain stage of his language development. But I had overlooked two events that influenced me to see language and gesture as intimately tied together. One was a conference in Paris, at the end of 1971, where I had something of a language-gesture epiphany. The conference was held in a lecture hall originally set up for diplomatic meetings, with translators at the back, overlooking the hall through a glass window from a soundproof booth. What I noticed, as I spoke (not then on gestures), was a sight that at first baffled me. I could see a young woman behind the glass vigorously moving her arms in an alarming way. She looked to be having some kind of fit, and this thought actually flashed through my mind, until it dawned on me that she was translating me into French! The process of going from one language to the other, or just speaking itself, stimulated these movements of her arms. I believe I saw then, in a sudden apprehension via this distant yet strangely intimate connection of my speech to another person's movements, that language and gesture were two sides of one 'thing'. I can date my revelation this precisely; I do not think I stopped talking, but it was in midsentence. The second force, which I am glad to acknowledge must have prepared me for this epiphany, was my contact at the time with Elizabeth Bates, whose voice has been tragically silenced at all too early an age at the end of 2003. Liz was then a graduate student at the University of Chicago and had just written papers on speech and gesture as twin factors in children's earliest language development (see Bates et al. 1979; also chapter 6 of this book). These papers, provocative and spirited as those who knew Liz would expect, got me to wonder how gesture could be linked to language; and then came the epiphany in Paris. I soon recorded my first video for the purpose of studying gesture (two mathematicians, described in *Hand and Mind*), but it took almost another decade to find the method of studying gestures I mentioned earlier; nevertheless, the insight that gesture and language are two parts of one entity had its origin back then.

PART 1

Preliminaries

CHAPTER 1

Why Gestures?

INTRODUCTION

This book is a companion to *Hand and Mind*, which appeared in 1992. The key ideas were planted in that earlier book and in numerous ways have been developed and extended in this one. In 1992 the emphasis was on how gestures reveal thought; now it is how gestures fuel thought and speech. The new step is to emphasize the 'dynamic dimension' of language—how linguistic forms and gestures participate in a real-time dialectic during discourse, and thus propel and shape speech and thought as they occur moment to moment. As in the earlier book, gestures, language, and thought are seen as different sides of a single mental/brain/action process. They are integrated on actional, cognitive, and ultimately biological levels. The difference is that now I present gestures as active participants in speaking and thinking. They are conceived of as ingredients in an imagery-language dialectic that fuels speech and thought.

The gestures I mean are everyday occurrences—the spontaneous, unwitting, and regular accompaniments of speech that we see in our moving fingers, hands, and arms. They are so much a part of speaking that one is often unaware of them, but if you look around and watch someone talking in informal terms you are likely to see the hands and arms in motion. Why? This is the question I propose to answer, ultimately in evolutionary terms.

To obtain an answer, in part, I carry forward an approach introduced by Vygotsky in the 1930s. Vygotsky is celebrated as an alternative to Piaget and, for many, as an antidote to a kind of sterile asocial cognitivism they imagine (not altogether inaccurately) dominates current linguistics and cognitive psychology. But Vygotsky had other themes. He argued for a different kind of psychology, one that is antireductionist, holistic, dialectical, and grounded in action and material experience. It is this sometimes overlooked Vygotsky that this book carries forward in ways that were not available in his day. Foremost among these is the systematic study of gesture and language as they occur spontaneously in daily speech.

The main theme of this book is that *language is inseparable from imagery*, a statement from Damasio (1994, 1999) somewhere. The imagery in question is embodied in the gestures that universally and automatically occur with speech. Speech and gesture occupy the same time slices when they share meanings and have the same relationships to context. It is profoundly an error to think of gesture as a code or 'body language', separate from spoken language. One message of this book is that gestures are *part* of language. It makes no more sense to treat gestures in isolation from speech than to read a book by looking only at the 'g's. It is also an error, in fact the same error, to think of speech as separate from gesture—as if to focus on just the 's's. The aim of the book is to present in full the arguments for the inseparability of language/speech and imagery/gesture, and to seek explanations for why this arrangement should be so. A précis of the book is given at the end of this chapter.

I suggest that language has two dimensions, static and dynamic, that combine in every speech event via the above-mentioned dialectic. This imagery-language dialectic (materialized in gesture and speech) is an interaction between unlike modes of thinking. The disparity of these modes is the 'fuel' that propels thought and language; the dialectic is the point at which the two dimensions intersect. The central part of the book describes how this dialectic takes form, how it propels thought and speech, and what must take place to resolve the tension between these unlike modes of cognition over the very brief intervals of time (just seconds) during which utterances are conceived and produced.

I should also stress what the book is not. It is not a comprehensive review of current gesture work, and it is not a commentary on all that has been discovered about gestures, which is by now a great deal. In particular, I say little about so-called emblems, or 'quotable' gestures as Adam Kendon has termed them, the very gestures that many people think of when they hear the word "gesture." Although I cover ample ground, I have kept my goal clearly in mind, and this has guided me in what to include and what not. It is accordingly a good idea

gesticulation → speech-linked gestures → emblems → pantomime → signs in primary sign
(accompanies speech) (substitutions (conventional (dumb languages)
within speech) gestures) WHY GESTURES? 5 (different
show) lexicon + syntax from speech)

to start by distinguishing among different kinds of occurrences that can be
called "gestures," and to specify the kinds that are in focus.

WHICH GESTURES? A CONTINUUM

Adam Kendon (1988a) once distinguished gestures of different kinds. I then
arranged these along a continuum that I named "Kendon's continuum" in his
honor (McNeill 1992). The gestures we are primarily concerned with are the
'gesticulations'.

'Gesticulation' is motion that embodies a meaning relatable to the accompanying speech. (The nature of this relationship is analyzed in Chapter 2.)
Gesticulation is by far the most frequent type of gesture in daily use, and it
covers many variants and usages. It is made chiefly with the arms and hands
but is not restricted to these body parts—the head can take over as a kind of
third hand if the anatomical hands are immobilized or otherwise engaged, and
the legs and feet too can move in a gesture mode (cf. McClave 2000).

'Speech-linked gestures' are parts of sentences themselves. Such gestures
occupy a grammatical slot in a sentence—"Sylvester went [gesture of an object
flying out laterally]," where the gesture completes the sentence structure.

'Emblems' are conventionalized signs, such as thumbs-up or the ring (first
finger and thumb tips touching, other fingers extended) for "OK."

'Pantomime' is dumb show, a gesture or sequence of gestures conveying a
narrative line, with a story to tell, produced without speech.

At the other extreme of the continuum, 'signs' are lexical words in a sign
language (typically for the deaf) such as ASL. Sign languages have their own
linguistic structures, including grammatical patterns, stores of words, morphological patterns, etc. The linguistic code of ASL is quite unlike that of
English. Sign languages have evolved without the requirement of being coordinated with speech. In fact, hearing signers find that producing speech and
signs simultaneously is disruptive to both.

As one moves along Kendon's continuum, two kinds of reciprocal changes
occur. First, the degree to which speech is an obligatory accompaniment of gesture *decreases* from gesticulation to signs. Second, the degree to which gesture
shows the properties of a language *increases*. Gesticulations are obligatorily
accompanied by speech but have properties unlike language. Speech-linked
gestures are also obligatorily performed with speech, but relate to speech in

a different manner—sequentially rather than concurrently and in a specific linguistic role (standing in for a complement of the verb, for example). Signs are obligatorily *not* accompanied by speech and have the essential properties of a language. Clearly, therefore, gesticulations (but not the other points along Kendon's continuum) combine properties that are unalike, and this combination occupies the same psychological instant. A combination of unalikes at the same time is a framework for an imagery-language dialectic.

FROM CONTINUUM TO CONTINUA[1]

On reflection, however, we can see that Kendon's continuum is actually a complex of separate continua, each based on an analytically distinct dimension along which the types of gestures (gesticulation, emblems, etc.) can be differentiated. I shall explain the points along the continua by reference to Figure 1.1.

Fig. 1.1. Spontaneous iconic gesture with "bends it way back."

The speaker was saying, "he grabs a big o[ak tree and <u>he</u> **bends it way back**]," with his hand moving through an arc, as shown. His hand rose from the armrest of the chair as he said "oak" (left bracket), reached its apex with "he," at which moment there was a brief prestroke hold (underlining); the hand then moved downward and to the side during the boldface section (the stroke—the part of the gesture depicting the actual 'bending back': the phase shown). At this point there was a poststroke hold and a new gesture began (not shown). Gesture transcription is explained in detail in the appendix.

During the stroke phase, the hand appeared to grasp and bend back an object with some thickness. Such a gesture has clear iconicity—the movement and the handgrip; also a locus (starting high and ending low)–all creating

---

1. An earlier version of this section appeared in the introduction to McNeill (2000).

imagery that is analogous to the event being described in speech at the same time (a comic book character bending back an oak tree).

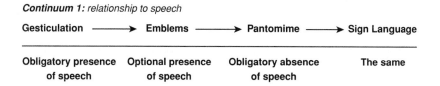

Continuum 1: *relationship to speech*

Gesticulation ⟶ Emblems ⟶ Pantomime ⟶ Sign Language

| Obligatory presence of speech | Optional presence of speech | Obligatory absence of speech | The same |

The first continuum controls the occurrence of gesture with speech. The bends-it-back gesture is meaningful only in conjunction with the utterance of "bends it back." An OK emblem can be made with speech or not. Pantomime, by definition, does not accompany speech (lack of speech is therefore trivial). With sign language, while it is possible to produce signs and speak simultaneously, doing so has a disruptive effect on both speech and sign. Speech becomes hesitant and sign performance is disrupted at the level of the main grammatical mechanisms of the language that utilize space rather than time for encoding meanings (Nelson et al. 1993).

Associated with the speech continuum is another continuum that reflects the presence vs. absence of the characteristic semiotic properties of a linguistic system. This is a second continuum on which gesticulation and sign language hold down the extremes, while pantomime and emblem have exchanged places:

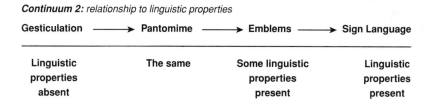

Continuum 2: *relationship to linguistic properties*

Gesticulation ⟶ Pantomime ⟶ Emblems ⟶ Sign Language

| Linguistic properties absent | The same | Some linguistic properties present | Linguistic properties present |

The bends-it-back gesture lacks all linguistic properties. It was nonmorphemic, not realized through a system of phonological form constraints, and had no potential for syntactic combination with other gestures. We can demonstrate the inapplicability of linguistic properties through a thought experiment. Imagine another person saying the same thing but with "it" meaning the corner of a sheet of paper. Then, rather than the hand opening into a grip, the thumb and forefinger would come together in a pinch; rather than the arm moving forward and slightly up, the pinching hand would be held slightly forward and down; and rather than pull the arm back, the pinching hand would rotate outward or inward. Also, this gesture would naturally be performed with two hands, the second hand 'holding' the paper that is being bent back. That is, none of the form properties of the first gesture would be present in the second gesture, bends-it-back though it is. Neither gesture in fact obeys constraints within a system of forms; there are only constraints that emerge from the imagery of bending itself—an oak tree versus a tab of paper. The handshape and position are creations of the moment and reflect the speaker's imagery—of a character from a story reaching up and forward to pull back a tree, of someone turning down the corner of piece of paper.

The ASL sign TREE (shown in Figure 1.2) in contrast *is* constrained by the phonological properties of the ASL language system.[1] The 5 handshape is a standard one of the language; the sign could not be formed and remain intelligible with a handshape that is not part of the language. While the 5 handshape has recognizable iconicity, it is a standardized selection of iconic features that other sign languages, with signs equally iconic, do not use (Danish Sign Language, for example, traces an outline of a tree). And the sign is what Okrent calls 'nonspecific' in that it is used equally well for all kinds of trees and tree shapes, not just trees with long bare trunks and fluttering leaves.

Fig. 1.2. ASL sign for TREE.

Pantomime, like gesticulation, does not seem to obey any system constraints (not considering theatrical pantomime, which does have its own traditional forms and rules; see Fischer-Lichte 1992). For example, showing what a vortex is with pantomime could be done by twirling a finger or by rotating the whole hand, and neither version would be unintelligible or seem to be a violation of a system constraint.

Emblems, on the other hand, do show system constraints. There are differences between well-formed and not-well-formed ways of making the gesture.

1. I am grateful to Arika Okrent for this example and analysis.

Placing the middle finger on the thumb results in a gesture with some kind of precision meaning, but is not recognizable as the OK sign. The OK gesture, like a word, is constrained to assume a certain 'phonological' shape. Yet these constraints are limited and don't by any means amount to a full language. There is no way to reliably reverse the OK sign, for example. Forming it and waving it back and forth laterally (another emblem that, on its own, conveys negation) might convey "not OK," but it also might be seen as meaning the opposite of negation—waving the hand could call attention to the OK sign, or to suggest that many different things are OK—a flexibility that is basically not linguistic in character.

Comparing Continuum 1, 'relationship to speech', to Continuum 2, 'relationship to linguistic properties', we see one of the basic facts of gesture life: the gesticulations, with which speech is obligatorily *present*, are the least languagelike; the signs, from which speech is obligatorily *absent*, have linguistic properties of their own. This is not so paradoxical as it may seem. It reveals that 'gesture' has the potential to take on the traits of a linguistic system, but as it does so it ceases to be a component of the spoken language system. This is the conclusion of thirty years of investigation of the sign languages of the deaf (see, for example, the collection of papers in Emmorey & Reilly 1995; Liddell 2003a,b). It is also the conclusion of research on the deaf children of hearing, nonsigning parents. These children are exposed to neither a sign language nor speech (in that they cannot hear the speech their caretakers produce) and they develop their own means of gestural communication, termed 'home signs', that manifest a number of important linguistic properties, such as a lexicon and basic syntax (Goldin-Meadow & Mylander 1984; home signs and cultural sign languages in general are discussed in Chapter 4.3). In effect, their gestures move to the right of the continuum. The conclusion is that nothing about the visual-manual modality per se is incompatible with the presence of linguistic properties. Yet gestures combined with speech lack linguistic properties.

The comparison of the first and second continua thus shows that when the *vocal* modality has linguistic system properties, *gesture*, the manual modality, does not take on these properties. And when it does not, speech tends to be *obligatory* with gesture. This is certainly one of the more interesting facts of gesture. It implies that speech and gesture combine into a system of their own in which each modality performs its own functions, the two modalities supporting one another. This book operates upon this premise.

Continuum 3: *relationship to conventions*

Gesticulation ⟶	Pantomime ⟶	Emblems ⟶	Sign Language
Not conventionalized	The same	Partly conventionalized	Fully conventionalized

Convention means that the forms of gestures and the meanings with which they are paired meet some kind of socially constituted or collective standard. It is because the gesture is ruled by convention that only forefinger and thumb contact are recognizable as OK. At the gesticulation end, in contrast, a lack of convention is a sine qua non. The bends-it-back gesture is conventional only in the broadest sense (e.g., that gesturing is acceptable in storytelling contexts). There are no conventions telling the speaker what form bending back is to take. The TREE sign, however, *is* constrained by the conventions of ASL. It must meet form standards according to which only an upright arm with a 5 handshape is TREE.

The fourth continuum concerns the semiotic differences between gesticulation and linguistic codes of all kinds (spoken as well as signed). This dimension further shows the richness that can emerge from combining gesticulation with speech in a unified speech-gesture system, a system that places contrasting kinds of semiotic properties into one vessel (in what sense *sign*-gesture systems might also exist is a topic of much current interest; see Liddell 2000, 2003a,b, and the discussion in Chapter 4.3).

Continuum 4: *character of semiosis*

Gesticulation ⟶	Pantomime ⟶	Emblems ⟶	Sign Language
Global & synthetic	Global & analytic	Segmented & synthetic	Segmented & analytic

Global refers to the fact that the determination of meaning in a gesticulation proceeds in a downward direction. The meanings of the 'parts' of the gesture are determined by the meaning of the whole. This contrasts to the upward determination of meanings in sentences. In the bending back gesture, we understand from the meaning of the gesture as a whole—a character bending something back—that the hand (one of the 'parts') equals the character's hand, the movement (another part) equals the character's movement, and the backward direction (a third part) equals the character's backward movement. These are not gestural morphemes. It is not the case that the hand in general means a hand or movement backward must always mean movement backward. Özyürek (2000) observed gestures for the same 'outward' meaning performed in different directions, dependent on the social context—whether the speaker was addressing one listener or two. The pairing of the outward meaning and the form (direction) of the gesture was not fixed, hence it is not listable as in a morphology, but varied depending on the context of communication. In speech, on the other hand, the character bending back the tree was constructed out of independently meaningful words or segments organized according to a standardized plan or syntax. The top-down global semiotic of gesticulation contrasts with the bottom-up mapping of the sentence. The linguistic mapping is *segmented*. Pantomime also appears to be global. A twirling downward pointing finger is understood to be a swizzle stick because the gesture, as a whole, has the meaning of a vortex. ASL signs are clearly segmented in their semiotic principles. The approbation meaning of the OK sign is not composed out of separately meaningful parts, but the precision image of the first finger–thumb contact is a component of the emblem, so it is probably correct to say that this gesture is analytic and segmented, in the sense that the meanings of at least some of the parts have an independent status.

Synthetic refers to the fact that a single gesticulation concentrates into one symbol distinct meanings that might be spread across the entire surface of the accompanying sentence. The single bends-it-back gesture displayed the actor, his action, and the path of the tree he acted upon. In the accompanying sentence, these same semantic functions were separated—"he," "bends," and "back"—and a meaning of extension was added ("way"). The mode of the sentence was analytic. Like English, ASL is also analytic. Emblems on the other hand are synthetic, like gesticulations. The OK meaning, bundled into one gesture, can spread over the full surface structure of a spoken equivalent ("a job well done," for example). Pantomime may also be analytic, though the lack of definition of pantomime makes the attribution uncertain. The twirl of a vortex gesture is the translation of a lexical term, which suggests analyticity. The issue of whether gesticulations characteristically map onto single lexical items or are not so constrained is a matter of some dispute (see Kita 2000, de Ruiter 2000, and Krauss et al. 2000). The issue is discussed in Chapter 2.

✓ Summary of Differences along the Continua

Gesticulation accompanies speech, is nonconventionalized, is global and syn-thetic in mode of expression, and lacks languagelike properties of its own. The speech with which the gesticulation occurs, in contrast, is conventionalized, segmented, and analytic, and is fully possessed of linguistic properties. These contrasting modes of structuring meaning coexist in speech and gesture, a fact of importance for this book's understanding of thought and language in general, and how they function in communication.

Signs in ASL, like words in speech, are conventionalized, segmented, and analytic, and possessed of language properties, while they are obligatorily not performed with speech. The presence or absence of speech with gesture is thus correlated with the absence or presence of conventional linguistic proper-ties.

Emblems are at an intermediate position on the various dimensions of con-trasting gestures. They are partly like gesticulations, partly like signs. For many individuals, emblems are the closest thing to a sign 'language' they possess, al-though it is crucial to emphasize the *non*-linguistic character of these gestures: they lack a fully contrastive system (there is no contrasting 'partly OK' gesture made with the second finger and thumb, for example) and syntactic potential (the impossibility of combining two emblems into a gesture sentence).

Pointing requires special mention. It has a form that is standardized within a given culture. Thus in North America, the standard is the G handshape (the index finger extended, the other fingers curled in), but in other societies one might use two fingers or an entire hand, or the face, lips, nose, etc. (cf. Enfield 2001). At the same time, however, the prescribed form is not required for the pointing act to take place—in appropriate circumstances, the two-fingers or full-hand alternatives (and even lip or nose pointing) would be understood in North America. Thus, pointing is less constrained than the OK sign. In some contexts the presence of speech with pointing may seem obligatory (de Ruiter 2000) but pointing is fully interpretable without speech as well. Haviland (2000) analyzes the semiotic foundations of pointing and describes in detail its use in the Guugu Yimithirr Aboriginal culture in Australia and the Tzotzil Mayan culture in Mexico, where it is an integral part of linguistic performance—in one case because the coding of directionality is obligatory in the language, in the other for the opposite reason, because such coding is outside the normal resources of the language.

HOW GESTURES HAVE BEEN REGARDED: SOME HISTORY

The next step in this introduction is to set this book in a framework of past understandings of gesture and what gesture does. Recent study has emerged via a twofold shift away from a tradition that dates to Roman times, when the whole emphasis was on rhetorical gestures—the mannered performances of orators with the hands and body comprising more or less deliberate gestured embellishments on spoken public performances (Quintilian wrote a treatise on gesture for the instruction of orators in first-century Rome; see a 1977 reprint, in Latin; for a history of gesture in the theater and many useful references, see Bremmer & Roodenburg 1991).

With the first shift, commencing with Efron (1941) in the 1930s, gestures have come to be studied in life, as they occur spontaneously during conversation and other discourse modes. This new approach has been greatly enhanced, one might say made possible, by the advent of slow-motion film and now video, without which the careful study of gesture in relation to speech and thought would scarcely be possible. All aspects of this book draw from modern audio-video recordings.

In the second shift, commencing with Kendon in 1972 and continuing with ever increasing vigor into the present day, gestures are regarded as parts of *language itself*—not as embellishments or elaborations, but as integral parts of the processes of language and its use. The development of this line offers new insights into the nature of speaking, thinking, remembering, and interacting with words in a social context. This book takes the point of view that language and gesture are integral parts of a whole and regards this multimodal unit as language itself.

For histories of gesture study, see, in addition to Bremmer & Roodenburg (1991), Kendon (1981) and Müller (1998, 2000). There is also a brief survey in McNeill (1992). An interesting discussion of gestures as inferred from classical texts and material artifacts is in Boegehold (1999). A major publishing event is Kendon's translation and introduction to Andrea de Jorio's *La mimica degli antichi investigata nel gestire napoletano* (Gesture in Naples and gesture in classical antiquity, 1832) (Kendon 2000). De Jorio, an antiquarian and archeologist in early nineteenth-century Naples, was greatly struck by the similarities of the gestures he saw around him in daily Neapolitan life and the gestures he found depicted in the wall paintings and other illustrative materials in the then recently excavated ruins of Pompeii and Herculaneum. He collected examples of current gesture use and organized them into a kind lexicographic compendium, together with a commentary whose foresight and modernity Kendon celebrates in his introduction.

The following sketch presents a few highlights from Cornelia Müller's (1998, 2000) account of the history of gesture study. She identifies five themes that have emerged throughout the two-thousand-plus-year history of commentary on gesture. Behind the themes are deeper underlying beliefs and attitudes, a number of which are still with us today.

First to appear is the 'domestication' of gesture and speech. Writers since antiquity have been concerned to suppress extensive and spontaneous gesture use. The underlying belief has been that gestures compete with language and therefore must be controlled. We shall see in the next chapter that, far from competing with language, gesture and language rise and fall in complexity and fluency *together*—this ancient belief, on current evidence, is mistaken.

Second, and almost as ancient, is the prescription of public and monologic gestures for oratorical use. The Quintilian text exemplifies this tradition. Again, there is behind the theme the belief that gesture and language compete; thus gesture must be regulated and defined prescriptively. Modern political speakers seem to be coached in the same vein, although in much simpler terms than their Roman counterparts. As recently as the nineteenth century, there were still elaborate expositions on the public performance of gestures and what gestures would be appropriate during speeches and sermons (Austin 1806, for example, and before him in the seventeenth century Bulwer 1974 wrote such guides for English-speaking audiences). This interest has declined in modern times but the ancient yet erroneous belief in language-gesture competition remains.

Third, since the Renaissance, there has been an interest in the private and dialogic use of gestures in conversation. This interest arose out of books on manners, and again there was a strong prescriptive component. The purpose was to state the things to do and not do in polite company (such as not losing control of your hands while speaking). However, rather than reject gesture out of hand, a concept of a suitably *restrained* gesture led to its use as an expression of education and nobility.

Fourth, dating from ancient times but becoming significant in the Enlightenment, philosophers such as Condillac and Diderot invoked the idea of gesture as the natural or original language of man (see Harris & Taylor 1989).

This idea has echoes in modern times in the gesture-first theory of language origins (e.g., Corballis 2002), which I consider at the end of the book.

(5) Fifth, and last to arise, is the study of gestures in everyday speech. De Jorio pioneered this approach, along with much else, but it was not until the current wave of interest in gesture study that it has truly blossomed.

There was a long hiatus in the twentieth century during which neither psychology nor linguistics saw gesture as a subject worthy of study, or of particular interest if they did stumble across it. I suspect that in both psychology and linguistics behaviorism was to blame for this long dry spell. Wundt discussed gesture in detail at the start of the twentieth century (Wundt 1970 [1912]) but after this strong beginning from the 'father of experimental psychology', curiosity and discussion simply disappeared for sixty years. It then reemerged in the 1970s and has been moving forward with accelerating energy ever since. Gesture studies is a developing new field at the intersection of the humanities, linguistics, psychology, social science, neuropsychology, and computer engineering/computer science. Young researchers across a wide range of disciplines are drawn to the topic. There are a new journal, *Gesture* (edited by Cornelia Müller and Adam Kendon and published by Benjamins), and a new scholarly society (the International Society of Gesture Studies, of which Jürgen Streeck is the first president) with international conferences (the first held in Austin in 2002, and the second currently planned for Lyon in 2005). Wundt's dream, a century later, is at last coming true.

THIS BOOK

The main theme of this book was stated at the start of the chapter and can be briefly repeated now at the end. It is that language is inseparable from imagery. The imagery in question is embodied in the gestures that universally and automatically occur with speech. Such gestures are a necessary component of speaking and thinking. The goal of the book is to elaborate this argument and explore it in depth. Most importantly, the book describes a mechanism of language-gesture integration, the growth point, and the moment-by-moment thinking that takes place as one speaks. The mechanism of this immediate ongoing thought process is that of an imagery-language dialectic, an intrinsically dynamic process. The concept of the growth point, in turn, enables us to branch out in a new way to the neuropsychology of gesture and language, including consideration of how the brain circuits creating growth points might have evolved. The resulting evolution model explains why, ultimately, language and imagery *are* inseparable: a joint system with these two components was part of the evolutionary selection of the human brain. I shall present evidence that languages have their own forms of dialectic, and that comparing speech and gesture across languages reveals partially distinct patterns of thinking for speaking. The important point for now is that the two frameworks of gesture and categorial content coexist and have the potential or, better, the *necessity* to combine.

The Chapters

The argument of the book is laid out in the following plan:

Chapter 1. Why gesture? The concept of language being inseparable from imagery; types of gesture on Kendon's continuum, revised to Kendon's continua; a brief history of gesture study; a précis of the argument.

Chapter 2. How gestures carry meaning. Speech-gesture synchrony and co-expressiveness; unbreakable binding; gesture anatomy; concept of the lexical affiliate; kinds of gesture, metaphor, and morphology; the question of who benefits from gesture; and the meaning of 'image'.

Chapter 3. Two dimensions. Contrasting traditions—the static, or Saussurian, and the dynamic, or Vygotskian—and their modern continuations.

Chapter 4. Imagery-language dialectic. Four subchapters:

4.1. Dialectic and material carriers. Vygotsky's concept of signs as material carriers of meaning applied to Merleau-Ponty, the 'H-model', Werner and Kaplan's organismic foundations, embodied cognition, etc.; gesture as such a material carrier of meaning.

4.2. The growth point as a model of the dialectic; inseparability from context (and how to portray it).

4.3. Extensions of GP to other languages and to different conditions of speaking, such as gesture-speech asynchronies and mismatches.

4.4. Social-interactive content. Analysis of a critical juncture in a conversation; the social shaping of growth points; gestures and growth point mimicry.

Chapter 5. Discourse. The catchment and discourse levels in single gestures.

Chapter 6. Children and Whorf. Ontogenesis of imagery-language dialectics; the shaping of visuospatial thinking by language.

Chapter 7. Neurogesture. Brain model and the orchestration of the brain for language and gesture; Broca's aphasia, Wernicke's aphasia, right hemisphere injury, and the split-brain.

Chapter 8. The thought-language-hand link and language origins. A case study (IW), and uncovering a dedicated thought-language-hand link in the human brain; the possible evolution of this link as a way of orchestrating brain action via mirror neurons and 'Mead's loop'; scenarios and time line for this selection.

In addition, the appendix describes methods for the collection, transcription, and coding of gestures.

Synopsis

For those who profit from a capsule summary, I have prepared the following précis. For those who prefer to plunge right in, this section can be skipped without loss; all its content, and much more, will unfold over the next seven chapters. However, the text in these chapters—Part 2 especially—is not, I realize, light reading. I have tried to write comprehensively and clearly, but the ideas are what they are and, when complex and novel, can be daunting. This précis can perhaps soften the blow.

Linguistics traditionally has focused on what can be termed the static dimension of language. In this tradition, language is regarded as an object, not a process. From Saussure on, the assumptions at the foundation of linguistics have been synchronic, and the goal has been to uncover the organization of the system of *langue*, or (in its modern version, with changes) competence. The static is a genuine dimension of language, experienced by speakers and listeners most directly through intuitions of well-formedness. However, there is another dimension, the dynamic. In this tradition, language is regarded as a process, not a thing. The figure most clearly exemplifying the dynamic approach is Vygotsky, but there are other historical figures as well—Wundt, Werner, Saussure himself at the end of his life–and the phenomenological tradition, especially Merleau-Ponty. The dynamic is also a real dimension of language, and gestures are a special route to accessing it.

I treat the static and dynamic therefore as real dimensions. Both are valid and necessary for a complete understanding of what Saussure called *langage*, or human language. Some phenomena are more accessible on one dimension, some on the other—linguistic forms, clearly, inhabit the static dimension but the linkage of language to discourse, narrative, and the focal consciousness of the speaker are phenomena more visible on the dynamic dimension. The conceptual challenge, after identifying the two dimensions, is to see how they combine in the cognitive and linguistic performance of speakers and hearers.

My starting point, as noted earlier, is that language appears to be inseparable from imagery. The imagery in question is 'gesture'. The first step, in this chapter, has been clarification of what kinds of gestures these are and how to characterize them. In Chapter 2, I describe how gestures carry meanings. Then, in Chapter 3, I analyze the two dimensions of language. In Chapter 4, I introduce the main concept for combining the static and dynamic, that of a dialectic, an idea first proposed by Vygotsky. Vygotsky lacked the critical data that modern gesture study provides and the dialectic model was accordingly not completed by him.

This dialectic is analyzed in various ways in the subparts of Chapter 4, but the chief approach is in terms of 'growth points'. A growth point, or GP, is a minimal unit of dialectic in which imagery and linguistic content are combined. A GP contains opposite semiotic modes of meaning capture—instantaneous, global, nonhierarchical imagery with temporally sequential, segmented, and hierarchical language. The GP is a unit with demonstrable self-binding power (attempts to disrupt it, for example, with delayed auditory feedback do not succeed), and the opposition of semiotic modes within it fuels the dialectic. The key to the dialectic is that the two modes are simultaneously active in the mental experience of the speaker. Simultaneously representing the same idea unit in opposite modes creates instability, a 'benevolent instability' that is resolved by accessing forms on the static dimension—constructions and lexical choices, states of repose par excellence. The GP and the unpacking of it into constructions and lexical items is how the two dimensions of language combine—the unstable growth point, itself a combination of imagery and linguistic content, is unpacked into an increasingly well-formed, hence increasingly stable, structure on the static dimension. This process continues until, eventually, a 'stop order' occurs (it stops only temporarily: a new cycle begins immediately or might overlap the earlier one). A stop order is an intuitively complete (or complete enough) static structure (intuitions of well-formedness being how one experiences the static dimension). Thus gesture and the imagery it embodies are an integral step on the way to a sentence.

Images vary materially from no apparent gesture at all to elaborate multidimensional displays; but, hypothetically, imagery is ever present. What varies is the amount of materialization. Materialization runs from little to much, depending on the predictability/continuity of the specific GP with its context of speaking. The concept of a 'material carrier' of meaning is also taken from Vygotsky. It is extended via the 'H-model', after Heidegger, according to which the materialization of one's meaning in a gesture (and speech) is, for the one speaking, not a representation but an updating the speaker's momentary state of cognitive being. The greater this contribution, the more the materialization, hence the more developed the gesture. The listener, in turn, inhabits the same meaning by updating in parallel his or her own momentary being, communication being a matter not only of signal exchange but of social resonance and inhabitance in the same 'house of being'.

Context, a notoriously slippery concept, is conceptualized as a field of oppositions. The more unpredictable/discontinuous the growth point in its field of oppositions is, the more elaborately materialized it tends to be in both speech and gesture; conversely, the more predictable/continuous the GP, the less the materialization, ultimately down to no gesture at all.

The GP model is congruent with Wundt, who, in a famous statement given in full in Chapter 4.1, emphasized that "the sentence is both a simultaneous and a sequential structure" (Wundt 1970, p. 21). In Chapter 4.2, I develop a detailed case study of a GP that, among other things, shows how a GP analysis incorporates the context of speaking as an integral part of the process of forming and unpacking growth points, and this leads to a way of modeling context and bringing it into a systematic relationship to growth point formation.

In all the above respects, this analysis is profoundly unlike the typical approach of psycholinguistics, which I regard as far too static in its assumptions and goals. The incorporation of context by GPs is one salient difference. Whereas context is integrated into the dialectic theory, it is the opposite—an external input—in these psycholinguistic models. Context is incorporated into the dialectic model automatically, because each growth point is what Vygotsky termed a psychological predicate—a point of differentiation of newsworthy content from a background; the background, or context, is an integral part of the growth point, without which it does not exist. Context is formalized in the GP model, as mentioned, as a field of oppositions. It is empirically recovered via 'catchments'—thematic discourse units realized in an observable thread of recurring gestural imagery. How, in GPs, idea units incorporate context, in the form of fields of oppositions, is one the central themes of the book.

I apply this theoretical framework to a very wide range of situations—discourse and gestures in different languages (Turkish, Spanish, and Mandarin, as well as my primary source, English); the gestures of children at the earliest stages of development; the Whorfian hypothesis, arguing that the impact of language on imagery is often a dynamic dimension effect that has been concealed by concentration on the static dimension; linguistic impairments (aphasia; right-hemisphere damage, which impairs discourse cohesion; and the split-brain state, all of which were described in *Hand and Mind* but are now integrated into a new neurogestural model). An important new source of observations is the case of IW. This is a man who suffered, as a young adult, complete deafferentation from the neck down and has relearned movement control, including gestures with speech, which he can do to perfection even without vision, a condition where it is difficult for him to carry out nongesture actions. His case suggests a partial dissociation in the brain of the organization of gesture from the organization of instrumental action and the existence of a dedicated thought-language-hand link that would be the common heritage of all humankind.

The book accordingly ends with an attempt to provide 'the ultimate answer' to the question of an imagery-language dialectic and why it exists at all, by proposing a theory of language evolution, focusing on this thought-language-hand link. I develop the hypothesis that what made us human crucially depended at one point on gestures. Without gestures, according to this hypothesis, language could not have evolved; some of the brain circuits required for language could not have evolved in the way they apparently have. The integration of gesture with language we observe in ourselves today is an essential part of the machinery that evolved. Gesture is not a behavioral fossil but an indispensable part of our current ongoing system of language. The theory is based on the IW case and the neurogestural model and employs recently discovered 'mirror neurons', supplemented with what I am calling Mead's loop, to explain how and under what conditions a thought-language-hand link could have evolved. According to the Mead's loop theory, what had to be selected is a capacity, not present in other primate brains, for the mirror neuron circuit to respond to one's own gestures as if they belonged to someone else (this produces the apparent social framing of gestures, even when they are invisible—talking on the phone, a blind person talking to another blind person). This reconfiguration of circuitry provided the thought-language-hand link and a way for language to co-opt the machinery of Broca's area. Contrary to the gesture-first theory, a model that has become popular with Corballis (2002), I am arguing that evolution selected the ability to *combine* speech and gesture under a meaning, and that speech and gesture emerged in evolution together. This combination was the essential property evolution chose; there would not have been a gesture-first step. Just as speech could not have evolved without gesture, gesture could not have evolved without speech.

TERMINOLOGICAL TANGO

Saying (as I do) both that gesture is 'part' of language and also that there is a 'language-gesture' dialectic led one reviewer of the book in manuscript to suggest that I was saying something absurd—that a part can be in a dialectic with its own whole. This is not what I mean, of course, but my locutions could be open to such a construal. The problem is terminological; the word 'language' is being used in two ways. It would be tedious to signal the shifts between them, so I use this section to call the reader's attention to the double usage and trust that so flagging it will suffice to keep the two senses apart. Nothing hinges on the ambiguity, and allowing it to stand seems harmless. First, I use 'language' in a technical-linguistic way, to refer to those static structures of language consisting of grammar, words, etc. In this sense, there is a 'language-imagery' or 'language-gesture' dialectic, implying that the dynamic meets the static in this process. Second, I also use 'language' in a traditional nontechnical way, to indicate what it is we know when we say we 'know a language' or what we 'use' when we speak, listen, read, etc. In this way, gesture is 'part' of language, implying that language consists of more than words, sentences, etc., and also includes spontaneous, speech-synchronized gestures. The reviewer suggested the term 'grammar' for the technical sense, but 'grammar' is too narrow. The static dimension includes many levels besides 'grammar', and such a term risks making nonsense of the second sense, since gesture is certainly not 'part' of grammar (it is linked to the context of speaking in ways that grammar, because it depends on repeatability, cannot capture). 'Speech' is also too narrow, and implies an unwanted division of speech and sign, contradicting what I regard as the deep similarities in their underlying dynamics (see Chapter 4.3). So I shall simply request that the reader tolerate and move along with the ambiguity—when a 'dialectic of imagery and language' is meant, language is understood in the technical sense; when 'gesture is part of language', it is in the traditional sense.

CHAPTER 2

How Gestures Carry Meaning

This chapter prepares the ground for the discussion in later chapters of an imagery-language dialectic and language origins. It lays out gesture form and gesture meaning; the strong temporal binding of speech and gesture; 'gesture anatomy', or the unfolding of gestures in time; how gestures package meanings; whether gestures occur in silence or with speech; the changes in gesture when speech is absent; gestural metaphor and conventions in general; and two chestnuts—the concept of a 'lexical affiliate' and the question of for whom the gesture is performed (the speaker or the listener). I conclude the chapter with an essay on what the term 'image' implies for gesture and what happens to an imagery-language dialectic when gestures do not occur.

CO-EXPRESSIVENESS AND SYNCHRONY

Two core features of gesture are that they carry meaning, and that they and the synchronous speech are *co-expressive*. Co-expressive, but *not redundant*: gesture and speech express the same underlying idea unit but express it in their own ways—their own aspects of it, and when they express overlapping aspects do so in distinctive ways. They are also *synchronous* at the exact point where they are also co-expressive. Co-expressive symbols, spoken and gestured, are presented by the speaker at the same time—a single underlying idea in speech and gesture *simultaneously*. The synchrony is crucial, because it implies that, at the moment of speaking, the mind is doing the same thing in two ways, not two separate things, and this double essence is a reason for positing a dialectic of imagery and language.

The gesture in Figure 2.1 illustrates this speech-gesture co-expressiveness and synchrony. The speaker was describing a cartoon episode in which one character tries to reach another character by climbing up through drainpipe. The speaker was saying, "and he goes up thróugh the pipe this time" (the illustration captures the moment at which she is saying the stressed vowel of "thróugh"). Co-expressively with "up" her hand rose upward; co-expressively with "through" her fingers spread outward to create an interior space. The upward movement and the opening of the hand took place concurrently, not sequentially, and these movements occurred synchronously with "up through," the linguistic package that carries the same meanings. The contrastive emphasis on "thróugh," highlighting interiority, is matched by the added complexity of the gesture, the spreading of the upturned fingers. What makes speech and gesture co-expressive is this joint realization of the idea of upward motion and interiority.

Fig. 2.1. Gesture combining upward movement and interiority.

But also note the differences. In speech, meanings are analyzed and segregated. Speech divides the event into semantic units—a directed path ("up"), plus the idea of interiority ("through"). Analytic segregation further requires that direction and interiority be combined, to obtain the composite meaning of the whole. In gesture, this composite meaning is fused into one symbol and the semantic units are simultaneous—there is no combination (meaning determination moves from the whole to the parts, not from the parts to the whole). The effect is a uniquely gestural way of packaging meaning—something like 'rising hollowness', which does not exist as a semantic package in the English lexicon at all. Thus, speech and gesture, at the moment of their synchronization, were co-expressive but nonredundant, and this sets the stage for doing one thing (conception of the cat's climbing up inside the pipe) in two forms—analytic/combinatoric and global/synthetic.

The example also illustrates the kind of gesticulation that I will call iconic, in that gesture form and movement expressed something analogous to the event being described. There are at least three other kinds of gesticulations (metaphoric, beat, deictic), all with their own properties. Moreover, the three kinds are not really kinds but are dimensions, and a given gesture can have loadings on several at once. For example, there is deixis in Figure 2.1, in that the speaker located the gesture at the bottom of her gesture space where the bottom of the drainpipe was. I return to the dimensionality of gestures later in the chapter.

THE 'UNBREAKABLE BOND' OF SPEECH AND GESTURE

Further observations show that such synchronized speech and gesture events comprise virtually unbreakable psycholinguistic units; unbreakable, as long as speech and gesture share meaning (repeating gestures by rote to they point where they begin to lose meaning can break the bond; cf. McNeill 1992, second DAF experiment). An observation to be described below also suggests that the bond can be overridden by rhetorical practices in which gestures are used as reinforcers or echoes of speech. But these exceptions aside, the connection of speech and co-expressive gesture appears to be inviolate. The very heterogeneity of the following observations shows the strength of the speech-gesture unit: (a) delayed auditory feedback (DAF) does not interrupt speech-gesture synchrony, (b) gesture inoculates against stuttering, (c) the congenitally blind make gestures to other blind, (d) in memory gesture exchanges information with speech, and (e) gesture number and gesture complexity vary with cognitive fluency.

Gesture Synchrony and DAF

Delayed auditory feedback involves hearing one's own speech played back continuously over earphones after a short delay (typically, 0.25 seconds or about a syllable). DAF has a dramatic effect on the flow of speech: speech slows down, becomes hesitant and is subject to drawling and metatheses (Spoonerisms). Nonetheless, despite the interruptions, speech and gesture remain in synchrony. The following is an illustration (McNeill 1992, pp. 276–277):

the next s-s-[scene] . . .   ha-a-as the [f-f-ront]   desk of a [ho . . .]tel

(1) points forward to   (2) slide right–left for the   (3) hand moves up and
the 'next scene'   shape of the desk   down for height of the desk

Despite the gross interference with speech by DAF, ideas of the next scene, the front desk and its height were all referenced in speech and gesture synchronously. DAF and its noneffect on synchrony shows speech-gesture binding. Speech and gesture form a unit that the outside force of DAF cannot break apart.

Inoculation against Stuttering

Clinical stuttering is characterized by syllable and sound repetitions and prolongations, potentially lasting for many seconds. It differs from normal dysfluencies, which create false starts, repetitions, and repairs on various levels and are fleeting. Mayberry & Jaques (2000), from whom this capsule summary comes, made two noteworthy observations. First, the onset of a gesture stroke inoculated against the onset of stuttering (the stroke is described later—it is the meaning-bearing phase of the gesture). No stuttering began when strokes were beginning, although stuttering could begin in other gesture phases or during a stroke once under way. Second, if stuttering began *during* a stroke, the speaker's hand immediately froze in midair or fell to rest. The stroke resumed as soon as the stuttering bout was over. In both observations, we see an incompatibility between the state of stuttering and occurrence of the meaningful part of the gesture. When this begins, stuttering is suppressed: when stuttering begins, the stroke goes into a holding pattern or ceases. Both effects imply a unit composed of speech and gesture jointly.

Gestures of the Blind

That the congenitally blind gesture at all as they speak is itself evidence of a speech-gesture bond. These speakers have never observed gestures in others.

Nonetheless, Iverson & Goldin-Meadow (1997, 1998) report that blind subjects do gesture, and gesture as frequently as sighted subjects do. They observed blind children talking to sighted subjects of the same gender and age and also to other blind children, also matched for gender and age. The children were informed whether their interlocutors were sighted or blind. To quote the authors, "[A]ll of the blind speakers gestured, and did so at a rate not reliably different from that of sighted-with-sighted or sighted-with-blind pairings" (p. 228). Lack of vision evidently does not impede thinking in gestural terms. This is dramatic evidence of a speech-gesture bond.

Information Exchange

Information that a subject receives in a gesture may be recalled later as speech only (not as a gesture). Information migrates from gesture to speech (McNeill et al. 1994, Cassell et al. 1999). For example, a subject watched a video of another person recounting an animated cartoon. The on-screen narrator, at one point, said "and he [came out] the pipe," and performed an up-and-down bouncing gesture. Thus, speech conveyed motion, but the gesture conveyed manner—bouncing. The subject, after viewing this filmed narration, described the scene by *saying* "and the cat bounces out the pipe," with a transverse non-bouncing gesture. Bouncing had been spontaneously converted in memory from gesture to speech, and this too demonstrates speech-gesture binding. The subjects were queried after the experiment if they had noticed the speech-gesture mismatches, and none had. In addition, Kelly et al. (1999) observed subjects recalling information actually presented in speech as having been gestural, suggesting that the binding of speech and gesture is symmetrical. Both experiments show that speech and gesture exchange information freely.

Gestures and Fluency

A common view of gesture is that it replaces speech. While gestures can fill in when words fail, gestures mostly do not have this function. Far more often, speech and gesture become complex or simple in tandem, even to the point of jointly disappearing (that is, the gesture disappears along with speech, rather than replacing it). The transcript below illustrates this correlation in one speaker's narration: her gestures *decrease* as speech fluency *decreases* and then *increase* as it *revives*. The curves are parallel, not reciprocal. The speaker loses the thread of her story and then finds it again. Concurrently, her gestures become simpler and stop, then reverse course and return in a series of increasingly elaborate gestures. The level of motor involvement via gesture parallels the fluency of speech and fullness of memory.

and then uh climbs up the build–the side of the building	*large iconic*
and jumps in the window	*deictic*
let's see what happens	***no gesture***
he tries to to find out where Tweety Bird is hiding in the house	*beats*
and she says here's a nice new penny for you little monkey or something and she	*large 2-handed iconic*
he holds out the can and she drops the the penny in the in the little cup	*large 2-handed iconics*
and he takes off his hat to her	*large full-body iconic*
and then it's obvious that he's really a cat	*metaphoric*
and she says ahhh! and whaps him with her umbrella	*large full-body iconic with 2 hands*

To Sum Up Binding

Speech and synchronous gestures form a tightly bound unit, capable of resisting outside forces attempting to separate them, such as DAF, stuttering, lack of visual experience of gesture, and loss of fluency. Speech and gesture also spontaneously exchange information in memory, so that when something is recalled the speaker cannot tell the original format. Tight binding clearly fosters an imagery-language dialectic by creating unbreakable psycholinguistic units within which it can take place.

Overriding Binding

However, binding is not inevitable. Cultural forces can override it. The Arrernte, a people of central Australia, appear to interrupt the binding of speech and gesture by consistently performing gestures after the co-expressive speech (de Ruiter & Wilkins 1998; see Wilkins 1999 for a description of the Arrernte in general). De Ruiter and Wilkins attribute the separation to a tendency of

Arrernte speakers to perform gestures at arm's length. Because the resulting gesture space is so large, they argue, the gestures require a longer preparation period, and the relevant speech segments are over before the hand is in position to perform the gesture stroke; thus, speech and gesture are not synchronous.

However, cause and effect in this situation may not be as de Ruiter and Wilkins surmise. An alternative hypothesis is that the delay is the cause, rather than the effect. This could occur if gesture delay, for example, was part of a cultural practice of deliberately putting gestures after speech, to add reinforcement and/or to echo speech (such a practice is seen in a film, *Lorang's Way*, about a native people in Kenya, the Turkana, to be discussed later). While we do not know if the Arrernte have such a practice, we do know that inducing arm's-length gestures from English speakers does not interrupt speech-gesture synchrony. English speakers do not have this rhetorical practice, of course, but they do have regular-length arms! We asked English-speaking subjects to retell our cartoon stimulus in a room prepared with still photos from the cartoon pasted at random places on the walls (Furuyama et al. 2002). The speakers were encouraged to point at the relevant pictures as they were describing the corresponding scene. Because of the distance from the subjects to the wall, this induced many arm's-length gestures. The English speakers, however, *maintained* speech-gesture synchrony, despite their arm's-length pointing. In other words, absent an overriding rhetorical practice, tight speech-gesture binding remained.

Gestures When Speech Is Not Allowed

A further implication of the tight binding of speech and gesture is that when individuals are not allowed to speak and must rely instead on gestures for communicating meanings, the gestures will change their character, because they are no longer integrated with speech. The change implies that speech-*synchronized* gestures have a specific character that exists when the system of speech and gesture is intact. In an experiment that Susan Goldin-Meadow, Jenny Singleton, and I carried out about a decade ago (Goldin-Meadow et al. 1996), we asked subjects to describe video-presented vignettes, in which small dolls were shown moving around and interacting with simple objects (items from Ted Supalla's Verbs of Motion Production Test for ASL; Supalla 1982). The subjects first described the vignettes with speech, and any gestures that occurred were recorded; such gestures were typical of gestures that occur with speech; co-expressive and synchronized, and semiotically not dissimilar to the gesture displayed in Figure 2.1. Then the tape was rewound and the subjects were asked to describe the same vignettes without speech, using only gestures. The differences between the two sessions are the interesting comparison here. Changes in gesture were immediate and dramatic. First, many more gestures occurred when there was no speech, since referential functions that would have been performed with words were now carried by gestures.

Second, the additional gestures in turn created the need to combine gestures to re-create descriptions. For example, a scene in which a small doll is shown somersaulting through the air into an adjacent ashtray (the ashtray proportionately the size of a sandbox to the doll) was rendered thus: First, the subject used two hands to form a circle: the ashtray; next, she formed a small vertical space between the forefinger and thumb of her right hand: the doll; then, still holding this posture, her hand rose up, circled in midair, and dropped down into the space where the ashtray-gesture had been: the somersault arc landing in the ashtray. This order, by far the dominant gesture sequence in the experiment, was first, S, a gesture for the stationary object (the ashtray), then, M, a separate gesture for the moving object (the doll), and finally, A, a gesture for the action (the somersault and arc). In other words, the three gestures combined into an S-M-A 'sentence', which presumably followed the iconic principle of increasing animation through the Stationary Object → Moving Object → Action sequence.

The S, M, and A gestures each captured a part of the total vignette. By combining them the vignette itself was re-created. Spontaneous speech-synchronized and co-expressive gestures, in contrast, have a global and synthetic semiotic, as described in Chapter 1, which ensures that gesture parts are meaningful without linear S-M-A type combinations, and indeed such combinations do not take place. This semiotic, and the resulting absence of combinations, is one of the characteristic design features of gestures in a speech-gesture system and shows how gesture is shaped to be a component of this dialectic (as opposed to the improvised sign language at the other end of Kendon's continuum that Goldin-Meadow, McNeill & Singleton 1996 observed).

GESTURE ANATOMY

Having established the unitary status of speech-gesture packages and the uniqueness of the gestures therein, as opposed to gestures divorced from language, we can now turn to the anatomy of gestures. This anatomy is temporal; it appears during the unfolding of a gesture. As an illustration I use the 'bends it back' gesture mentioned in Chapter 1 (Figure 2.2). This gesture includes all phases of the temporal anatomy except the final, retraction phase, which did not occur in this case because a new gesture followed immediately after the one described here. The speaker had been given a comic book to read and was retelling the story to a listener from memory (Marslen-Wilson, Levy & Tyler 1982). The transcription is as follows:[1]

so he gets a / hold of a big o[ak tree / and <u>he</u> **bends it way ba<u>ck</u>**]

so he gets a/hold of a big   [oak tree/and <u>he</u>

Fig. 2.2. Gesture phases of the "and he bends it way back" gesture. The insert is a frame counter (1 frame = 1/30 sec.). The total elapsed time is about 1.5 secs.

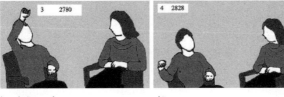

bends it way ba   <u>ck</u>]

Panel 1. **Pre-preparation position.** Hand is shown just prior to lifting off from the armrest.

Panel 2. A **prestroke hold** occurs while saying "he"—the hand waiting for "bends." This figure depicts the hand at the start position of the stroke (ready to pull down and to the rear). The preparation interval was slightly less than 1 second.

Panel 3. Middle of **stroke**—"way" (also illustrated in preceding chapter). The hand has closed around the 'oak tree' and is moving downward and to the rear. Note how the speaker's own position in space defines the location of the oak tree and the direction of the bending back movement—the gesture framed according to a 'first-person' or 'character' viewpoint (CVPT).

Panel 4. End of stroke and beginning of the **poststroke hold** in the middle of "back." Hand is at its farthest point to the rear. After the poststroke hold, the hand immediately launched into a new stroke, showing how the character used the tree to catapult himself onto a nearby building.

1. Transcription by S. Duncan.

Unfolding in Time

As this example illustrates, gestures pass through a series of phases, each with its own position and role in the gesture. The phases enable us to peer into performance dynamics. Kendon (1972, 1980) differentiated among what he termed gesture units, gesture phrases, and gesture phases. A gesture unit is the interval between successive rests of the limbs. In the bends-it-back example, the gesture unit includes not only the interval from "oak," all the way to "back," but also further speech and later gestures not shown here. A gesture unit is the largest interval in Kendon's hierarchy and may contain one or more gesture phrases. (To me, it has always seemed that Kendon's terminology was inverted at this point—a gesture 'phrase' sounds like an ensemble of gestures and a gesture 'unit' a single gesture.) A gesture phrase is what we intuitively call a 'gesture'. In our notation, left and right brackets [ ] mark gesture phrases. A gesture phrase in turn consists of up to five gesture phases (without an "r"), in sequence. Among the phases, Kendon distinguished *preparation, stroke,* and *retraction,* defined below. Sotaro Kita (1990) added *pre- and poststroke hold* phases, and Susan Duncan (personal com.) has added *stroke hold* phases for motionless strokes, both also described below.

Gesture Phases

Preparation (optional): The limb moves away from the rest position into the gesture space where it can begin the stroke. "Oak tree and" coincided with the preparation phase in the illustration. The onset of preparation also suggests the moment at which the visuospatial content of the gesture stroke actually starts to take form in the cognitive experience of the speaker. There is no reason for the hand to shoot into the upper gesture space other than to get ready for the upcoming stroke and the imagery it embodies. We can conclude, accordingly, that the bending back image was taking shape as the speaker said "oak tree." Notice that it thus arose during the preceding clause; it has long been supposed that a subsequent clause could be organized during an antecedent clause (Levelt 1989), and here we find direct evidence. It was also the moment at which the speaker first introduced into the narration the referent "oak tree." Thus, we can suppose that the first memory retrieval and reference to the oak tree also triggered the next image in line, namely the event in which the oak tree was bent back, etc.

Prestroke hold (optional): A temporary cessation of movement before the stroke. In the illustration, a prestroke hold occurred at "he." A prestroke hold delays the stroke until a specific linguistic segment is ready to be articulated (in this case, "bends"). The hold suggests that this speech segment was targeted by the gesture image, something that could occur if the image and the linguistic segment were in fact co-generated and combined from the onset of the preparation phase, and became separated only through the separate mechanical unfolding of manual and vocal movements, the asynchrony of which the prestroke hold repaired.

Stroke (obligatory in the sense that absent a stroke, a gesture is not said to occur): The stroke is the gesture phase with meaning; it is also the phase with effort, in the dance notation sense of focused energy (Dell 1970). In the example above, the stroke was the bending back motion, the hand in a grip around something thick, timed with the co-expressive "bends it way back." The stroke meaning was not identical to the speech meaning, however, since the gesture was bending an object fastened at one end (the movement was one-handed), whereas speech, although implying bending such an object, did not mention it (the pronoun indexes oak tree but "bends it way back" could equally describe bending back a tab of paper, for example).

In a large sample of gestures, the stroke is synchronous with co-expressive speech about 90 percent of the time (Nobe 2000, Valbonesi et al. 2001). When strokes are asynchronous, they precede the speech to which they link semantically, usually because of brief hesitations, and the time gap is small. Strokes rarely if ever follow their co-expressive speech (Kendon 1972); asynchronies in such a direction are seen in neurological anomalies, such as split-brain commisurotomy, described in Chapter 7, and in the IW case study described in Chapter 8. There is no basis for the continued assertion that gestures 'occur during hesitations'; this point is discussed in greater detail below.

Stroke hold (obligatory if static): Such movements are strokes in the sense of meaning and effort but occur with motionless hands.[2] The illustration does not include such a phase, but an example would be raising a hand into the upper

---

2. Stroke holds are not 'holds'. Kita, van Gijn & van der Hulst (1998) distinguish between 'independent holds' (= stroke holds) and 'dependent holds' (= pre- and poststroke holds). Dependent holds are so termed because they are dependent on their strokes. Independent holds stand on their own.

gesture space (preparation) and then holding it in place with the meaning of the upper floor of a building. There is no motion, but there is content and 'effort' in terms of focused energy.

Poststroke hold (optional). The hand freezes in midair before starting a retraction, thereby maintaining the stroke's final position and posture. In the illustration, there was a poststroke hold during the final part of the word "back," shown with underlining. As in the prestroke hold, meaning takes active charge of speech-gesture timing. A poststroke hold occurs if the speech co-expressive with the stroke continues to roll out, while the stroke itself has completed its motion. In the example, the relevance of "back" to the pulling back gesture was registered by freezing the hand in midair until the word was fully articulated. Both the pre- and the poststroke holds thus ensure synchronization of the stroke with its co-expressive speech.

Retraction (optional). The hands return to rest (not always the same position as at the start). There may not be a retraction phase if the speaker immediately moves into a new stroke, as was the case in the illustration. The retraction phase, especially its end, is not without significance, contrary to what I have written about it in the past (McNeill 1992). It is of interest because it shows the moment at which the meaning of the gesture has been fully discharged. The hand ceases motion as it vacates its motivating force, the meaning it carried as a symbol. The end of retraction can thus show the full temporal reach of the co-expressive speech with the gesture.

The Significance of the Phases

Gesture phases are organized around the stroke. The stroke is the object being presented. It is accordingly prepared for, withheld if need be via a prestroke hold, and held again if need be until the linked speech is over.

As described, the prestroke and the poststroke holds ensure that the synchrony of the stroke and the co-expressive speech is attained. In the prestroke hold, the gesture is ready and 'cocked' (Schegloff 1984) but waits for a specific linguistic segment. In the poststroke version, the hand holds the posture and locus of the stroke until speech fully expresses the co-expressed meaning. In both cases, the hold arises from the tight binding of gesture strokes and their co-expressive speech; they appear when differences in the rates of gesture and speech flow attempt to divide them.

The full span of gesture phases, from the beginning of preparation to the end of retraction, describes the lifetime of a particular gesture and its language-linked imagery. We see the image in a state of activation that did not exist before and will not exist after this span. This activated state is where an imagery-language dialectic can occur.

GESTURAL VIEWPOINTS

Broadly speaking, there are two viewpoints in gesture. In the third-person point of view or *observer viewpoint*, or OVPT, the hand(s) represent one or more of the entities in the narration—for example Sylvester as a rising fist-hand: the fist is Sylvester as a whole, not his hand or other part, and the gesture space before the speaker is the space of the action, a kind of a stage or screen on which it takes place. In the first-person point of view or *character viewpoint*, or CVPT, the hand(s) represent the character's hands and the speaker him/herself is inside the gesture space, performing the part of the character. The bends-it-back gesture was CVPT. In some gestures the two viewpoints are combined. When combinations occur each viewpoint typically has its own component(s) of the gesture. For example, describing an event where Sylvester had propelled himself upward on a catapult, grasped Tweety in his hand at the apex, and then fell back to earth (indestructibly of course), all the while still holding Tweety, a speaker's gesture consisted of (a) a grip hand around Tweety (Sylvester's hand in CVPT) and (b) a simultaneous downward thrust (the trajectory as seen from the outside in OVPT) (see McNeill 1992, fig. 4.13).

WHEN EXACTLY DO GESTURES OCCUR?

The interpretation of gesture phases in relation to timing with respect to speech brings up the vexed question of when gestures occur—something that would seem easy to establish, but in fact has been the subject of much contro-versy. Basically, the question is this: Do gestures tend to anticipate their linked linguistic material, or do they coincide with this material? The anticipation view is often accompanied by a further idea—that gestures take place during pauses in speech. The synchrony view, clearly, implies that gestures and speech are co-occurring. This whole discussion is a tempest in a teapot that displays disagreement not about the facts of timing, but about the definition of the 'be-ginning' of a gesture. When the question is examined with careful attention to the distinction among the three principal gesture phases—preparation, stroke, and retraction—the facts are clear: The *preparation* for the gesture precedes the co-expressive linguistic segment; the *stroke* coincides with this segment; and any pre- and poststroke holds ensure that this speech-stroke synchrony is preserved (Nobe 1996).

Onset of Preparation

Butterworth & Beattie (1978) is usually the cited source for the claim that gestures tend to be launched during brief pauses and that they anticipate speech. Butterworth and Beattie examined films of college tutorial sessions and looked specifically at where gestures began. Presumably, though they do not say so, gesture beginning meant for them the onset of preparation. Concentration on the 'fluent' phases of speech (utilizing definitions of fluent and hesitant phases from Goldman Eisler 1968), they found that gestures, *per unit of time*, started during pauses about three times more often than during phonation: this is the factoid that has become part of the folklore of gesture-speech timing. It is often repeated in the following version: gestures tend to take place during pauses, not during speech. However, note the shift in meaning from the original to the legendary claim, highlighted by my italicization of the crucial phrase 'per unit of time'. Butterworth and Beattie did not demonstrate that gestures occur during pauses. This would be false—most gestures, by far, occur during phonations. What they said is that the probability, per unit time, of a gesture launch is greater during pauses than during phonation. This may or may not be so (see below), but without doubt it is a fact that far more time is spent phonating in discourse than pausing, and accordingly, more gesture onsets also occur during phonations than pauses, even if more per unit time occur in pauses. To see this point, imagine that Figure 2.3 represents a series of units of time, with the gray boxes representing pause (pse) units and the white boxes representing units during which phonation occurred. In such a situation, the claim could

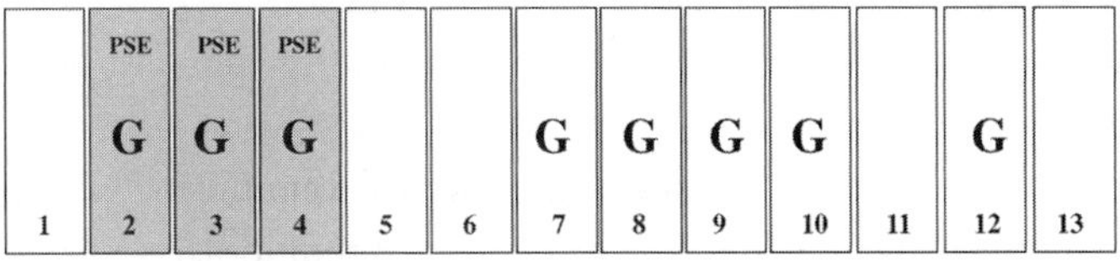

Fig. 2.3. Hypothetical gestures during pauses and phonations.

Table 2.1. Gesture rates (onsets per 1000 secs.) in fluent speech (from Nobe 1996).

	Butterworth & Beattie (Phases Unknown)	Nobe (Onsets of Preparation Phases)
During silent pause	280.1	321.7
During phonation	106.9	372.3

be made that a gesture (G) was initiated in 100 percent of all pause units, but in only 50 percent of all phonated units. However, it is also the case that almost twice as many gestures occur during phonation as pauses. Thus, because pause units of time are less frequent than phonation units of time, examining the initiation of gesture by comparing units of time can lead to a deceptive result.

Furthermore, the probability per unit of time of a gesture launch during a pause may not, in fact, be higher than during phonation. Using the same definitions of fluent speech and pause, Shuichi Nobe compared onsets in pauses and onsets in phonations in the narrations of six subjects delivering a narration of our standard cartoon stimulus, with the results shown in Table 2.1.

Contrary to the 3:1 predominance of initiations during pauses in the Butterworth & Beattie column, Nobe finds a slight predominance during phonation (nonsignificant). In Nobe's case, we know these are the onsets of preparations. The strokes to which the preparations led occurred during phonations to an even greater degree—90 percent of strokes did so.

To explain this difference between the studies, Nobe speculates that the original Butterworth & Beattie result could have been related to the specific speech situation from which their data come (tutorials). The hypothesis suggested by Nobe is that the dialogic situation resulted in a higher occurrence of "turn attempt–suppressing signals" (Nobe 1996, p. 45, quoting Duncan & Fiske 1977). A gesture with a turn-attempt suppression function is obviously more likely during a pause. Given the ambiguity of what the pause signifies, a listener may incorrectly think a turn has ended, and the speaker then uses a gesture to retain the floor. Such a gesture would automatically precede the linked speech—and hence both aspects of the Butterworth & Beattie result are explained by Nobe's hypothesis. This gesture strategy would not have been called for in the cartoon narrations that Nobe examined.

To sum up, there is no basis for claiming that gestures occur during pauses in speech to any particular degree, and the strokes, the meaning-bearing phases of the gesture, only rarely anticipate speech. Preparations, the first sign that the meaning to be presented in the stroke is becoming organized in the speaker's thought, do (necessarily) anticipate the speech segments with which the stroke will ultimately synchronize, and some of these anticipation onsets (less than half) occur during pauses. However, the extent to which gesture onsets occur in pauses can be grossly overestimated if such gestures in pauses are confused with other functions of gestures, specifically the use of gesture as a turn-attempt suppression signal.

THE LEXICAL AFFILIATE

A *lexical affiliate*, a term introduced by Schegloff (1984), is the word or words ✓ deemed to correspond most closely to a gesture in meaning. Schegloff introduced the concept to localize the moment at which, during a conversation, a lexical meaning was first put 'in play'. He observed that gestures tended to precede the words that lexically corresponded to them and that the gesture could therefore signal the introduction of the new meaning into the conversational stream before it surfaced in speech. Apart from the problem of whether it is the gesture preparation or stroke that anticipates the lexical affiliate, it is important, lest there be confusion, to distinguish this concept from speech-gesture co-expressivity, as this term is used here.

A lexical affiliate does not automatically correspond to the co-expressive speech segment. A gesture, including the stroke, may anticipate its lexical affiliate but, at the same time, be synchronized with its co-expressive speech segment. Whereas a lexical affiliate can be recognized by comparing gesture and word, co-expressive speech can be defined only in relation to the context of speaking (since such speech, along with the gesture stroke, is what the speaker is differentiating from the context as significant). It is possible that a co-expressive linguistic segment might be a lexical affiliate, but there is no necessity for it to be.

A clear illustration of the lexical affiliate/co-expressive speech distinction appears in Engle (2000). A gesture anticipated a lexical affiliate, consistent with Schegloff's original observation, but the immediate context of speaking suggests that the gesture and the *co-expressive speech* were actually synchronous. This is the example: Attempting to explain how a lock-and-key mechanism works, the subject said, "lift them [tumblers] to a // height, to the perfect height, where it [**enables**] the key to move," and appeared to turn a key as he said "enables." The lexical affiliate is "key" or "key to move" and the key-turning gesture clearly occurred in advance of it. But from the vantage point of what would be newsworthy content in context, the synchrony of "enables" with the key-turning gesture embodies an idea this speaker might be expected to highlight—that by lifting the tumblers up, you are *able to turn the key*; and this thought is what the combination of a turning gesture plus "enables" captured.

TYPES OF GESTURES

Gesture classification plays little role in the dialectic analysis to follow; gesture *content*, regardless of type, is far more significant. At the end of this section I will explain what replaces gesture categorization in the upcoming dialectic analysis. Nonetheless, it is useful to describe the diversity of gestures. Systems for classifying gestures have been proposed for decades, and many gesture workers have provided ideas for this (e.g., Efron 1941, Ekman & Friesen 1969). The systems differ mainly in the number of categories they use. I myself participated in creating one such system (McNeill & Levy 1982, McNeill 1992). The search for categories, however, now seems misdirected. Most gestures are multifaceted—iconicity is combined with deixis, deixis is combined with metaphoricity, and so forth. Rather than categories we should think in terms of dimensions. One practical effect of shifting to a dimensional framework is that gesture coding is simplified. Coders are not forced to cram a gesture into a single box—say, the iconic—when it also seems deictic, and so forth. Difficulties with intercoder reliability are often traceable to such forced choices. A new dimensional approach was first described in Duncan et al. (1995).

An advantage of the dimensional approach is that we can combine dimensions without being forced to posit a hierarchy of them. A given gesture can have its own loadings across dimensions, and in this way can contain space for all the meanings—semantic, pragmatic, and poetic—that it may embody. I will explain this idea by reviewing our own efforts, and then describe the problems that arose from them.

The Iconic-Metaphoric-Deictic-Beat Quartet

The dimensions I will describe below are based on the original categories we described in McNeill & Levy 1982 and McNeill 1992. Inspired by the semiotic categories of C. S. Peirce (1960), Elena Levy and I proposed a classification scheme with four categories: *iconic, metaphoric, deictic,* and *beat.*

Iconic: Such gestures present images of concrete entities and/or actions. They are gestures in which the form of the gesture and/or its manner of execution embodies picturable aspects of semantic content (aspects of which are also present in speech). An example is the gesticulation example described above (Figure 2.2 and Chapter 1). Various aspects of the gesture—form, hand (standing for the character's hand, and opening it as if grasping an object with some thickness), trajectory (a curved path), direction (backward), etc.—correspond to aspects of the event, a character bending back a tree. The gesture as a referential symbol functioned via its resemblance to this event, iconically. Speech and gesture were not identical, however. As noted before, the gesture was made with a single hand, reflecting the fact that the tree was fastened down at one end. Speech did not mention this fact; being fastened at one end was implied by the use of "it" (a tree), but this was not built into the verbal description itself. Speech and gesture were *co-expressive* in the sense that they portrayed the same event but were not redundant, since each articulated its own aspects of it.

Metaphoric: Gestures can also present *images of the abstract*. Some gestures involve a metaphoric use of form—the speaker appears to be holding an object, as if presenting it, yet the meaning is not presenting an object but rather that she is holding an 'idea' or 'memory' or some other abstract 'object' in her hand. There is an iconic component (the form of the gesture resembles holding an object) and a metaphoric component (holding or presenting something is a metaphor for presenting a meaning). Other gestures involve a metaphoric use of space. A speaker, for example, divides the gesture space before him according to an appearance-reality dimension of morality being attributed to story character (McNeill 1992, p. 155; cf. Cienki 1998). The division is not necessarily along the lines of such a cultural stereotype as good to the right (cf. 'dexterous') and bad to the left ('sinister'). The metaphor may well assign good and bad in the opposite direction. In a metaphoric gesture, an abstract meaning is presented as form and/or space, but not necessarily in terms of stereotypic linkages. The topic of metaphoricity will be taken up in greater detail below.

Deictic: Although the prototypical deictic gesture is the ☞ hand with an extended index finger, almost any extensible body part or held object can be used for pointing. If the hands are employed otherwise we can improvise pointing with our heads, noses, elbows, feet, etc., as well as with abstractions like the 'eidola' or gaze of ancient ophthalmology. Indeed, some cultures prescribe deixis with the lips (Enfield 2001). Deixis entails locating entities and actions in space vis-à-vis a reference point, or what Bühler called an origo (Bühler 1982a,b; Hanks 1996; Haviland 2000). The deictic property of the bending back gesture was in its locating the tree in relation to the speaker, who was acting as a surrogate for the character, and served as the origo for the gesture and whole scene. Pointing is one of the earliest gestures to develop in children (Bates et al. 1979). But much of the pointing we see in adult conversation and storytelling is not pointing at physically present objects or locations but is instead *abstract pointing* (McNeill et al. 1994). Bühler (1982a,b) referred to abstract pointing as *deixis at phantasma*. The emergence of abstract pointing is a milestone in children's development. In striking contrast to concrete pointing and its appearance before the first birthday, abstract pointing is a late acquisition not much in evidence before the age of twelve (McNeill 1992).

Abstract pointing is a species of metaphoric gesture, where space and a locus within it are used to present a nonspatial meaning. The metaphoric division of space according to morality mentioned above was accomplished via pointing. The speaker said, "they're supposed to be the good guys" and pointed to the central space; then said, "but she really did kill him" and pointed to the left space; next, "and he's a bad guy" and pointed again to the central space; and finally, "but he really didn't kill him" and pointed left. The difference between the central space (attributed morality) and the left space (actual morality) became the speaker's metaphor, a temporary one, for the appearance/reality contrast.

Another example involves a speaker differentiating loci for ideas which instantiate a type-token relationship—(type) that something is difficult (near space), and (token) that there was an instance of it today (farther space), with his hands shifting to a new locus between the first and second references.

Abstract deixis reverses the relationship that gesture has to reference from what is found in concrete pointing. Abstract deixis *creates* new references in space; concrete deixis *finds* references in it. I analyze a case of abstract pointing in Chapter 4.4, where it played a crucial role in reorienting a conversation.

Beats: Levy and I called gestures 'beats' when they took the form of the hand beating time. Others have alluded to the same musical analogy with the term 'baton' (Efron 1941). Beats are among the least elaborate of gestures formally. They are mere flicks of the hand(s) up and down or back and forth that seem to 'beat' time along with the rhythm of speech. However, they have meanings that can be complex, signaling the temporal locus in speech of something the speaker feels is important with respect to the larger discourse (Cassell & McNeill 1990, McNeill 1992), the equivalent to using a yellow highlighter on a written text. A beat may accompany the first mention of a character or highlight words whose occurrence is relevant for a larger narrative purpose. Here is an example of the latter kind:

he* <um> you see him dr^áwing up l^óts of bl^úeprints.

The three beats, one after each ^, placed emphasis on the words "drawing," "lots," and "blueprints," as each was produced (each beat's downward thrust coinciding with the prosodic peak of the word). What the beats in this case seem to be highlighting is the elevated effort by the character being described. The speaker went on to relate how the character had constructed a kind of rope on which to swing across a street from one building to another and enter a window, only to discover that his effort—the significance of which was highlighted by the beats—was in vain, as he smashed into the wall instead. The speaker of course knew this outcome in advance, and the larger discourse purpose the beats served was to create the contrast of Sylvester's effort to the anticipated result.

With these four categories, Levy and I were able to classify nearly all gestures in the narrative materials we collected (McNeill & Levy 1982). Other researchers have proposed more finely subdivided categories (Ekman & Friesen 1969). Bavelas et al. (1992) has identified a category, 'interactive gesture', whose function is to ensure smooth turn-taking exchanges in conversations.[3]

Dimensions Rather Than Kinds

I wish to claim, however, that none of these 'categories' is truly categorical. We should speak instead of *dimensions* and say *iconicity, metaphoricity, deixis,* *'temporal highlighting'* (beats), *social interactivity,* or some other equally unmellifluous (but accurate) terms conveying dimensionality.

The essential clue that these semiotic properties are dimensional and not categorial is that we often find iconicity, deixis, and other features mixing in the same gesture. Falling under multiple headings is not impossible in a system of categories, but simultaneous categories implies a hierarchical arrangement. We cannot define such a hierarchy because we cannot say in general which

---

3. In our original classification scheme there was also a category of 'cohesive gestures'—gestures that functioned somewhat like anaphoric linguistic elements. This category has been supplanted by the concept of the catchment—which applies to any gesture. The catchment is introduced in Chapter 4 and enlarged upon in Chapter 5.

categories are dominant and which are subordinate. Consider the bends-it-back example again. The hand pulled backward; this much is iconic. But the gesture was also deictic. It located the tree in relation to the speaker as origo. So how should we categorize it? If we call it iconic, then deixis is lost. If we are to say it is iconic and deixis is a subordinate element in it, we can include both categories, but then we posit a hierarchy in which iconicity dominates deixis, and this is a hierarchy that we have no reason to posit. In another gesture, we may wish to put deixis on top, and this requires yet another hierarchy. In a dimensional framework, we think of every gesture as having a certain loading of iconicity, metaphoricity, deixis, temporal highlighting, and social interactivity; these loadings vary from zero upwards. The bends-it-back gesture carried loadings on at least two dimensions: iconicity and deixis.

Because a multiplicity of semiotic dimensions is an almost universal occurrence in gesture, it makes sense to shift from categories to dimensions. This is the case even in an obviously 'iconic' gesture like bending back. In this conception, gestures are not flattened into categories but are accepted as rotund, multidimensional.

Saliency of the Dimensions

Table 2.2 suggests that in cartoon narrations, at least, the four gesture dimensions are not equally salient. The more frequent a dimension, the more salient we infer it to be. Saliency depends, however, on discourse demands. The counts in Table 2.2 are extracted from cartoon narrations and are accumulated from six adult English speakers (based on Table 3.7 of McNeill 1992). Thus, they are counts for one discourse genre and one language, but because they are averages they are relatively free of speaker idiosyncrasies. For these kinds of narrations, at least, iconicity predominates in clauses that present steps in the plot line, or narrative clauses. Such clauses are subject to the constraint that the

Table 2.2. Gestures in narrative and extranarrative contexts (cartoon narrations).

Type of Clause	Estimates of Gesture Saliency					
	Iconicity	Beat	Metaphoricity	Deixis	None	N
Narrative	41%	25%	2%	5%	27%	543
Extranarrative	14%	54%	13%	1%	18%	247
N	261	268	43	28	190	790

sequence of clauses corresponds to the sequence of events (Labov & Waletsky 1967, Hopper 1979, Hopper & Thompson 1980). Metaphoricity predominates in extranarrative clauses, or clauses which do not add to the plot line but add to the structure of the narration itself. The position in the discourse flow of such clauses is not subject to a sequentiality constraint—they describe the setting, summing up, introducing characters, references to the video, its quality, etc., and appear without interrupting the plot line.

Saliency has theoretical interest as well. It can affect the dialectic of imagery and language because saliency influences the kind of imagery that occurs. We can accordingly expect a dialectic to show predictable differences as genre changes. Most of the later examples are from narrations, where the above pattern should emerge, but others are from conversations and here deixis seems far more salient. Living space descriptions seem equally divided between deixis and iconicity. A dialectic can be formed in any genre, but we predict differences in the kind of dialectic that emerges (see Chapter 4.4 for a case in point—the conversation between Mr. A and Mr. B).

'Poetic' Factors

Roman Jakobson, perhaps too trenchantly, wrote that "the poetic function projects the principle of equivalence from the axis of selection into the axis of combination" (Jakobson 1960, p. 358). The 'axis of selection' is the paradigmatic axis in Saussurian terms (see Chapter 3)—contrasts established when one linguistic form is selected from a set of alternatives ("sheep" vs. "mutton" is a classic illustration). The 'axis of combination' is the syntagmatic axis, the organization of linguistic elements into a sequence. By the poetic function, Jakobson means a process whereby syntagmatic sequences come to have paradigmatic or oppositional values. Recursion is the mechanism of this function (Silverstein 1985), and it works for gesture as well as for speech or writing. A phonetic rhyme signals that the lines linked by recursion, the rhyming lines, have a paradigmatic contrast; for example, "His big tears, for he wept full well/Turned to mill-stones as they fell" (Shelley, "The Mask of Anarchy").[4] The rhyming "-ell"s project a new semantic opposition—"well" to "fell"— cluing us to seek meaningful linkages (probably ironic). 'Rhymes' of gestures can also occur (Furuyama 2001). An example is the use described earlier of

---

4. Thanks to Randall L. B. McNeill for this example.

the central space for the attributed morality of two sets of characters and the left space for their true morality. These repeated 'selections' corresponded to the moral status of the characters. The sequence, center-left, acquired a new albeit temporary significance—apparent versus real morality. Poetic factors, so understood, are omnipresent in gesture. In Chapter 5 I discuss the part played by gestural poetics in creating the kind of discourse segments termed 'catchments' and how they contribute to the dialectic of imagery and language.

HOW GESTURES WILL BE INTERPRETED IN THIS BOOK

The categorization of gesture is useful for statistical summaries but plays little role here in recovering gesture meaning and function; for meaning and function I rely on the form of the gesture and its deployment in space and through time, and on the context of speaking, but not its type. I have already illustrated this form of interpretation with the opening example of this chapter (Figure 2.1). The gesture depicts the cat rising up inside a drainpipe as a 'rising hollowness'. We can be confident of this interpretation for two reasons— because the speaker was concurrently saying "he tries going up thróugh the pipe this time," and because we know the source of the gesture, an event from the animated cartoon in which the character is climbing up a drain on the inside (as opposed to on the outside, his route in an earlier attempt). Speech indicates which event from the cartoon this was but speech is not the source of the interpretation. We interpret the gesture's content purely on the basis of our knowledge of the event in the animated cartoon stimulus and the properties of the gesture itself (shape, trajectory, etc.). In this way, the gesture is free to show information that is co-expressive with speech, rather than being merely redundant (cf. the earlier discussion of the lexical affiliate). It is the gesture's content that we compare to the content of speech to determine co-expressivity. Having identified this content, we observe that it is timed exactly to coincide with the co-expressive speech; a factual observation, not something imposed by the methodology.

METAPHORICITY IN GESTURE

Lakoff & Johnson (1980) considered metaphor to be a means of expanding human conceptualization. Metaphors are characterized as the presentation of some (usually abstract) content as something else, often a concrete image.

The image also becomes part of the meaning. Metaphoricity in gesture is important for extending the process of an imagery-language dialectic to abstract meanings that lack imagery of their own. The gestures provide imagery for the non-imageable. The image is the vehicle of the metaphor, in the parlance of I. A. Richards, where the vehicle is the form that is doing the presenting and the topic is the abstract content being presented. Cornelia Müller, in her new book, *Metaphors, Dead and Alive, Sleeping and Waking* (Müller 2004a), emphasizes the triadic character of metaphor, with the third element being a process of 'seeing as' (a term Müller employs in part to replace the static framework of vehicle-ground-topic with a new dynamic framework; cf. Richards 1936; also, Fauconnier 1994, Fauconnier & Turner 2002, for 'blending theory', which Müller regards as a dynamic model but which I still consider as beholden to a synchronic conception of language; cf. chapter 3 for full discussion). A useful set of terms is Sign-Base-Referent, introduced originally to describe sign language semantics (Mandel 1977; Cohen, Namir & Schlesinger 1977). The Referent is the idea presented by the metaphor; the Base is the image in terms of which the Referent is presented; and the Sign is the overt form of the Base, here a gesture (a Sign is a sign language lexeme in the original version).

Sign, Base, and Referent—and gestural metaphor in general—can be illustrated by Figure 2.4, taken again from a narration of the cartoon. As the speaker said, "and the next scene is," his left hand appeared to be supporting/presenting something. This was a gestural version of the *conduit metaphor*, the verbal version of which appears in such expressions as "I gave you that idea": this abstract notion shown as an entity that can be 'given' by one person to another (Reddy 1979, Lakoff & Johnson 1980). In the same sense, the upturned open hand is 'presenting' or 'holding' an idea. In terms of Sign, Base, and Referent, the

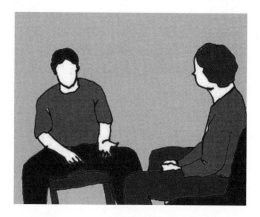

Fig. 2.4. Typical conduit 'cup of meaning' gesture with "and the next scene is," in which the idea of 'the next scene' seems to be present in the open hand.

Sign is the upturned open hand, the Base is the conduit-inspired image of a bounded entity, and the Referent is the abstract idea of the next thematic unit of the story. In terms of Müller's triadic structure, the gesture (the Sign) in Figure 2.1 induces one to see a container or a manually supported entity as an abstraction—the "next scene" of the narration. (See Chapter 5 for the role of metaphors in organizing discourse.)

Note that gesture and speech are here again co-expressive. The co-expressive aspect is not a shared depiction of a narrative event—the gesture but not the speech embodies the image of an entity or container—but there is mutualness on a metadiscourse level. Both gesture and speech convey information about the organization of the narration itself, qua a discourse. In speech, the reference is to a thematic division of the cartoon and its retelling into scenes. In the gesture, this division—the 'next scene'—is held in the hand. (The gesture also had had a deictic component—placing the next scene metaphorically on the left side of space, implying a time line in which events parade from left to right in front the speaker.)[5]

Metaphoric gestures thus extend gesture imagery beyond depictions of concrete entities. The metaphor is a way to extrapolate imagery to a range of meanings that are not themselves imageable. If language is inseparable from imagery, then metaphors and metaphoric gestures are crucial for bringing abstract content into contact with imagery, and hence for the ability of language to present this kind of information itself.

Metaphors as Cultural Adaptations

In many cultures, including our own, there is a belief that *form and content are different; form has an existence of its own that is separate from its content.* Gestures embody this belief when abstract concepts are made into bounded containers, with 'content' a substance in the hand, as in the 'next scene' gesture, and the hand itself a 'form'. Metaphoric imagery is culture-specific: the images and their metaphoric extensions embody some of the most deeply entrenched ontological beliefs of a given culture.

---

5. Another common time line for English speakers is from front to back, with the past behind. Núñez & Sweetser (in press) describe an Andean culture, the Aymara, for whom past is the space in front, future the space behind, so that indicating the next day could be via a gesture over the shoulder.

We can demonstrate that metaphoric gestures incorporate cultural beliefs by showing the presence of cross-cultural variation in the beliefs they imply. In contrast to the 'next scene' conduit gesture by the English speaker, Figure 2.5 (drawn from the film *Lorang's Way* by MacDougall & MacDougall 1977) shows a gesture by a speaker of Turkana (spoken in northwestern Kenya) in which 'knowledge' is depicted, not as a substance in the hand, but as something the hand releases into the air. All in one motion, the speaker's hand plucked 'knowledge' from his brow; then dipped down, fingers pinched; then rose again, fingers opening; and at the end (the moment pictured) released 'knowledge' aloft. It is clear that knowledge is not something supported in the hand, as in the conduit.

Fig. 2.5. Turkana nonconduit metaphoric gesture for knowledge.

Similarly, speakers of Mandarin Chinese do not appear to create metaphoric gestures with a built-in form/content distinction. In Chinese the imagery is of substances *without* form. Gestures show the locus of 'knowledge', e.g., patting on it, but do not support it in the hand or suggest a container, as an English speaker might (English speakers also use the formless substance metaphor of knowledge and meaning).

Japanese has a number of metaphors of anger that it conventionally localizes within body parts (the chest for example) or depicts as conventional objects, such as bursting balloons (Ishino 2001a). The metaphors have corresponding gestures that appear to incorporate the form-content distinction. Such a conclusion is consistent with casual observation and native speaker reports (by Nobuhiro Furuyama and Mika Ishino), that speakers of Japanese generate conduit gestures in quantity. Thus two cultures, Chinese and Japanese, despite geographic proximity and long historical contact, have different metaphoric traditions, as would be anticipated on the grounds that metaphors are cultural adaptations adopted in part to render the invisible visible.

Such examples point to cultural norms for metaphoric imagery. Local standards establish guidelines, showing how images are to be created and what belief systems they embody. In the Western tradition, the conduit metaphoric gesture, with its built in form/content distinction, is long-standing. A quote from Montaigne (already back to the 16th century) attributes an elaborate series of conduit gestures to Zeno of Elea (6th century B.C.):[6]

> Zeno pictured in a gesture his conception of this division of the faculties of the soul: the hand spread and open was appearance; the hand half shut and the fingers a little hooked, consent; the closed fist, comprehension; when with his left hand he closed his fist still tighter, knowledge. (Montaigne 1958, p. 372)

GESTURE AND CONVENTION

The above discussion has introduced the topic of convention. It is now time to focus on this aspect, and it will be helpful to have a model gesture that possesses it unquestionably. An emblem, such as the "OK" sign, can provide this model. The gesture is made by placing the tip of the first finger in contact with the tip of the thumb, thereby forming a circle, the other fingers extended out more or less straight; the meaning is bestowing approbation. "OK" illustrates a number of hallmarks of conventionalization: its form is (a) obligatory, (b) arbitrary, and (c) culturally specific. Moreover, its meaning is (d) prespecified (an act of approbation), not contextually driven.

Obligatory form: This can be seen in the consequences of altering the form, e.g., making the circle with the thumb and middle finger. Such a gesture conveys precision but it is not recognizable as "OK." The specific requirement of forefinger-thumb contact is part of the convention for the emblem.

Arbitrary form: This implies that the meaning of approbation does not determine the form. A metaphor of precision is possibly present in the form, and clearly precision is not in conflict with approbation, but precision, which could motivate either the first or other finger-thumb contact, is not approbation itself; that meaning is due to convention.

6. Josef Stern of the University of Chicago Department of Philosophy brought this passage to my attention.

Cultural specificity: The ring has different meanings in other places (it is a sexual insult in North Africa, for example). For a description of this gesture and its diversity and history, see Morris et al. (1979). Diversity is to be expected with conventionalized gestures.

Prespecified meaning paired with the form: This implies the form-meaning pair is fixed, listable, and morpheme-like. Such a pairing of form and meaning is expected from convention, since it is the combination of a certain form presenting a certain meaning that the convention specifies.

These hallmarks can be tested when a gesture is suspected of conventionalization—such a gesture should show the traits of having an obligatory form, an arbitrary form, cultural localization, and prespecified meanings.

Convention and Metaphoric Gestures

So what, then, are metaphoric gestures? Are they also conventional, like emblems? Purely iconic gestures are minimally conventional. The distinctive form of the "up through" example is driven by the 'rising interiority' meaning in a specific narrative context and not by context-independent conventions of form. But the status of metaphoric gestures is less clear. Cornelia Müller (to appear) has carefully analyzed a gesture that she labels the Palm Up Open Hand (using nomenclature suggested privately by Kendon, which I shall abbreviate PUOH), a gesture whose functions appear closely allied to the conduit gesture. The prototypical meaning of PUOH is the hand presenting a 'discursive object'. Müller writes, "Variations [in PUOH] seem to be limited"; that the gesture combines with other gesture features, such as moving the hand through a wide space to convey a range of objects being presented, and "the incorporated features appear to be semiotically unrelated to the features of the hand shape and orientation." The fact of limited and independent forms "suggests indeed that two independent form-function [viz. signifier-signified] elements are joined in one gesture," an arrangement that "points towards a rudimentary morphology based on purely iconic principles."

The PUOH shape is a case of what Müller (2004a) terms a 'performative gesture'—one that enacts what it performs; here it performs the presentation of a discursive object. How does PUOH compare to the prototype of a conventional gesture, the "OK" sign? The PUOH form is obligatory in the sense that altering aspects of it (e.g., the palm forward rather than up), although it is not necessarily devoid of meaning, fails to present the PUOH's discursive object meaning; so on this criterion PUOH resembles the emblem. It is also culturally specific (although the cultural area is very wide), as its absence in the Turkana gesture demonstrates. However, it is not arbitrary. The surface of the hand is a natural platform for presenting discursive (indeed, any) objects, and its upward orientation is an essential part of the platform image.

The question is not whether there are conventions but the level at which the conventions apply. In the "OK" sign, they apply at each of the following: the form of the gesture, the pairing of the form and meaning, and the meaning of approbation. In PUOH, with its 'discursive object' meaning, it seems plausible that the *metaphor* is all there is—this alone generates PUOH. That is, the convention of the metaphor suffices, and no further conventions specify the form itself. The processing implication would be that each time a speaker imagines some conceptual content as a discursive object or a container or a substance in the hand, the PUOH form results; the form is not prespecified but is an online product of thinking in terms of the metaphor.

Some indication that the metaphor hypothesis may hold is that minor variations of form don't categorically change meaning, the way that changing from first finger to second finger-thumb contact cancels the "OK" meaning or (to take a word example) that adding the single phonetic feature of voicing deletes the meaning of "fly" (*"vly"). With real morphemes, tiny form changes can have radical all-or-none effects on meaning, and this is due to the fixed status of the form. Variations of PUOH in contrast—in finger tension, finger spread, degree of curvature, beatlike added movements, etc.—correlate with nuances on the root meaning, which is clearly retained throughout the changes. A strongly presented discursive object can be signaled in a PUOH via added tension, finger curvature, added beats, etc. The Zeno gestures cited earlier formed a continuous series, starting with PUOH and ending with the fist closed and further clenched by the opposite hand. The gestures left the PUOH form itself entirely behind but the progression was matched by a progression of meanings—from 'appearance' (PUOH), through 'consent' (the fingers hooked), to 'comprehension' (closed fist), and finally to 'knowledge' (more tightly closed by the second hand). With true morphemes, in contrast, something of form survives no matter how extensive the variation of meaning.

Consider a continuum of *form conventions* in gesture. At the "up through" pole, form is determined 100% by meaning, 0% by preestablished standards (approximately). At the "OK" pole, it is 0% by meaning and 100% by preestablished standards (these are idealizations). PUOH is like "up through" in that its form is driven by meaning but is like "OK" in that this meaning is itself a product of convention, the cultural metaphor. Viewed in this way, the metaphoric gesture is in the middle of yet another continuum, conventional at one level, created at another. It is this layering of the conventional and the created that makes metaphor so useful in an imagery-language dialectic. It can generate imagery for meanings that would otherwise not be imageable, yet does so in a culturally specified way.

Some Tests That Could be Tried

To settle the form question, and at what level conventions apply, several probes of conventional forms could be attempted:

1. Do people *recognize violations of gesture form*? Comparable to the rejection of the "OK" sign made with the second finger, would they recognize and reject modifications of the gesture form? Conversely, do they consider variations of form to correspond to noncategorial variations of meaning, as in the Zeno variations of PUOH?

2. Also, if two gestures have different meanings but similar forms, is there some form difference, however minor, added to at least one of the gestures to *maintain distinctiveness*? The addition should have no iconic function of its own for such a test. Form additions are found in the Aboriginal sign languages that Kendon (1988b, p. 189) described, a gesture code where the status of form conventions seems secure. For instance, the signs for TRUCK and CHILD are made in the same way in one of these languages, except that the little finger in TRUCK extends outward and has the effect of maintaining the distinctiveness of the sign vis-à-vis CHILD.

3. And finally, do people *have intuitions of good form*? Most English speakers probably could say that contacting the second finger with the thumb is not the proper way to make the "OK" sign, but could they say the same for PUOH as the presentation of an idea if the handshape varies somewhat? And can they describe the form requirement, and do different speakers give the same description?

Until very recently, no one has used these probes and the answers to such questions have not been sought. Now, Fey Parrill (2003) has carried out a study of this kind, apparently the first. She compared conduit metaphoric gestures across a range of handshapes—the thumb bent across the palm to varying degrees and varying amounts of finger curl. Participants rated the gestures for naturalness. The same procedure was followed for the "OK" sign (the ring), again across a range of shapes. Surprisingly, subjects did not agree on their judgments of naturalness for either kind of gesture—"the same gestures were rated as both very natural (1) and very unnatural (5)," a result that is especially surprising with the emblem. Parrill points out the paradox that, while people produce conduit gestures and "OK" signs with similar forms, they don't seem to recognize that the forms are restricted. And this in spite of the fact that participants' comments showed them to be familiar with these gestures, often calling the emblem by name. While this may seem to raise the question of whether it is warranted to apply form conventions even to emblems, let alone to the PUOH/conduit, it is possible that this surprising result, rather than revealing an opacity of conventions, reflects difficulties in attempting to obtain judgments of forms alone from naïve observers (cf. further discussion of linguistic intuitions in Chapter 4.1).

McCullough's Thesis: Basic Semiotic Components

A rather different take on the question of conventions of form is Karl-Erik McCullough's thesis of basic semiotic components (ongoing thesis research). In his view, there may be combinable, stable elements in PUOH that comprise conventions of form.

In McCullough's view, the PUOH has two features: deixis, which resides in the orientation the hand (facing up), and a surface, which resides in the shape of the hand (a flat surface). These components are inherent in the anatomy of the hand, but in the PUOH they are semiotic, not anatomical as such. The hand facing up is meaningful, not as the palm up, but as *an orientation*; and the open palm is meaningful, not as a handshape, but as *a surface*. Surface and orientation are significant in the gesture as components of the gesture's iconicity (cf. Peirce 1960).

The deictic and shape components impose a kind of granularity of the possible meanings of PUOH; the palm means a surface, for example, but it is unlikely that the side of the hand would ever have this meaning. Also, the direction of the palm and the meaning of orientation are fixed, valid no matter the direction. Likewise, the palm paired with the meaning of a surface is valid under all conditions. These pairs cannot be deemed arbitrary (far from it— iconicity is their raison d'être), but there is a pairing of form and meaning.

But there is also a critical difference between these pairs and a putative convention of gesture form-meaning pairing. The difference is that the semiotic components of upward orientation and a flat surface are *not* the speaker's intended meanings. McCullough points out that what the speaker *intends* is the idea of presenting a discursive object; not the iconic primes of orientation and a surface. We can add that the intended meaning becomes attached to the orientation and surface components *through metaphoric extensions*, presumably something like those provided by the conduit cultural metaphor. The combination of up-facing + surface does not, on its own, constitute a presentation; this requires a metaphor that endows the iconic image of an upward facing surface with the presentation meaning. Thus, there is no fixed form–meaning pairing at the level of intention, and we again encounter metaphor as the possible source of the association of gesture form and meaning.

Conventions: Conclusion

To conclude, what recurs in recurrent metaphoric gesture forms are semiotic components, but the conventional components are those of a cultural metaphor, not of form qua form. This reinforces the earlier conclusion, that metaphoric gestures lie on a continuum between the fully conventional emblems at one end and the fully meaning-driven gestures like "up through" at the other.

WHO BENEFITS?

A long-running controversy in the gesture-study field revolves around the issue of whether gestures are 'for the speaker' or 'for the listener'—that is, whether gestures primarily perform an internal function that aids the speaker, e.g., to carry out lexical retrieval and/or to boost fluency, or an external function of communicating information to a listener. (Among those who support the former hypothesis are Krauss, Chen & Gottesman 2000, Butterworth & Hadar 1989, Hadar & Butterworth 1997, and Rimé 1982. Those arguing for the latter hypothesis include Kendon 1994, Cohen & Harrison 1973, Cohen 1977, Alibali et al. 2001, Özyürek 2002, and Bavelas et al. 1992, who distinguish a class of 'interactive gestures'; and Beattie & Shovelton 2000, who present evidence against one version of the 'for the speaker' position.)

Despite its long run, I believe the speaker-benefit/listener-benefit controversy rests on a false or, at best, simplistic distinction. The fact is that every gesture is simultaneously 'for the speaker' and 'for the listener'. I do not mean this in a bleached ecumenical way. I mean that an individual-social duality is inherent to gesture. A gesture is a bridge from one's social interaction to one's individual cognition—it depends on the presence (real or imagined) of a social other and yet is a dynamic element in the individual's cognition. This fact will be discussed in full in Chapter 4.4 and will be a clue to the origin of gesture and language in Chapter 8. The implicit social other gives the gesture a sense of being for the other even while it is part of one's own speech and thought. Said differently and with a more explicit reference to Vygotsky, every thought (intrapsychic) passes through a social filter (interpsychic). If such is the nature of thought, and of gesture, the opposition between a speaker versus a listener benefit is a false or at best simplistic distinction.

PRESENCE VERSUS ABSENCE OF GESTURE

If there is an imagery-language dialectic, mediated by gesture, what happens when there is no gesture? To provide an answer, it is useful to see a gesture as a 'material carrier' of imagery (the material carrier concept is borrowed from Vygotsky 1986). Chapter 4.1 provides a detailed discussion and theory of the material carrier, but the concept is useful here in discussing the implications of gesture absence. Imagery can exist without gesture but then it is in its least material form, without actional substance. A lack of materialization occurs under predictable conditions. A material carrier has enhancing power, and the absence of gesture appears when this 'enhancing power' is neither used nor wanted.

A Continuum of Materialization

We have a continuum of imagery materialization:

$$no\ gesture \rightarrow beats \rightarrow points \rightarrow iconics\ (simple) \rightarrow$$
$$iconics\ (complex) \rightarrow two\ different\ hands,\ etc.$$

An absence of gesture is expected if there is memory failure or its opposite, a complete predictability of the next step in discourse. We saw earlier in this chapter that as memory faded gestures declined proportionately and finally disappeared, and then, as memory returned, gestures revived in steps to full iconic form. The second factor of discourse predictability (Givón 1985, Firbas 1971) is described in the following.

Communicative Dynamism

A continuum of continuity/discontinuity of reference was defined in Givón (1985), in which more elaborate noun phrases (NPs) corresponded to greater discontinuity or novelty. For example, a Ø NP subject (as in the subject slots in "he ran and Ø got a bowling ball and Ø dropped it down the pipe") is strongly indexed as a presupposed reference, implying high continuity or predictability. Such a NP should not require the material carrier support of a gesture. A full clause converted to a NP, on the other hand, implies the opposite—maximal discontinuity, for example, "the next thing he did was," where the whole underlined clause is an NP that implies a break in continuity; such discontinuity should be accompanied by the highest degree of gesture materialization. In *Hand and Mind* I showed that that indeed gestures in narrative discourse vary in complexity along Givón's continuity/discontinuity continuum (repeated here in Table 2.3).

It is clear that the two streams—the spoken and the gestured, both of which are material carriers—correlate in terms of the amount of elaboration or 'substance' each provides as we move along the communicative dynamism scale. The most elaborate NPs are accompanied by the most developed gestures, the least with the least, and middling amounts in between.

Table 2.3. Gestures, speech, and communicative dynamism.

Most Continuous/Predictable	———————>		Least Continuous/Predictable	
Linguistic Form Continuum				
Ø	Unstressed Pronoun	Noun Phrase	Modified Noun Phrase	Clause or Verb Phrase
Gesture Form Continuum				
Referring term included in ongoing iconic that covered full clause	Referring term excluded from adjacent iconics	Iconics that cover the clause or VP	OVPT iconic with an NP	4 deictics with clause or VP 3 OVPT iconics (one handed) 3 OVPT iconics (two asymmetric hands) 3 CVPT iconics

WHAT IS AN IMAGE?

I conclude this chapter with an essay on the concept of an 'image' in an imagery-language dialectic. One conclusion of this essay is that 'imagery' is not to be equated with photo realism.

Gesture Imagery as Action

Images, however, are often equated with photographs or realism in painting (e.g., Kosslyn 1980, who begins his book by asking the reader to imagine, among other things, the shape of a German shepherd's ears), but mental imagery of this photographic kind is just one form and is a form not required or likely to be present in an imagery-language dialectic. Spatial-*actional* imagery is a more accurate term. For our purposes, a definition of imagery is that form directly embodies meaning. In a similar vein, Emmorey & Herzig (2003) define an 'analogue system' as "one in which there is . . . an iconic relation between the linguistic forms and their meaning" (p. 222). To make a gesture, then, is to iconically materialize a meaning in actional and spatial form.

Gesture Imagery Is Shaped by Proximity to Language

Gesture imagery so described has the semiotic properties defined on Kendon's continuum 4 (Chapter 1) plus two more, which collectively ensure that gestures can mesh with language in an imagery-language dialectic and each medium presents the same underlying idea unit in unlike forms.

Global. The meanings of the parts of a gesture are determined by the meaning of the whole, in contrast to the determination of the whole from the meanings of the parts in speech.

Synthetic. A single gesture's meaning is broken down in speech and separated in different segments.

Instantaneous. The gesture stroke does not build up meaning sequentially, even when it takes time to unfold; the meaning is present from the beginning, in contrast to the ordered accumulation of meanings in speech.

Noncombinatoric. Globality also affects how the parts of gestures combine. Two gestures can co-occur, each depicting different aspects of the scene to be described, but not combine syntagmatically, to use the Saussurian term for rule-based linguistic combinations (see Chapter 3). Instead, they *coexist*, and their meanings are united globally, the parts meaningful within the whole. An example is a two-handed gesture in which the left hand creates an opening that means an interior space, while the right shows a character moving upward (the left hand may or may not envelop the right—the hands can be side-by-side in their own locations). The total meaning is the same as in Figure 2.2—a character rising upward inside the drainpipe—with interiority and upward motion separated (literally, spatially) to the two hands, each with its own share of the meaning. The meanings are determined by the roles of the hands within the whole gesture, in the typical gesture-style top-down direction.

Dynamic. Gesture imagery is shaped by the immediate context of speaking, both the linguistic context (the co-expressive, synchronous speech) and the speaker's representation of the larger discourse context, including memory and intention. The image reflects this context as much as it does the event being depicted, and contextual shaping is a feature of imagery in an imagery-language dialectic.

Image and Communicative Dynamism

Dynamically shaping imagery implies it is tied to communicative dynamism, as Table 2.3 demonstrates. The higher the newsworthy content, the more elaborate the image. In some cases a conduit cup of meaning hand merely flicks upward but never quite reaches a palm-up posture. The gesture embodies minimal imagery (approaching the level of a beat) and would be expected in conditions of high discourse continuity or predictability. In other cases, the image is more elaborated and provides greater discourse differentiation. For example, a gesture described by Rebecca Webb (1996) as a 'claw' hand positioned next to the head during a lecture was part of a reference to the contents of the mind/brain. The mind/brain was newsworthy content in the lecture flow. The claw appears to be the conduit cup of meaning, combined with a specific orientation, conveying a complex image of the contents plus the locus of the contents. The claw shape itself, rather than a more standard conduit cup of meaning, might also have been motivated to provide imagery of compactness or confinement, the contents at a particular locus in the mind/brain.

Images Are Nonrepresentational

Finally, imagery is not the same as iconicity (iconicity being a hallmark of photo-like mental imagery). I can show the distinction by citing Nelson Goodman's ingenious arguments against iconicity, in which he enunciated the idea that iconicity does not explain how images represent objects or events in the world. However, imagery—gesture imagery—is immune to Goodman's critique, and this immunity will demonstrate the distinction.[7]

Goodman at the start of his classic *Languages of Art* (1968, pp. 4–5) presented three arguments against iconicity, or 'resemblance', as a mode of representation. He asked: Does a painting of some historical figure represent this figure by *resembling* him/her? And he answered that resemblance could not explain how the painting does its job of representing. The conclusion is not that the painting does not represent, but that the representation does not depend on iconicity:

> For one thing, an object resembles itself to the maximum but it doesn't represent itself.
>
> A second argument is that while resemblance is symmetrical, representation is asymmetrical—the painting and the person resemble each other equally but the painting represents the person and the person doesn't represent the painting.
>
> Finally, resemblance is neither sufficient nor necessary for a painting to represent the object. No degree of resemblance is enough to make something represent something—the painting of a building resembles another painting more than it resembles the building, yet it represents the building and not the other painting. And resemblance is not necessary for representation since almost any arbitrary signifier (a dot, say) can represent anything else. (Goodman 1968, p. 93)

We are compelled to accept these arguments in general. However, they do not apply to gestural images. Gestures differ from photos, paintings, etc. in two ways that remove them from Goodman's arguments.

First, iconicity adds reality as a *material carrier*. By moving the hand up, upness is materialized. Iconicity has a different explanatory status in a first- and third-person perspective. It can be a causal force in a first party's gesture and, for this person, more iconicity equals greater materialization or reality of meaning, even though iconicity is unable to explain how a gesture represents something to a third party.

Second, for the party performing a gesture, a gesture does not represent at all; the gesture is *created* by the speaker as a materialization of meaning. This fact alone removes it from Goodman's critique.

7. I am grateful to Jürgen Streeck for alerting me to this approach.

The 'Image': A Picture

Putting these properties together—images are global, synthetic, instanta- ✓✓
neous, noncombinatoric, and dynamically shaped by context; they are actions,
nonrepresentational for the one creating them, and vary from simple to elaborate depending on the need for materialization; and we have a creation of
meaning in action that is imagistic but not the experience of photo realism.

PART 2

Dialectic

CHAPTER 3

Two Dimensions

In this chapter I commence the dialectic topic with a description of two traditions for approaching language—the static and the dynamic. The following
chapter will combine these approaches in a new way, utilizing the concept of
the growth point, which is proposed as a minimal unit of an imagery-language
dialectic.

langue
v.
parole

CONTRASTING TRADITIONS

Classically, the traditions are called 'linguistic' and 'psycholinguistic', but much
psycholinguistics remains static in its underlying assumptions, and more accurate terms are *dynamic* and *static*, with psycholinguistics mainly in the static
camp. These terms refer both to scientific traditions and to what can be called
dimensions of language, each the specialty of one of the traditions.

In the *static* tradition, language is regarded *as a thing, not a process*. A homely
but not inaccurate word for this dimension is the 'thinginess' quality of language. Thinginess is the framework of nearly all contemporary work on grammar as well as the classic Whorfian hypothesis (Whorf 1956), with its focus on
'habitual thought' (a static infrastructure of thought). The Whorfian hypothesis is considered in Chapter 6.

In the *dynamic* tradition, language is regarded as *a process, not a thing*.
This dimension could be termed the 'activity' of language, but I will call it
(somewhat mysteriously, at present) the 'inhabiting' of language. A historical

figure associated with this tradition is Vygotsky. Vygotsky provides a framework well-suited for the version of the Whorfian hypothesis that focuses on the online effects of language on thinking, termed 'thinking for speaking' by Slobin (1987). Thinking for speaking too is considered in Chapter 6. The word 'inhabiting' echoes Merleau-Ponty (1962), whose connection to the dynamic dimension is explained in Chapter 4.1.

The approach I am following requires combining the static and dynamic. The definition of the dynamic dimension of language as a process rather than a thing is incomplete. The static dimension is equally a component of the dialectic. Only in this way can we understand the inherent dynamics of an imagery-language dialectic. In every speech event both dimensions are active and need to be taken into account. The growth point model I shall propose combines the static dimension with the dynamic.[1]

It is to be expected that some phenomena are more accessible or prominent on one dimension, others on the other, but the dynamic dimension cannot be isolated: it intersects and interacts with the static. As we shall see, the essence of thinking *for* (and thinking *while*) speaking is that the static and dynamic combine at every moment. This dialectic begins in an unstable state in which the speaker's idea unit is simultaneously in two unlike forms (imagery and linguistic categorial) and ends by attaining a stable state, achieved through resolution of the dialectic, a step called the 'unpacking' of the growth point into a conventional linguistic form or approximation thereof. The dialectic is brought to a halt by the speaker's intuitive recognition of a linguistically well-formed utterance. Every speech event accordingly occupies both dimensions. A reliance on intuition is often criticized in linguistics, but in our case it is a positive feature. The linguist isolates, clarifies, and formalizes the very intuitions that have a systematic role in the dialectic.

THE STATIC TRADITION

We start with the static approach. As an effective force on the development of current linguistics this tradition can be traced to Ferdinand de Saussure in the

---

1. It should be evident that I am not trying to derive linguistic structure from imagery or any other underlying psychological mechanisms. This would undercut the entire dialectic concept.

early twentieth century. I argue in this section that, to the present day, much of modern linguistics remains Saussurian (cf. Newmeyer 2003).

To quote Jonathan Culler (1976, p. xiii), "Ferdinand de Saussure is the father of modern linguistics, the man who reorganized the systematic study of language and languages in such a way as to make possible the achievements of twentieth-century linguistics." The Saussurian tradition, however, after reigning for the better part of a century, may have reached a limit, its insights into language finally running dry. (Interestingly, Saussure himself might have agreed with this assessment, but much earlier; see the later section on the 'new' historical Saussure.) The field is characterized by a quality of recycling already developed ideas. What Paul Postal in his *Skeptical Linguistic Essays* (2004) derides as faddish changes of theoretical claims in the generative linguistics tradition displays this—it's not that we see new concepts emerging with great speed but repackagings of familiar Saussurian concepts (hence the speed). Is linguistics ripe for a new paradigm? If the Saussurian tradition is at an impasse, a breakthrough might come over either of two routes.

One approach is radical and attempts to dissolve the competence-performance distinction (the modern counterpart of Saussure's langue-parole, as discussed below) and replace it with a new paradigm, in which, somehow, features of langue and parole are unified and replaced by something that is dynamic, yet retains the idea of standards of form. A number of recent 'usage-based' grammars can be explicated in this light—a reaction, within linguistics, to the barriers inherent in the old paradigm. But it is far from clear that a breakthrough has been achieved or is at hand from this direction. Versions of cognitive grammar still seem wedded to the synchronic axiom, described below. Another approach, connectionism, also aims to accomplish a meltdown of competence-performance (see Rummelhart & McClelland 1986, for example), but seems able to do this only by relinquishing standards of form. Moreover, from a dialectic perspective, connectionism goes too far. The programs developed to date, including those with preprogrammed 'innate' constraints, are designed to take varying inputs and reduce them to a single pattern or set of patterns, not to set up simultaneous modes of meaning with unlike semiotic properties. The result is that the 'essential duality' of language (to use a phrase of the 'new' Saussure) is erased, and with it the possibility of modeling an imagery-language dialectic. Perhaps the boldest effort yet to break away from the Saussurian tradition is 'emergent grammar' (Hopper 1998, in press), but this is still a work in progress, achieving a mixture of static and dynamic elements but not yet the kind of radical dissolution of competence and performance the first approach envisions. Finally, I am intrigued by the potential in Cornelia Müller's dynamic metaphor theory for overcoming the competence-performance distinction, but at this early stage of its formulation the theory is limited to conceptual metaphors.

The other, more conservative approach is the one I follow here. It retains the notion of langue, viewed statically and distinct from parole, but makes it into a special case. Perhaps, for the time being, this approach is radical enough (for example, it inverts the continuing tradition in psycholinguistics, dating from the 1960s, in which performance depends on competence; here, instead, competence will occupy a functional role within 'performance').

Saussure's Foundations for Modern Linguistics

Saussure's concepts are known to us through the class notes of his students, later compiled and published as his *Course in General Linguistics* (original in 1915; the earliest English edition I know of is Saussure 1959). The goal was to capture the *fundamentals of language form* in terms of a set of dichotomies:[2]

langue-parole (competence-performance in modern form)
synchronic-diachronic approaches to langue
signifier-signified within the linguistic sign
oppositions on two axes: syntagmatic and paradigmatic
arbitrariness vs. motivation/predictability/determinedness
social vs. individual facts.

These dichotomies in turn relate to each other, as suggested in Figure 3.1.

I now turn to a discussion of the dichotomies, and, where available, their modern counterparts. These dichotomies comprise an interlocking set of axioms that have supported the work of linguistics for nearly a century. Some of this discussion will cover very familiar ground, but I hope to cover it in a new way. Also, how the axioms interconnect is not often discussed, and the existence of modern counterparts of the syntagmatic and especially the paradigmatic axes is not always noticed.

2. This draws on Greeno (1981).

Saussurian Square

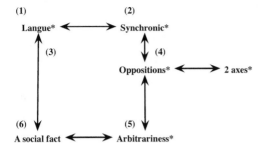

* With a modern counterpart. Only the social fact axiom lacks a current equivalent.

Fig. 3.1. Saussurian square. The parenthetical numbers are the order of discussion.

Theoretical Separation of Langue (Competence) from Parole (Performance)

Langue-parole. Human language ('Langage' or L) has two aspects, as illustrated in Figure 3.2.

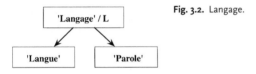

Fig. 3.2. Langage.

Langue is everything that is 'systematic' (pertaining to the regularities of the 'system') in human language (langage). Parole is everything else—the aspects of langage that don't pertain to the system of language (parole is 'nonsystematic', not 'unsystematic'—that is, not random and unpredictable, but it also is not part of the system of langage). The speaker must at some level know the regularities of the language—this is his/her *competence*, in Chomsky's (1965) reformulation. The goal of an adequate linguistic description is to capture what a speaker/hearer knows when he/she 'knows' a given language. The emphasis in the case of Saussure's langue was on the social system or institution of language itself. In the case of competence, this system is regarded as internalized, lodged in the mental storehouse of individuals. Competence thus attributes langue—the social system of language—to individuals as a personal property, and this loss of the social fact axiom is one of modern linguistics' major departures from the original Saussurian system.

Synchrony-diachrony. The dichotomy between the synchronic and the diachronic methods is the best starting point for this exposition.

Synchrony is a simultaneous view of all the patterns of langue at a single theoretical instant. This synchronic view is an invention needed to identify *linguistic relations.* The idea is that langue is a *system of relations.* This idea in turn engenders the concept of the frozen-in-time synchronic view, the view in which all the relations of langue are available to the linguist at the same panoramic instant.

Diachrony is the opposite concept—change on some timescale (the actual scale to be specified). To Saussure, change meant historical change—changes over decades, if not centuries. (Language ontogenesis is also diachronic with a time scale of months, while microgenesis, the process of concern here, is diachronic on a scale of seconds.) Synchrony and diachrony are different approaches to language. Only the synchronic is concerned with the system of langue. Thus, to Saussure, linguistics was necessarily committed to the synchronic method.

This is because historical change can break the relationships that connect words within the system of L. As a result, facts are lost from the system of langue—e.g., a word is no longer felt to be derived from another word. In Latin, the word for 'enemy', *inimicus,* derived from that for 'friend', *amicus,* by adding a negative prefix:

amicus $\Rightarrow$ in + imicus (phonetic adjustment of 'a' to 'i').

Historical vicissitudes then impacted the words separately, so that by the time we reach French all sense of negation has been lost:

ami $\nRightarrow$ ennemi ('en' is no longer a negative prefix—it is now simply the first syllable of a monomorphemic word, and this is also the case for English "enemy," which derived in turn from French "ennemi").

Saussure's conclusion: to see the true relationships of L, it is necessary to *halt the historical process* and look at the relations that obtain at a given theoretical moment—that is, to shun the diachronic and use the synchronic method. Thus Saussure sees language as a static system of some kind.

What are the consequences of this view? Some qualities that the synchronic view highlights are:

elements in L oppose each other
the pairing of signifiers and signifieds is arbitrary

the value of a linguistic sign reflects what it is not
the arbitrariness of the sign requires social convention.

These interconnect in ways that I'll explain.

Oppositions

In language, Saussure said, *difference is everything.* The system of L consists of elements that define each other by differing from one another. This entails that linguistic elements stand in negative or contrastive relations.

Words (the sounds of language) stand for *distinctions.* In addition to whatever they stand for in themselves, they also stand for *not* being something else.

The English words "mutton" and "sheep," to use a classic example, define one another by such contrasts—cooked sheep vs. sheep on the hoof. French "mouton" does not have this distinction. It thus enters into different oppositions from its translation equivalents, and actually could never provide an exact translation of either "sheep" or "mutton."

The picture of L that results is a mosaic with the somewhat unusual feature of squishable tesserae. Subtracting "mutton" from English would plausibly lead the adjacent "sheep" to expand and turn itself into something like French "mouton."

Each sign is thus opposed to other signs. The oppositions take place along two axes simultaneously: the *syntagmatic* and the *paradigmatic.*

Syntagmatic. Such oppositions are between signs in the same 'syntagm'—a sequence of signs producing some syntagmatic value or values. Syntagmatic values arise from contrasts of the words in sequences. A sentence is one kind of 'syntagm'; values arise from combinations of subjects and predicates. Being a subject or predicate is not a property of any word; it is a product of entering into a certain syntagmatic opposition. A predicate itself is another syntagm that defines a main verb and a direct object (in the case of a transitive construction like "hit the ball"). These are also syntagmatic values and are purely relational, arising out of oppositions within this syntagm (hence such examples as "the boy talked to the girl" and "the girl talked to the boy," where reversing the order of words induces an exchange of syntagmatic values).

Paradigmatic. These are relations between signs with something (a 'paradigm') in common. Both English and French have a word for woolly barnyard animals. However, in the two languages, they have different paradigmatic oppositions. Again, an axis of opposition, now paradigmatic, creates linguistic value. In English, "sheep" and "mutton" contrast on a dimension that English encodes but lexically French does not: on the hoof vs. on the table.

How the Concepts of a Relational System, Linguistic Value, and Oppositions Interlock

Linguistic value is the essential 'substance' of language, in the Saussurian paradigm, because it encapsulates the relational organization of the system. Value arises on both the syntagmatic and paradigmatic axes; for this reason they are foundational to all the structures of langue. Linguistic value also reflects reference or word meaning. The value of "sheep" is determined in part by what the word refers to in the world but also, crucially, by what it is not (viz. not "mutton"). Another part of its value is its role in a specific syntagm. And it is value, of both kinds, that the synchronic method, and only the synchronic method, reveals. Finally, value in general will differ from language to language, even for translation 'equivalents'; this is because value is a product of the relations that constitute langue, and langues differ.

Current Versions of Syntagmatic and Paradigmatic

In keeping with the Jonathan Culler (1976) statement quoted at the start of this chapter, linguistics as an academic field has remained true to the Saussurian tradition for the past century. The extrapolation of Saussurian concepts to current linguistics is evident in several modern grammatical theories. L continues to be conceptualized as a system of differences along the syntagmatic and paradigmatic axes and is still conceptualized as a static object. The axes of contrast are not always on the surface and the Saussurian pedigree is not always acknowledged in terms that make it evident.

Syntagmatic

The syntagmatic axis is the most straightforward extrapolation. The tree diagrams or their bracketed equivalents familiar in grammars sketch syntagmatic values. For example:

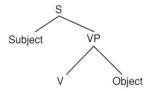

VP (verb phrase) is one syntagm and V (verb) and Object contrast syntagmatically within it—the V makes the object *into* an object (in other words, 'object' exists only relationally—that is, syntagmatically). The sentence as a whole is another syntagm, within which the V-Object syntagm contrasts with the Subject, and this makes it into a predicate, another syntagmatic value. Thus, phrase structure, as classically described, portrays syntagmatic values—each node is a focus of a specific labeled value, and the branches are the syntagmatic contrasts themselves.

Paradigmatic

The extension of the paradigmatic axis is less obvious but is more characteristic of the current state of formal linguistics. The paradigmatic examples that Saussure offered were words: "mouton," "sheep," "mutton," and the like. He had thought of the possibility of extending the paradigmatic axis to larger linguistic units, and in this way define the linguistic values of phrases and sentences, but he apparently never carried this program out and only mentioned it as a possible line of future development. In the first of what came to be known as transformational-generative grammars (Chomsky 1957, 1965, 1981a,b, 1995), a major breakthrough was to extend the idea of a paradigmatic opposition to larger units, specifically phrases, clauses, and sentences. The transformations after which the theory was named made the paradigmatic relations between such larger units explicit by stating the relations or contrasts between them. A good illustration is the active-passive sentence opposition ("John hit the ball" vs. "the ball was hit by John"). In the syntax, the contrast was originally stated by a 'passive transformation' and this transformation made the paradigmatic contrast between the two forms of sentence explicit. A more complicated example is the analysis Chomsky developed in his original presentation of the new linguistics, *Syntactic Structures*, to analyze the ambiguity of the sentence, "John found the boy studying in the library." The analysis was, in effect, that this string of words belongs to two possible—without using this term—*paradigmatic contrasts* and thus has two sets of such oppositions. This was taken to be the basis of the ambiguity.

Parameters Example

Transformational grammars have continued to evolve and recent versions have done away with even the eponymous transformations. Nonetheless, the basic Saussurian assumptions remain. In particular, paradigmatic oppositions remain, although they are often now buried (even from their authors, one imagines). Indeed, it is unlikely that the static model that (despite its name) transformational-generative grammar is, could be formulated without paradigmatic oppositions occurring somewhere within it.

The concept of a *parameter* has become an important construct in recent versions of these grammars, as described in Chomsky (1981a, 1995) (see Baker 2001). Old-style transformations like the passive described oppositions on paradigmatic axes, but did not identify the axes themselves. Parameters do identify paradigmatic axes: this seems to be at least one important difference. The array of constructions sharing a given parameter is then the oppositions. The theory envisions each separate langue in a particular state within a universal 'parameter space', or set of paradigmatic axes, a unique configuration of on and off values (Chomsky 1995). The parameter space is imagined to be hugely complex, but ordered. While this program breaks in some ways with the past, the theory stays entirely within the Saussurian framework.

To give an example, one parameter defines where the head of a phrase goes.[3] The particular setting of the head direction parameter—whether initial in the phrase or at the end—captures a paradigmatic axis. Instead of transformations, the parameter setting maps across a range of syntactic environments, and these are the contrasts. Baker (2001) presents an interesting table listing opposite word orders in English and Japanese over a range of syntactic environments. For example, verbs precede direct objects in English and follow them in Japanese; verbs precede prepositional phrases in English and

---

3. The head is the controlling element of the phrase, such as the head noun of a noun phrase. It determines the syntagmatic value of the larger phrase of which it is a part—thus a noun phrase, regardless of its internal complexity, still has the syntagmatic value of a noun.

follow postpositional phrases in Japanese; complementizers ('that', 'which', etc.) precede embedded clauses in English and follow them in Japanese; and so forth (Baker 2001, table 3.1). These contrasts comprise one paradigmatic axis in both languages—in English, part of the paradigmatic value of a direct object derives from its contrast on the head-initial setting with other head-initial forms, prepositional phrases, complementizers preceding clauses, etc. In Japanese, part of the paradigmatic value of the same entity derives from *its* contrast across the same range with head-final forms, postpositional phrases, clauses preceding complementizers, etc.

The point here is simply that the paradigmatic axis has a certain inevitability and shows up repeatedly (and in unexpected places) over a range of grammatical theories. It is this continual reappearance of the Saussurian paradigm that, by now, may be acting as a brake on further insights into language itself.

Cognitive Grammar

The approach known as cognitive grammar arose in strong reaction to the generative tradition and seems motivated by the same sense noted at the start of this chapter, that the Saussurian paradigm is facing an impasse. Departing from Saussurian arbitrariness (see below), forms are not treated as separable from meaning, and an ability to conceptualize grammars in which the arbitrariness axiom is relaxed is an important achievement of this new paradigm. Langacker (2000), for example, describes the foundations of clausal transitivity as follows:

> There is, then, a natural correlation between this idealized cognitive model [the 'canonical event conception'] and the structure of a transitive finite clause. When a canonical event is coded linguistically in the maximally unmarked way, the clausal head is a verb that designates the agent-patient interaction, the agent and patient being coded by the subject and direct object nominals, respectively. Non-focal participants to the profiled interaction . . . are expressed as obliques. (p. 25)

Langacker identifies the dynamic dimension and considers accessing it a long-range goal of cognitive grammar. With welcome intellectual honesty he recognizes that this has not yet been achieved, but feels that accessing and describing this dimension is only a matter of time (in this he moves beyond the generative school, which does not even appear to recognize a dynamic dimension). However, I do not agree that cognitive grammar is equipped to handle this problem or that it is necessarily on the right track to doing so. In critical respects it remains wedded to the Saussurian synchronic axiom. Its achivement is to discover how the *forms* language, seen as objects, incorporate solidified images and metaphors.[4] I will explain this by reference to Langacker's discussion of a true dynamic phenomenon, the updating of discursive focal points. My point will be that, while the phenomenon is dynamic, the grammatical model confronting it does not provide the tools with which to understand or portray such updating on the dynamic dimension.

Langacker writes, "Invoking a reference point is thus an inherently dynamic process involving a shift of focus from the more readily accessible reference point to a target accessed through it," and provides invented examples such as "in the kitchen, on the counter, next to the toaster, sat a cute little mouse," which requires constantly shifting foci and reference points (pp. 363–364). There is here a succession of reference points, but note where the locus of change lies: it is not at the level of the emerging forms; the forms are treated as static objects in the Saussurian sense (as suggested in the long quote from Langacker above, forms are fixed configurations with meaning paradigms like the canonical event representation, which can be matched up with communicative intentions but whose own emergence is not regarded as part of the grammar). The succession of focal points is driven merely by the speaker's perceptual experience. There is nothing of the forms themselves emerging nor of an imagery-language dialectic. I consider this analysis therefore to address the engagement of perception with linguistic objects but not the dynamic dimension itself, in which thought and speech develop through time (in later chapters I make crucial use of two cognitive linguistic models, Talmy 2000 and Goldberg 1995; although perhaps not 'grammars', they also are tied to the synchronic axiom).

In presenting the synchronic axiom and its role in current linguistics I run some risk of drawing the contrast of the static and the dynamic too starkly. Aspects of the dynamic dimension might conceivably develop their own recurring 'grammars' (or, better, *grooves*) of change. For example, asymmetric

---

4. Cognitive grammar includes categories like 'image' and other seemingly dynamic elements. However, they remain, as far as I can tell, fundamentally static in conception. They do not emphasize the concept of change but instead treat 'images' as synchronic summations or templates. The concept of a blend found in Fauconnier & Turner (2002) is an ingenious innovation in this vein, a kind of snapshot of the outcome of a dynamic process, but is not the process of change itself; neither does it provide theoretical space for this kind of process to occur; the synchronic axiom remains. For a recent extension of blending theory to gesture, see Parrill & Sweetser (2004).

two-handed gestures, in which one hand is motionless and provides thematic coherence for the other hand, which is active—an arrangement codified in the form standards of many sign languages—illustrate such recurrent grooves (see Chapter 5, subsection "Layering with two hands"; also Enfield 2004).[5] But cognitive grammars—those open to the dynamic dimension—remain static in their basic assumptions, and do not capture these kinds of dynamic accommodations.

THE LINGUISTIC SIGN

A sign for Saussure has two parts: the *signifier*, or 'sound image'; and the *signified*, or the concept it conveys. For example, the English word "tree" consists of the sound we make when we say "tree" (the signifier) and the idea of a tree (the signified), as illustrated in figure 3.3.

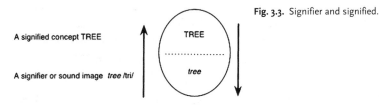

A signified concept TREE

A signifier or sound image *tree* /tri/

Fig. 3.3. Signifier and signified.

Arbitrariness and Binding

The bond between the sound and idea halves of the linguistic sign is 'radically arbitrary'. This means that the form of the signifier sound image is unpredictable from the identity of the signified concept. "Tree" is not predictable

5. Enfield proposes that gestural layering is a 'construction' that exhibits 'segmentation' and 'combinatorics', yet I do not see that the layering in his examples involves static forms, as he suggests they might. In his Lao examples, speakers create gestures that depict the construction and function of native fish traps. The gestures start as two symmetric hands and then switch to two asymmetric hands, in which the static hand shows the presence of the trap while the active hand depicts various events involving the fish inside. This organization of the gesture pretty clearly derives from the shape and functionality of the trap itself, not from standards of form for gestures qua gestures. There is undeniably recurrence of form but it seems fully explained by the imagery, and one can equally find situations commencing with a single hand, then shifting to two asymmetric hands, if the imagery warrants, violating a presumed 'symmetry-dominance grammar' of gesture. See the discussion of conventions in Chapter 2; also, the catchment discussions in Chapter 4.2 and Chapter 5.

from TREE. Because the connection is arbitrary, both signifier and signified must be specified. In a motivated sign, the signifier would predictable from the signified, and a new signifier could be generated whenever the speaker wished to convey the concept (similar to gestures). The up and down arrows of the diagram, however, show that in arbitrary signs, there is binding in both the direction of the signifier and the signified. The word "tree" is a sign only insofar as it is connected to the idea of a tree. Similarly, the concept of a tree is a sign only when attached to a signifier, "tree"; without the connection, it remains a concept but is not part of language. Saussure said the two sides of the sign are unsplittable, and likened signifier and signified to the two sides of a coin.

Semantic Satiation

One can directly experience the unsplittability of the sign. If you stare continuously at a word (alternatively, listen to it over and over), the signifier and signified eventually appear to fall apart. The aim of the exercise is not to alter vision or hearing but to disrupt the internal organization of the sign. At first the word is just the familiar "tree" but soon it changes character. You continue to see the letters but they no longer make the word; it, as such, has vanished. The phenomenon is called 'semantic satiation' (first identified by Severance & Washburn 1907), or loss of the signified concept from the signifier (visual or acoustic). This loss is in keeping with Saussure's dictum that a sign is unsplittable. Since the signifier remains in place and present to perception, the word ceases to function as a linguistic sign; the unsplittable has split, and the sign disappears. The result is an unsettling mixture of the familiar (letters) and the unfamiliar. It's not that the content of the word has been forgotten. The satiation effect is confined to the modality being satiated—if you stare at TREE until satiation sets in, you are still able to *hear* "tree" as a word in the normal way; and vice versa, if you satiate on the sound image /tri/, you can still *read* the word. It is specifically the signifier-signified link that is satiated, and this fact establishes the existence of such links in the internal composition of signs.

LANGUAGE AS A SOCIAL FACT

To Saussure langue was irrevocably a *social fact.* This Durkheimian idea was current when Saussure lectured; in a more current idiom it would be that langue is a socially constituted norm. By social fact Saussure meant a sociocultural institution. Langue, he argued, exists at the level of the social collectivity. It is held together by the glue of conventions. Arbitrariness in fact requires this glue. He wrote, for example, "The community is necessary if values that owe their existence solely to usage and general acceptance are to be set up; by himself the individual is incapable of fixing a single value" (1966, p. 113). The social fact axiom is missing from many present-day analogues of Saussure, having been replaced in the concept of 'competence' by a kind of individual psychology (see below).

Arbitrariness and Social Fact

It is the 'opacity' of the linguistic sign that requires social conventions; and signs must be arbitrary in order to have space for social facts. These axioms support each other. In the absence of constraints from the signified concept, *only convention (social facts) can hold signifier and signified pairs together.* By the same token, *the arbitrariness of the sign is a critical component of what makes language into a social fact.* Saussure put it this way, together with the earlier remark that the individual is powerless to fix any linguistic value: "The arbitrary nature of the sign explains in turn why the social fact alone can create a linguistic system" (1966, p. 113).

Signs are arbitrary in two senses:

1. The *pairing* of signifier and signified is arbitrary in that the concept of a tree, for example, doesn't specify the sound image of the word, *tree*. On a structural level, cognitive linguistics claims that meaning does specify form.
2. The signified *concept* is an arbitrary way of dividing up reality. "Mouton" divides the world differently from "mutton" or "sheep," and neither division is given by the world.

Both senses of being arbitrary arise from the underlying reality that *forms* are not generated from *meanings*.[6] This statement distinguishes linguistic signs from iconic, metaphoric, and other nonconventionalilzed gestures.

---

6. On the whole, but Saussure also identified partially motivated signs, such as some English number terms; "nine" and "ten" are arbitrary but "nineteen" is not.

Competence and Social Fact

What do we say, then, about the modern concept of competence? As a technical concept, 'competence' is langue attributed to the individual mind, converting it from a social to a psychological fact. This weakening of the Saussurian paradigm occurred without substituting something of value in return; the social fact axiom was, and remains, a pillar of the entire interconnected set of axioms, without which the static edifice totters on the edge of collapse. Moreover, to psychologize the social reality of langue obscures the very psychology it claims to include. Müller, in *Metaphors, Dead and Alive, Sleeping and Waking* (2004a), lucidly explains the effect of this shift from social fact to individual psychology on the role assigned to the very psychology it purports to move to center stage; in fact it reduces it to a kind of markup of langue structures; she writes,

> [L]anguage use is the defective realization of the competence of an idealized speaker. Thus, the relation between the level of the system and the level of the individual is conceived of as relatively unproblematic, and merely a question of how to model the facets of the linguistic system so that they are all accessed and processed in a plausible order. Use is instantiation of a linguistic system, not a possible point of theoretical and empirical departure. (pp. 0.16–17)

In this book, the system of language is presented as a "possible point of theoretical and empirical departure" by considering 'competence' as one dimension of a multidimensional dialectic process, assigning it a functional role within the process. Although it seems an oxymoron to say that langue is *both* an individual and a social fact, this is what we must conclude, despite the modern silence concerning the social fact side of language. And moreover the peeling off of the social fact axiom is conceptually unnecessary. The key to resolving the paradox is that the social system of langue is internalized by the person during his/her psychological development. What individuals are competent *at* is a system that has sociocultural reality, a set of 'social facts'. The reality of this dependence on the social constitution of langue is seen from the course of events in linguistic innovation. As Saussure noted, a new word is easily coined—I once attempted to invent, with the help of Nobuko B. McNeill, a new term for 'gesture studies', "temaniotics," half Japanese, half (ancient) Greek! However, our word did not become an element of English langue precisely because it did not make the leap to the realm of 'social facts'; it remained stubbornly ego-bound. It would be of interest for linguistics as a field to consider once again the implications, in a modern context, of Saussure's original conception of langue as a social fact.

PUTTING IT ALL TOGETHER: THE STATIC DIMENSION

To see langue (or competence) a static view is crucial. Even cognitive linguistics must assume it. All the features of langue—langue rather than parole, synchronic rather than diachronic, oppositions, the arbitrariness of signs, and language as a social fact—imply a static view. The concept of competence, in which langue is claimed to be a property of the individual, also implies the same static view. The picture of language that emerges from the static axioms is one view that we consider. It differs from the dynamic view to be described below. Ultimately, we must find a way to combine them.

THE 'NEW' HISTORICAL SAUSSURE

At the time of his death Saussure was working out a further and more nuanced view that combines the structuralism of langue with the more dynamic requirements of parole (Saussure 2002). Roy Harris, in a *Times Literary Supplement* review (26 July 2002), describes the recent publication in France of notes written by Saussure that sketch an emerging view that is not unlike the theory to be presented in the following chapters, but worked out on a completely different basis, Saussure's contemplation of the reality of linguistic forms.[7]

Saussure was apparently preparing to replace the langue-parole opposition in favor of "l'essence double du langage" (this and all following quotes from Harris 2002, p. 30). The dialectic to be described later also starts from the observation of the 'dual essence of language', and there are further similarities. Harris writes, "Saussure is inviting us to see language (not languages) as having a dual structure," and further, the system of language itself, as the synchronic method reveals it, "exists only in the praxis of verbal communication, which is seen as presupposing and dependent on contextual factors of all kinds." And

7. Harris has revised his own statement on Saussure to take into account this discovery of an 'integrative' approach (Harris 2003).

still further, crucially, "Words and their meanings exist, [Saussure] tells us, only in the awareness we have of them, or bring to bear on them, in any given instance."

We shall see all these prescient statements echoed in other terms in the dialectic of imagery and language to follow.

THE DYNAMIC SIDE OF LANGUAGE

The next tradition—the 'dynamic' or 'processural'—is not meant as a replacement of the classic Saussurian static view. It is, rather, another dimension of language. But ultimately, we have to consider how the static and dynamic dimensions combine and in this way recover Saussure's essential duality. It is then that we shall see, in the form of a dialectic of unlike cognitive modes, the explanatory value of Saussure's insights into the dynamic and contextually dependent nature of language. In addition, the imagery-language dialectic depends on speakers' intuitions of linguistic form at specific points, fulfilling Saussure's further insight, that the reality of linguistic form is not independent of the awareness of the speakers and the listeners who are using them. The way to combine the static and dynamic is to find a role for linguistic awareness in the imagery-language dialectic, and this role is stopping the process: in a dynamic process a growing awareness of intuitively complete forms ultimately brings the imagery-language dialectic to a close. This role I take to be consistent with Saussure's remark that "words and meanings exist only in the awareness of the speaker."

The historical figure who best articulates the dynamic view in all its richness is Vygotsky, writing in the 1930s (1986). Vygotsky argued that meaning is a process; that language impacts thought; that thought impacts language; and, finally, that these mutual impacts are outcomes of a developmental process that occurred once in the history of homo sapiens and occurs again in the development of each child.

Some quotes give the gist of Vygotsky's conception of language and thought: *Language impacts cognition:*

> Each word is . . . already a generalization. Generalization is a verbal act of thought and reflects reality in quite another way than sensation and perception reflect it. (1986, p. 6)

Meaning is a process in both thought and language:

> [M]eaning is an act of thought in the full sense of the term. But at the same time, meaning is an inalienable part of the word as such, and thus it belongs in the realm of language as much as in the realm of thought. (1986, p. 6)

The topic is verbal thought:

> Verbal thought...does not by any means include all forms of thought or all forms of speech. There is a vast area of thought that has no direct relation to speech....Nor are there any psychological reasons to derive all forms of speech activity from thought.... [T]he fusion of thought and speech, in adults as well as in children, is a phenomenon limited to a circumscribed area. (1986, pp. 88–89)

The result of joining speech and thought is a new form of thought and action:

> The use of signs leads humans to a specific structure of behavior that breaks away from biological development and creates new forms of culturally-based psychological processes. (Vygotsky 1978, p. 40)

Scope of the Dynamic Model: The Fusion of Thought and Speech

Figure 3.4 illustrates the scope of the dialectic model is the overlapping region of thought and speech; excluded are thought without speech and speech without thought. (An example of speech without thought is rote repetition; thought without speech might be the immediate perception of musical forms without verbal description; many other examples can be found.)

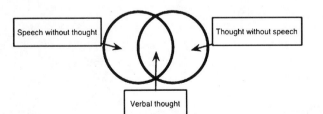

Speech without thought

Thought without speech

Verbal thought

Fig. 3.4. Verbal thought.

Structure, Function, and Inner Speech

Inner Speech

Inner speech for Vygotsky is not merely speech without articulation. It has a unique structure, closer to pure thought, but thought shaped by its intimate involvement with language. Egocentric speech, as seen in children, is contextualized and reduced. Inner speech, Vygotsky believed, was similar to egocentric speech, yet more evolved in its dependence on context and its reduction to cognitive essentials. In its final, most 'inner' form, inner speech consists of *psychological predicates*, in effect, pure differentiations of significant information from the immediate context.[8] These concepts will prove invaluable in the explication of the imagery-language dialectic and the growth point in Chapter 4.

Growth Points

Growth points are considered to be psychological predicates and are, accordingly, units of inner speech, in Vygotsky's terms. However, unlike inner speech, they are not spoken or even necessarily speakable—to get to speech, something further takes place, and this is what will be termed *unpacking*. Growth points are 'unpacked' into surface linguistic forms, such as constructions (Goldberg 1995). Vygotsky considered inner speech to be autochthonous, speech for oneself, while external speech was connected to the social interactive discourse. Another difference accordingly is that a growth point is always connected to the discourse context, including any social interactive aspects. In the growth point version, the distinction between inner and social speech blurs. But there is still a difference of function between them, which for Vygotsky was the most important distinction. Functionally, the growth point is where a new verbal idea unit takes form in the stream of the speaker's experience; external speech reconfigures this idea to fit the demands of langue. The context of speaking, including the social-dynamic context, affects this process throughout, including the growth point itself. This cross-cutting role of the social context of speech is

---

8. Comparable to 'rhematic' content (Halliday 1985), but unlike this linguistic concept, a psychological predicate is not tied to particular sentence components and can be any linguistic element or elements, with or without articulation, that capture the point of differentiation within the immediate context of speaking.

the dynamic counterpart to the importance given by Saussure to 'social facts', now formulated as a socially geared *process* of meaning creation. The social dimension of the growth point is discussed specifically in Chapter 4.4.

Minimal Psychological Units

A minimal unit in Vygotsky's sense is the smallest psychological unit that *retains the essential properties of being a whole*. In the case of gesture and speech, a 'whole' entails a gesture and the linguistic category or categories carried by its synchronous co-expressive speech. The concept rules out either speech or gesture as fundamental; only their *joint presence* is a minimal psychological unit.

A minimal psychological unit in Vygotsky's sense should not be thought of as an element in an information processing analysis. The aim of information processing is to reduce complex processes to simpler processes that are *unlike* the whole (Palmer & Kimchi 1986). The minimal psychological unit for Vygotsky is *like* the whole. In contrast to Vygotsky's approach, the information processing approach is reductive—some 'intelligent' process is boiled down to a concatenation of simpler processes. The reduction is carried out recursively until a defined theoretical limit is reached, the level of primitive terms for the model.

However, terminology here is confusing. In information processing the primitive to which reduction is brought is often called a 'unit'. Vygotsky calls this level that of the 'element' and terms his own minimal unit the 'unit' as well. I will continue to employ Vygotsky's terminology.

The following quotes elaborate upon Vygotsky's definition of a minimal psychological unit. He speaks of *two analytic methods*:

> The first method analyzes complex psychological wholes into elements. . . . It leads us . . . into serious errors by ignoring the unitary nature of the process under study. . . . Psychology, which aims at a study of complex holistic systems, must replace the method of analysis into elements with the method of analysis into units. (1986, pp. 4–5)

A *unit* here means

> a product of analysis which, in distinction from elements, possesses all the basic properties of a whole. Further, these properties must be a living portion of the

unified whole which cannot be broken down further. (Vygotsky, *Thinking and Speech* [Russian, 1934], p. 9, quoted in Zinchenko 1985, p. 97)

And this definition identifies *a unit in which a dialectic can take place:*

> A psychology . . . must discover the indissoluble units that preserve the properties inherent in the unified whole. It must find the units in which contradictory properties appear. (Vygotsky, *Thinking and Speech* [Russian, 1934], quoted in Zinchenko 1985, p. 97)

Vygotsky also maintained that the minimal unit was 'word meaning'. However, for our purposes, word meaning is too tightly linked to a static view of language. I will propose that the *growth point*, in which the 'contradictory properties' of imagery and language appear, is a unit better suited to Vygotsky's own definitions. We take advantage, in this way, of the empirical data of speech and gesture that Vygotsky, working in the 1920s and 1930s, could not have been aware of. I believe this change is true to Vygotsky's overall conception and analysis of complex processes into the smallest units that retain the essential property of being wholes (the whole being, in our case, a speech-gesture combination).

The Dynamic Dimension

Two further quotations from Vygotsky relate the dynamic dimension of language to two essential emergent features: the interpenetration of language and thought and the fact that meaning is not fixed but rather is continually developing. Vygotsky's thoughts are similar to Saussure's final efforts to define an essential dual essence of language (there is no reason to suppose that Vygotsky was aware of Saussure's notes):

Language and thought impact each other:

> The meaning of a word represents such a close amalgam of thought and language that it is hard to tell whether it is a phenomenon of speech or a phenomenon of thought. (1986, p. 212)

Word meanings are dynamic entities:

> Word meanings are dynamic rather than static formations. They change as the child develops; they change also with the various ways in which thought functions. (1986, pp. 212, 217)

VYGOTSKY ON DIALECTIC

Definition

A dialectic implies ✓

(a) a conflict or opposition of some kind, and
(b) resolution of the conflict through change.

A dialectic is inherently dynamic. It presupposes Vygotsky's concept of a minimal unit—a smallest unit retaining the property of a whole. It is within this unit that the dialectic opposition takes place.

Vygotsky writes about the dialectic in a number of places; the most famous statement is:

> The relation of thought to word is not a thing but a process, a continual ✓
> movement back and forth from thought to word and from word to thought. In
> that process, the relation of thought to word undergoes changes that themselves
> may be regarded as development in the functional sense. Thought is not merely
> expressed in words; it comes into existence through them. (1986, p. 218)

And he *ties the dialectic to change:*

> Thought undergoes many changes as it turns into speech. It does not merely
> find expression in speech; it finds its reality and form. (1986, p. 219)

And finally, he brings out an insight not unlike Saussure's, that in a dynamic ✓
process it is *impossible to pick out preestablished elements:*

> Thought, unlike speech, does not consist of separate units. When I wish to
> communicate the thought that today I saw a barefoot boy in a blue shirt
> running down the street, I do not see every item separately: the boy, the shirt,
> its blue color, his running, the absence of shoes. I conceive of all this in one
> thought, but I put it into separate words. . . . In [the] mind the whole thought
> is present at once, but in speech it has to be developed successively . . . the
> transition from thought to word leads through meaning. (1986, p. 251)

Necessity of the Minimal Psychological Unit

The upshot of the concept of a minimal psychological unit is a different approach to meaning. In an information processing model, meaning is broken down into primitives, or 'atoms' of meaning. The converse process is composition, in which primitives are assembled to construct meanings during production. An information processing theory is thus structured by composition and decomposition.

In a dialectic, on the other hand, meanings maintain the property of a global whole. Composition or decomposition don't apply, because the whole remains intact. Unpacking into articulated linguistic forms continues this process through modification of the whole, by relating lexical items and grammatical patterns to it; but the whole is never lost.

The Role of Context

There is also a contrasting treatment of context. In information processing, context is outside the model and treated as one among many 'inputs'. In Levelt's *Speaking* model, for example, context is an input along with the speaker's intention, his situational and encyclopedic knowledge, and other data streaming into the construction of the 'preverbal message' (Levelt 1989). This fits the ethos of information processing, where modular units combine according to networked links. Context, which is inherently noncategorial and therefore not reducible to a module, must necessarily be excluded. In the dialectic model, on the other hand, context is not 'input', it is an essential component of thinking for and while speaking, inseparable from the process itself. This is a fundamental difference: an information processing framework is unable to put context at the core. It is not a matter of having overlooked context; the conceptual foundations are not present to include it. Context in this scheme is necessarily 'preverbal', because the model fundamentally lacks the machinery to incorporate context into the utterance generation process itself.

PUTTING IT ALL TOGETHER: THE DYNAMIC DIMENSION

In the following chapters, Vygotsky's ideas will appear in a new guise. For Vygotsky, language is a *process* in which thought and language interact over time in a dialectic and change according to context. The result of merging thought and language is *a new psychological function*—both phylogenetically new, and ontogenetically new in the growth of the individual child. These concepts are developed by means of a phenomenon that was inaccessible to Vygotsky, the tight coordination of language and gesture, a coordination so tight that they can be usefully regarded as two sides of a single thing/process.

Imagery-Language Dialectic

This 'chapter' is a family of four subchapters (4.1–4.4). The subchapters logically comprise a single extended discussion of the imagery-language dialectic, presenting it conceptually and as a phenomenon on the dynamic dimension of language. The discussion begins with this dialectic; then it turns to the growth point as the proposed minimal unit of it, including a detailed case study; the discussion then elaborates it with various linked issues under the heading of 'extensions'. The final subchapter is a further 'extension' that relates the growth point to the social-interactive experience of the speaker. I have divided the discussion into parts primarily for ease of access, breaking up in this way a twenty-five-thousand-word behemoth. The chapters correspond to natural subunits and can be read independently; but they need to be understood as a whole and should be read in the order presented. Collectively, they look at Saussurian parole, or performance, from a new angle. The fresh approach consists in regarding performance as organized as a dialectic of unlike cognitive modes. This dialectic, I suggest, is the key to the evocation, organization, and ultimate execution of meaningful actions shaped to take form in discourse. Both modes, static and dynamic, are essential components of performance. A dialectic, moreover, naturally incorporates the context of speaking, and we shall develop a theoretical description of context as part of the analysis. Such a dialectic model is self-motivating and self-directed and does not need the guiding hand (hidden or otherwise) of an executive.

Chapter 4.1 presents the concept of dialectic and relates it to the concept of a material carrier of meaning. It also describes how the two dimensions of language—the static and the dynamic—combine within this dialectic framework.

Chapter 4.2 presents the growth point as a minimal unit of imagery-language dialectic and gives a detailed case study. This case study shows, among other things, the necessity of incorporating context to explain the imagery-language dialectic.

Chapter 4.3 considers various extensions of the growth point concept, including some seeming exceptions (which are explained); gesture-speech mismatches; the role of affect; gestures in sign language; how gestures improve other cognitive performances; and others.

Chapter 4.4 is the place of intersubjective content and how it enters thinking and speaking without reducing the mind to a mere cognitive scratchpad.

Dialectic and Material Carriers

This subchapter introduces concepts that will be important in the next sub-chapter on the growth point, and in the two subsequent subchapters on extensions of this concept. First is the concept of imagery-language dialectic itself. Next is the concept of a material carrier, which will be used to elaborate a theory of the role played by gesture in a dialectic. Third is the 'H-model' and the concept of 'cognitive being' as a replacement of 'representation'. Finally, I ◄— will consider what it means, from a material carrier viewpoint, for gestures to be absent from speech.

OPENING EXAMPLE

Figure 2.1 on p. 23 illustrates how we can interpret a gesture, together with its co-occurring speech, as the embodiment of an individual's thinking at a specific moment. The speaker was describing one of the episodes from an animated cartoon stimulus she has just seen. A character is entering a drainpipe on the side of a building and climbing up it on the inside (previously, she had described how he climbed up the same pipe on the outside). The speaker described this event with, "and he goes **up thróugh** the pipe this time." Synchronously, in the boldfaced section, she raised her right hand upward, her palm up and fingers and thumb spread apart: a kind of open basket shape moving up, as illustrated (the moment she is saying the vowel of "through").

The gesture embodies several meanings—the character (the hand itself), rising up (the trajectory), and interiority (the open shape). Such a combination of meanings in a single symbol is imagistic: ideas that require temporal sequencing and combination in speech are concentrated and instantaneous in the gesture. The gesture has a unitary meaning, something like 'rising hollowness', which is not a meaning cataloged in the lexicon of English but appropriate in the immediate context of speaking. The gesture does not seem to have been a conscious communicative effort. The speaker's gaze was not directed at it nor was there any indication that it was something other than an unconscious movement with semantic significance, produced with a speech segment conveying the same significance.

When we see a gesture like this, what are we actually seeing? Motion, to be sure: something going on while the person is speaking, but I propose that we are also seeing verbal thinking in the form of action (cf. Beattie 2003). The gesture and its synchronous speech are components of verbal thinking, separate but combined, and they merge into minimal units of a Vygotskian kind, termed here 'growth points' (GPs). The growth point is the minimal unit of an imagery-language dialectic. The combination of "up through" and the rising hollowness meaning is an example of a GP (though its context also must be defined; how to do this is the focus of Chapter 4.2). This subchapter lays the ground for a discussion of the growth point and its role as a minimal dialectic unit.

WUNDT'S INSIGHT

How gesture might contribute to linguistic performance can be seen in a description of speech production written a century ago by Wilhelm Wundt, the 'father of experimental psychology' who also worked across many other areas, including what we would now call the psychology of language. Wundt observed that sentences include two modes of cognition simultaneously: the 'simultaneous' and the 'sequential'.

> From a psychological point of view, the sentence is both a simultaneous and a sequential structure. It is simultaneous because at each moment it is present in consciousness as a totality even though the individual subordinate elements may occasionally disappear from it. It is sequential because the configuration changes from moment to moment in its cognitive condition as individual

constituents move into the focus of attention and out again one after another. (Wundt 1970, 21).[1]

When co-expressive speech and a gesture synchronize, we see something that is both simultaneous and sequential, as Wundt envisioned. There is a combination of two semiotic frameworks for the same underlying idea, each with its own expressive potential. Speech and gesture are co-expressive but nonredundant in that each has its own means for packaging meanings.

How do the semiotic frameworks differ then? One way, obviously, is how they distribute information in time. In speech, ideas are separated and arranged sequentially; in gesture, they are instantaneous in the sense that the meaning of the gesture is not parceled out over time (even though the gesture may take time to occur, its full meaning is immediately present). In the example above, upward motion and interiority were distributed across time in the words "up" and "through" but were concentrated in a single gesture. As Wundt described, these contrasting modes are themselves simultaneous, and are exactly so.

The upshot is that the synchrony of gestures and speech puts different semiotic modes together at the same moment of the speaker's cognitive experience. This is the key to the dialectic. The modes are opposites in multiple ways—global meaning with analytic meaning; idiosyncratic and created on the fly with prespecified form-meaning pairings; imagery with forms regulated by conventions. Figure 2.1 illustrates all of these dualities: the gesture components (the hand, the trajectory, the shape) are meaningful only because of the meaning of the whole. In speech, conversely, the words, "goes," "up," and "through" are meaningful on their own; by combining, they compose the meaning of the whole. The gesture is idiosyncratic and had just been created, original both as a form and as a conceptual object (the new idea of an 'upward going hollowness' or somesuch); and, finally, the gesture form is motivated by imagery, in contrast to the largely arbitrary morphology of the words.

'INHABITING' GESTURES

The entire conception of speech and gesture is moved to a new level when we draw on Merleau-Ponty (1962) for insight into the duality of gesture and

1. I am grateful to Zenzi Griffin for alerting me to this passage.

language and what we can expect of gesture in a two-component process. Gesture, the instantaneous, global, nonconventional component, is "not an external accompaniment" of speech, which is the sequential, analytic, combinatoric component; it is not a "representation" of meaning, but instead meaning "inhabits" it:

> The link between the word and its living meaning is not an external accompaniment to intellectual processes, the meaning inhabits the word, and language 'is not an external accompaniment to intellectual processes'.[2] We are therefore led to recognize a gestural or existential significance to speech.... Language certainly has inner content, but this is not self-subsistent and self-conscious thought. What then does language express, if it does not express thoughts? It presents or rather it *is* the subject's taking up of a position in the world of his meanings. (p. 193)[3]

The dialectic unit, the GP, is a mechanism for this "existential content" of speech—this "taking up of a position in the world." Gesture, as part of the GP, is inhabited by the same "living meaning" that inhabits the word (and beyond that, the discourse). Thus, a deeper answer to the query—when we see a gesture, what are we seeing?—is that we see part of the speaker's current cognitive being, her very mental existence, at the moment it occurs.

IMAGERY-LANGUAGE DIALECTIC

The Dialectic

As defined in Chapter 3, a dialectic implies:

(a) a conflict or opposition of some kind, and
(b) resolution of the conflict through change.

The combination of imagery and language creates conditions for this dialectic. The combination is of unlike modes of cognition and this fact produces instability. It is this unstable combination of opposites that fuels thought and speech. Instability is an essential feature of the dialectic and is the key to the dynamic dimension.

2. Merleau-Ponty's quotation is from Gelb and Goldstein, 1925, p. 158.
3. I am indebted to Jan Arnold for this quotation.

The dialectic also creates not merely a descriptive but a *systematic* role for the static dimension. This is because change seeks repose. A grammatically complete sentence (or its approximation) is a state of repose par excellence, a natural stopping point, intrinsically static and reachable from instability. Such is the origin and explanation for organized speech output in this theory. But how is the static dimension integrated with the dynamic?

Relation of Static Forms to Dynamic Change

Neither language nor gesture is primary in this dialectic, nor is one more basic than the other. Both are necessary; gesture is not input to speech, nor is speech input to gesture; they occur together.

The Role of Linguistic Intuition

[*cf. Vygotsky*]

Formal linguistic properties, as they emerge from the dialectic, are the *outcome* of the dialectic. This outcome registers to the speaker as growing intuitions of linguistic form. The outcome has in this way psychological reality. 'Intuition' has long been an object of linguistic description.[4] Traditionally, it has been regarded as a topic in linguistic methodology, with questions having to do with its accuracy, stability, and vulnerability to expectations (the entire topic is thoroughly reviewed by Schütze 1996). Intuition, however, is also how the individual experiences the system of langue. It is the direct perception of linguistic form. Intuitions are accessible to consciousness and can play a role in the process of speaking. They do so, specifically, by *stopping* the dialectic processes: intuitions of well-formedness provide stopping points. There is a growing sense of completeness that functions as a kind of stop order, as the dialectic moves forward to its state of repose.[5]

[*She's prolixity: resists stopping too soon! Wants to get it right. | hence also his propensity to coin new words and to breach grammatical categories*]

4. A classic example is Chomsky's 'sentence' without coherent meaning but with grammatical form, which we recognize intuitively: "colorless green ideas sleep furiously" versus its ungrammatical twin, "furiously sleep ideas green colorless" and other permutations. How do we know which is grammatical and which not? Our experience of the static dimension in the form of intuitions of well-formedness distinguishes them. A dialectic sifting through a series of possible forms (and stopping points), each rejected before achieving an intuitively acceptable solution, is described in Dray and McNeill (1990) (the 'nurturing' example).

5. Linguistic form also registers in other ways psychologically. Syntactic induction (Bock 1986) is the tendency to reuse syntactic patterns in continuing discourse, patterns

In an imagery-language dialectic, intuition therefore plays an active role. Its evocation is as an element of speaking and of verbal thought, and this is the point at which the static and dynamic intersect.[6] Such a role of intuition does not presume that it is 'accurate', a question more critical for its use as a methodological probe in linguistics. It is not dependent on technical ratings of grammatical form and is not required to be invariant.

What does matter, and what gives it special status, is that during speech performance intuitions of language form are present to consciousness and, as they emerge, are able to put a brake on the dialectic. Intuitions must be accessible and graded, providing a sense of well-formedness in degrees. Intuitions tell us that *this* seems familiar and means more or less the right thing; doesn't mean the wrong thing; and can acceptably be the end to the process of change. That intuitions arise as we speak seems undeniable and a dialectic exploits them. Newmeyer (2003), in his defense of the Saussurian tradition against 'usage-based' grammatical revisions (e.g., connectionism), comments that "[g]rammar is such a poor reflection of usage because we have many more meanings to convey than could ever be supported by our grammatical resources in a reasonable period of time" (p. 693). However, intuitions as stop orders would be a good use of an underdetermined grammatical system. For intuitions to stop the process of the dialectic they are required only to approximate idea units, and as they cross the threshold of adequacy (which might vary with conditions), bring the process to a halt.

Example of Effective Stopping Points

'Effective' stopping points are those intuitively complete structures that assert themselves as stopping points even when the process of change can go further. Elena Levy (pers. com.) is carrying out a research project in which she collects (from child speakers) repeated narrative retellings of an animated cartoon stimulus. A child recounts the same story on successive days (each day to the

[margin notes, handwritten:]
✓

cf. Vysobky
re: inner
speech vs.
external
speech
|
so Sh's
prolixih →
grammatical
abondon
have the effect
of performing
inner speech

---

like the passive or ditransitive. Once used they tend to recur with elevated probability. Presumably these recurring uses are out of awareness. Natural occurrences of syntactic induction, not those in experiments, may be aspects of social mimicry (see Chapter 4.4 for examples of gesture mimicry).

6. The growth point, as explained in Chapter 4.2, models this intersection.

same listener, a feature that encourages increasingly compact descriptions). Looking across the days, we see different stopping points, with each day's stopping point a well-formed structure (intuitively recognizable), but not the structure the child is ultimately capable of reaching.

Day 1 found a stopping point in two nonsuccessive sentences that contained all the information relevant to a narration of the story. Day 2 compacted this into two successive sentences, and day 3 into a single sentence. In each case, we can interpret the stopping point as an intuitively recognized well-formed structure. The rule seems to be that the dialectic stops if it hits an intuitively complete form without degradation of significance. Day 2 is the clearest illustration. It shows compactness, but is not complete. Figure 4.1.1 is the record (a girl, seven years old).

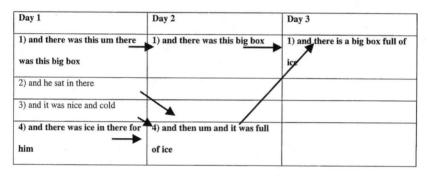

Fig. 4.1.1. Intuitively well-formed stopping points.

The process of speaking revealed in this example is not atypical. Often, it seems, we reach not the limit of some process of resolving the tension between imagery and form, but what is just good enough, as the child was doing here on days 1 and 2, with stopping points that are adequate but not the last possible such points.

Distinguishing Intuitions

Not all intuitions are plausible dialectic stop orders. To consider the possibility that some intuitions are better at this than others, I propose that intuitions can be classified under two headings. 'Intuitions-1' are one's sense of completeness or familiarity when performing or encountering linguistic performances; they are immediately apprehended and imply stop orders. 'Intuitions-2' are *examined* intuitions by a linguist-analyst. Intuitions-2 are really meta-intuitions, opinions about intuitions, informed by theoretical goals and standards, and collected in a contemplative mode. It is implausible that intuitions-2 would, or even could, be stop orders. Cumbersomeness and an activation and registration process that is fundamentally different from that engaged during an imagery-language dialectic would rule them out—meta-level reflection and contemplation versus an emerging familiarity online. Intuitions-2 have a different function: to expose and articulate the structures of which we become sensible via intuitions-1. Moreover, intuitions-1 can arise with structures that, from an intuitions-2 point of view, are imperfect. Paul Hopper, in his Chicago Linguistic Society lecture (Hopper, in press), comments on the difficulty of finding canonical examples of the English pseudocleft in actual speech corpora:

> We have seen that the canonical pseudocleft is a biclausal construction with a *wh-* part and a focus part consisting of an NP. But this pattern is seldom fully exemplified. Instead the pseudocleft typically has a more fragmentary appearance.

Hopper cites examples such as, "Of course what they're talking about this is helping the national team," which clearly is not canonical (viz., not meeting expectations for intuitions-2), but nonetheless could, with its structure of a full sentence in the second position, provide sufficient intuitions-1 to provide a stop order.

Formulating Intuitions Critically

What kinds of intuition-2 descriptions mesh gracefully with an imagery-language dialectic, to define intuition-1 stopping points? As far as I can determine, no current model is equal to this task. Each meets some requirements but misses others. In a sense, therefore, it matters little which grammatical model we refer to. One form of analysis, however, construction grammar, for a special reason to be described, comes close to what is needed.

Here are the requirements:

First, the description must transparently exhibit the speaker's sense of well-formedness (intuitions-1). Ever since Chomsky's breakthroughs (cf. Chomsky

1965), most synchronic models of the generative variety attempt to systematize the linguistic intuitions of native speakers. Such models are directly applicable to a dialectic insofar as they are interpreted as descriptions of intuitions-2, since they define potential stop orders. The field of candidate models, however, is drastically narrowed (essentially to zero) by two further goals:

Second, each derivational step must also exhibit well-formedness in that:

(a) it is not a violation of good form and
(b) it opens a commitment to a constituent that is also well-formed.

A third constraint is that each constituent, as it appears, must be ratable as a stopping point in terms of:

(c) how well it corresponds to an intuition of completeness and
(d) how well it corresponds to the opposite, an intuition of incompleteness—leading to a continuation of the dialectic and search for good form.

No current analysis meets all of these requirements, especially the second and third. However, it is possible to bypass them, and this is what construction grammars are able to do. Such grammars (Goldberg 1995, 1997), together with frame semantics (Fillmore 1985), accomplish this feat by treating constructions/frames as conventional form-meaning pairs, similar in having a signifier-signified structure to words but with an internal organization and open slots for lexical inserts. So doing provides a logic for considering the meaning of a construction as a whole (caused-motion, for example, is a construction-semantic frame pair, in which "the S Ved the N off the table," as a whole, signifies that S caused N to move off the table). Sentence derivation is flattened, and the second and third requirements are met effectively by default. I shall make use of a construction grammar formulation in the case study to be presented in Chapter 4.2, to illustrate how a dialectic of imagery and linguistic categorial content can be resolved through the activation of the caused-motion construction in this case study. Paul Hopper (2004) is exploring 'open ended' and 'emergent' synchronic systems that may eventually meet conditions two and three, but no current grammatical model, other than construction grammar, meshes well with an imagery-language dialectic.

MATERIAL CARRIERS

We get a deeper understanding of the imagery-language dialectic by introducing the concept of a 'material carrier'. A material carrier—the phrase was used by Vygotsky (1986)[7]—is the embodiment of meaning in a concrete enactment or material experience.[8] A material carrier appears to enhance the symbolization's representational power. The concept implies that the gesture, *the actual motion of the gesture itself*, is a dimension of meaning. Such is possible if the gesture *is* the very image; not an 'expression' or 'representation' of it, but *is* it. From this viewpoint, a gesture is an image in its most developed—that is, most materially, naturally embodied—form. The absence of a gesture is the converse, an image in its least material form.[9] I describe here a theoretical model of how materialization has an effect on representational power and when gestures do and do not occur with speech (cf. Goldin-Meadow 2003a). A striking illustration of the material carrier is what Cornelia Müller (2004a) terms the 'waking' of 'sleeping metaphors'—new life given to inactive metaphors, in which a gesture acts as an enhancement of the metaphor's original source. This enhancement shows the effect of gesture as a material carrier. Müller gives an example of a German metaphor ("gefunkt," 'sparked', the equivalent to English 'clicked', for suddenly falling in love). The metaphor is inactive, not apprehended through the metaphor source, but is seen as a literal term in most uses. However, it can be awakened by a gesture. A speaker, describing her first love, said "between us somehow it sparked ['clicked']" (Müller's translation). As she said "between us" her hand rose upward next to her face in a ring shape but with an unusual orientation—the fingers pointing at her own face; then, as she uttered the metaphor itself, "gefunkt," her hand abruptly turned outward—her gesture materializing the 'dead' metaphor as a sudden event, an electrical spark.[10]

7. Pointed out by Elena Levy.

8. As suggested by the semantic satiation effect demonstrated in Chapter 3: the material form of a symbol appears to change perceptually when it temporarily ceases to be a material carrier.

9. The material carrier helps explain a lack of gesture. When no gesture occurs, we witness the *lowest level of materialization*. This issue is addressed at the end of this subchapter.

10. Müller views the metaphor dynamically, as a *process* by which the speaker and her listener generate metaphoricity in the context of the speech event; clearly a conception

The 'H-Model'[11]

By performing the gesture, a core idea is brought into concrete existence and becomes part of the speaker's own existence at that moment. The Heideggerian echo in this statement is not accidental. Following Heidegger's emphasis on being, a gesture is not a representation, or is not only such: it is a form of being. Gestures (and words, etc., as well) are themselves thinking in one of its many forms—not only expressions of thought, *but thought, i.e., cognitive being, itself.* The H-model is in this way an extension of Merleau-Ponty's "existential content of speech" (and gesture). It gives existential content an interpretation on the level of cognitive being. To the speaker, gesture and speech are not only 'messages' or communications, but are a way of cognitively existing, of cognitively being, at the moment of speaking.[12]

The speaker who creates a gesture of Sylvester rising up fused with the pipe's hollowness is, according to this interpretation, embodying thought in gesture, and this action—thought in action—was part of the person's being cognitively at that moment. Likewise the woman who gestured a sudden transformation with "gefunkt." To make a gesture, from this perspective, is to bring thought into existence on a concrete plane, just as writing out a word can have a similar effect. The greater the felt departure of the thought from the immediate context, the more likely is its materialization in a gesture, because of this contribution to being. Thus, gestures are more or less elaborated depending on the importance of material realization to the existence of the thought.

---

germane to the position of this book. The activation of the metaphor, and the semiotic impact of the sparking image, is a variable, dependent upon the speaker's thought processes and the context of speaking. The gesture, as a material carrier, is an active component of this process.

11. The 'H-model' was inspired by a lecture at the 1995 Linguistics Institute, "On the embodied nature of grammar: Embodied being-in-the-world," by Barbara Fox. I am grateful to Jürgen Streeck for detailed e-mail discussions in 1996.

12. The H-model avoids anomalies that arise in models where significance is via some form of representation, specifically the 'theater of the mind' problem highlighted by Dennett (1991). The theater of the mind is the presumed central thinking area in which representations are 'presented' to a receiving intelligence. The possibilities in this theory for downward spiraling homunculi inside other homunculi are well-known. In the H-model, there is no theater and no extra being; the gesture is, rather, part of the speaker's momentary mode of being itself.

There are, however, deep and hitherto unexplored issues here, and possibly some contradictions with Vygotsky as well.[13] If gesture and linguistic form are themselves forms of being cognitively for the speaker, there would seem to be no room in this process for the presentation of symbols; the signifier-signified distinction that constitutes semiosis is lacking. This semiotic relation appears when an observer is taken into account—this could be a listener who participates in, or a coder who looks at, the communication. Dreyfus (1994), in his invaluable exposition of Heidegger, explains Heidegger's treatment of symbols in a way that suggests a rapprochement with a Vygotskian semiotic. To cope with signs is not to cope just with them but also with the whole interconnected pattern of activity in which they are embedded (this still has the viewpoint of a listener/observer; from the speaker's viewpoint, we should say that producing a sign *carries the speaker* into a 'whole interconnected activity'). Heidegger, according to Dreyfus, says that signs point out the context of a shared practical activity—and this is the key to the rapprochement. To have your thoughts come to exist in the form of signs is to cause them to exist in a context of shared practical activities (for example, in conversations bodily processes, such as breathing, come into synchrony and the physiological records of two individuals can actually be superimposed; McFarland 2001). A sign signifies only for those who 'dwell' in that context. In this we can recognize a recipe for a dialectic: sign and image are inseparable and jointly form a context to dwell in; the two combine to create the possibility of shared states of cognitive being. This description brings the GP and the social Other together as joint inhabitants of the context (and it is the speaker who always is the one dwelling there the best). The communication process is then getting the Other to dwell there too. Heidegger spoke of language as the *house of being* (cf. Dreyfus 1994, pp. 217–224),[14] just as Merleau-Ponty spoke of inhabiting it. Their metaphors dovetail, in that the imagery-language dialectic inhabits this house and brings it to life.

13. Vygotsky's concept of mediated cognition, in which the sign serves as a 'cognitive tool', inserts a step of manipulation and resource exploitation into the linkage of speech to thought. This residual of behaviorist thinking, I believe, can be and in this work *is* dissociated from other indispensable Vygotskyian concepts—dialectic, verbal thought, the minimal psychological unit, and the separation of functions between the social and individual planes (on this last, see Chapter 4.3).

14. I am grateful to Shaun Gallagher for calling my attention to this phrase.

Werner and Kaplan's Organismic Foundations

A related dimension of the material carrier is its *organismic* grounding in symbol formation. In an organismic approach, the symbol's material qualities (sound image, gesture action) are an integral part of its semantic qualities. It is 'organismic' in that meaning is never dissociated from the body; indeed, it is impossible ('unthinkable') without engagement of the body.

Werner & Kaplan (1963) wrote specifically of the organismic foundations of symbol formation; of our capacity to represent the world symbolically by capturing the world in a kind of imitation carried out in bodily movements. Symbols are made possible by

> this *transcendence of expressive qualities*, that is, their amenability to materialization in disparate things and happenings. (p. 21, emphasis in the original)

According to Werner and Kaplan, the development of an individual child is a process of adding semiotic *distance* between movement and the expressive qualities that the movement can have:

> The act of denotative reference does not merely, or mainly, operate with *already formed* expressive similarities between entities. Through its productive nature, it brings to the fore latent expressive qualities in both vehicular material and referent that will allow the *establishment of semantic correspondence* between the two entities. It is precisely this productive nature of the denotative act that renders possible a symbolic relation between any entity and another. (pp. 21–22, emphasis in the original)

We see this kind of creation of meaning in a gesture-language interaction. As a material carrier a global, instantaneous gesture is a further creation, beyond infancy, of the organismic foundations of which Werner and Kaplan spoke. In the case of gesture, the material carrier interacts with the fully distanced symbols of the linguistic code.[15] The growth point formalizes this interaction of image and linguistic code.

15. The Werner and Kaplan idiom suggests that an interaction of imagery and language is not a given, that young children must develop it. Until there is 'distancing' between signifier and signified, there is a single mode of meaning creation: organismic imitation of the world. The other principal implication of this framework is that an organismic

Semantic Phonology

William Stokoe (1991) had a similar insight into the material carrier when he wrote (also Armstrong et al. 1995):

> The usual way of conceiving of the structure of language is linear: First there are the sounds (phonology), these are put together to make the words and their classes (morphology), the words in turn, are found to be of various classes, and these are used to form phrase structures (syntax), and finally, the phrase structures, after lexical replacement of their symbols, yield meaning (semantics). A semantic phonology ties the last step to the first, making a seamless circuit of this progression. The metaphor for a semantic phonology that jumps to mind is the Möbius strip: the input is the output, with a twist. (Stokoe 1991, p. 112)

The term 'semantic phonology' suggests the material carrier concept. In Stokoe's version, all the steps of an intervening synchronic description are also implied, which suggests a kind of continuous inching from the dynamic to the static. The dialectic we shall explore sees the static and dynamic joining in a different way—the dynamic is fueled by the dialectic, which is where materialization plays its part (adding to the speaker's cognitive being, the meaning inhabiting the speaker's gesture). The static dimension manifests itself to the speaker in the form of intuitions-1 of form and completeness, which is what the phonology, morphology, and syntax state analytically. In this dialectic view there is not a continuous progression around a Möbius strip of language, to use Stokoe's metaphor; instead, each domain retains its own ontological status, with intuitions linking them.

Embodied Cognition

The concept of a material carrier connects to the idea of embodied cognition, as described by Johnson (1987) and Lakoff & Johnson (1999). Johnson, though not mentioning gesture, links the embodiment of conception to modes of meaning organization similar to gesture—nonpropositional and figurative,

---

mode of meaning creation does not disappear but continues alongside the symbolic mode, organized in an imagery-language interaction. See Chapter 5.

with provision for imagery and analogic meaning construction. Lakoff and Johnson (1999) cite the phenomenon of gesture, but consider only gestures embodying listable metaphors. Nonetheless, a far more wide ranging materialization in gesture appears to be the essence of embodiment.

PRESENCE VERSUS ABSENCE OF GESTURE

The H-model explains why gestures sometimes are absent—under what conditions, and what the absence implies for an imagery-language dialectic. Various factors influence the extent and/or complexity of the materialization at any moment, and when these factors are diminished or absent, gesture should dwindle or disappear.

Memory is one factor. An absence of gesture is expected if the activation of one's cognitive being is not updated because of memory failure. We saw in Chapter 2 that as memory faded the speaker's gestures declined proportionately, ending with no gesture at all; then, as memory returned, gestures revived in degrees to full iconic form. The fall and recovery reflects degrees of materialization in the speaker's moment-by-moment state of cognitive being in the H-model.

Low communicative dynamism is another factor. Absence of gesture is expected if the opposite of memory failure occurs, a complete predictability of what comes next, as was also described in Chapter 2 (table 2.3). The greater the continuity with the immediate past, the less the elaboration of the present.

With either a lack of memory or high predictability, the materialization of imagery is predicted to diminish and, as this happens, an imagery-language dialectic shrinks to purely verbal formulas. At some point, the dialectic ceases and pure verbalism remains (cf. "let's see what happens" in the memory example, with no gesture; it is tempting to say that political speeches, given over and over, in nearly identical form, tend in this direction as well). In terms of the Vygotskian overlapping speech-thought circles, a decline of gesture, under these conditions, moves thought out of the overlapped zone and into the circle of speech without thought.

All this implies that the dialectic itself varies proportionately with communicative dynamism and memory, and when these conditions are absent speaking is no longer merging with thinking.

SUMMARY

Speech-synchronized gestures produce conditions for a dialectic of unlike cognitive modes. In this dialectic, the dynamic and static dimensions of language intersect, with the static dimension experienced via linguistic intuitions; these intuitions develop out of the dialectic and ultimately become the stop order to further development. Gesture and speech, as material carriers of meanings, provide an alternative to representation. Via materialization, meaning 'inhabits' the speaker; in the H-model specification of this process gesture and speech contribute to his/her momentary cognitive being. This being is the ultimate reality of verbal thought embodied in speech and gesture.

The next subchapter further develops the Vygotskian concept of a minimal unit of the dialectic, called there the growth point, and explores this concept and its relationship to context via a case study.

The Growth Point[1]

As described in Chapter 4.1, the *growth point* is proposed as the minimal unit of an imagery-language dialectic. A growth point is a package that has both linguistic categorial and imagistic components, and it has these components irreducibly. It is a minimal unit in the Vygotskian sense, the smallest package that retains the property of being a whole; in this case the imagery-language whole that we see in synchronized combinations of co-expressive speech and gestures.

Growth points are inferred from the totality of communicative events, with special focus on speech-gesture synchrony and co-expressivity. Semiotically a combination of opposites, image and form, the growth point creates a benign instability that fuels thought and speech. We call the combination a growth point because it is meant to be the initial form of thinking for (and while) speaking, out of which a dynamic process of organization emerges. It is also called a growth point because it is a theoretical unit in which the principles that apply to the mental growth of children—differentiation, internalization, dialectic, and reorganization—also apply to real-time utterance generation

1. Earlier versions of this chapter were given as the Gustaf Stern Memorial Lectures, Göteborg, Sweden, in 1999, and in a series of talks at the University of Copenhagen, in 2001; some of the material also appeared in *Cognitive Studies: Bulletin of the Japanese Cognitive Science Society* in 2000 and *Acta Linguistica Hafniensia* in 2002. I am grateful to Jens Allwood, Department of Linguistics, Göteborg University, and Elisabeth Engberg-Pedersen, Department of Linguistics, University of Copenhagen, for hosting me at their respective institutions. Randall L. B. McNeill provided valuable comments.

(in both adults and children). A final reason for the name is that a growth point addresses the concept that there is a specific starting point for a unitary thought. Although an idea unit may emerge out of the preceding context and have ramifications in later speech, it does not exist at all times. It comes into being at some specific moment; the growth point is this moment, theoretically. One reviewer of this book in manuscript seemed to regard the growth point as a kind of alternate linguistic unit, but the growth point is not such a unit. Linguistic concepts like the phrase or clause pertain to the static dimension of language. The growth point is a <u>minimal dynamic unit</u> in which imagery and linguistic categorial content are equal parts.

'Dynamic' implies change, and the change is due, in theory, to two sources. First is the inherent instability of simultaneously conceptualizing the same idea in opposite semiotic modes. Second is the shaping of growth points by context. The force of context brings us to the concept of a psychological predicate, which enables us to illuminate this source of dynamism.

The Psychological Predicate

The concept of a psychological predicate (a term from Vygotsky 1986—not always a grammatical predicate) provides the theoretical link between the GP and the context of speaking. Defining a psychological predicate (and hence a GP) requires reference to the context; this is because the psychological predicate and its context are mutually referring. The <u>psychological predicate</u>

(1)   marks a significant departure in the immediate context; and
(2)   implies this <u>context</u> as a <u>background</u>.

Regarding the GP as a psychological predicate thus suggests a mechanism of GP formation in which differentiation of a focus from a background plays an essential part. Such differentiation is validated by the very close temporal connection of gesture strokes with the peaks of acoustic output in speech (see discussion in Chapter 2). Shuichi Nobe (1996) has documented this connection instrumentally: "The robust synchrony between gesture strokes and the peaks of acoustic aspects suggests that the information the gesture stroke carries has an intrinsic relationship with the accompanying speech information prominently pronounced with these peaks. The manifestation of the salient information seems to be realized through the synchronization of these two modalities" (p. 35).

What, Then, Is 'Context'?

[handwritten margin note: a kind of figure/ground Silvelism, in which the speaker striving to establish & communicate ✓ the figure]

I will use the terms *field of oppositions* and *significant (newsworthy) contrast* to refer to the constructed background and the differentiation of psychological predicates within it. All of this is meant to be a dynamic, continuously updated process in which new fields of oppositions are formed and new GPs or psychological predicates are differentiated in ongoing cycles of thinking for speaking.

A significant contrast, and the field of oppositions within which it appears, are linked meaning structures under the creative control of the speaker at the moment of speaking. The field of oppositions indexes and is constrained by external conditions, both social and material, but an essential fact is that it is also *a mental construction, part of the speaker's effort to construct a meaning.* The speaker shapes the background in a certain way, in order to make possible the intended significant contrast within it. Background and contrast are both necessary, and are constructed together. Control by the individual ensures that GPs establish meanings true to the speaker's intentions and memory. Regarding the GP as a psychological predicate in a field of oppositions clarifies the sense in which we are using the term 'context'. This word has a host of meanings (cf. Duranti & Goodwin 1992), but for our purposes 'context' is the background from which a psychological predicate is differentiated.

Meaning of 'Meaning'

Finally, the concept of a psychological predicate, or significant contrast, and its relationship to background or a field of oppositions, amounts to a hypothesis of what it is to create a meaning, in a psychological sense. The meaning is two things taken jointly, including both the point differentiated and the field of oppositions from which it is differentiated. This concept of meaning as irreducibly a relationship of a point to a background, both of which are constructed in order to make the relationship possible, contrasts with the classic view of meaning as 'association' or 'habit strength' or 'content' at a mental address. These latter conceptualizations share a quite different metaphor wherein meaning is a substance that can be accumulated, stored, or lost (in this traditional concept of meaning as substance we again see the conduit metaphor; Reddy 1979).

Gestures and Psychological Predicates

An important observation is that gestures correspond with psychological predicates. The alignments are in two domains. First, when gestures and speech *synchronize* they jointly form the contrast underlying the psychological predicate. Second, the *form* of the gesture embodies the content that makes this differentiation meaningful—along with the synchronous speech segments, it embodies the elements of meaning that are being differentiated at this moment.

We can demonstrate the alignment of gestures and psychological predicates by exploiting a quirk in the cartoon stimulus that we have employed. One of the characters (Sylvester) attempts to reach a second character (Tweety) for culinary purposes; Tweety is in a window of a hotel some stories above the street where Sylvester is standing. Luckily, a drainpipe runs up the side of the building from street level to the very window where Tweety is perched. Sylvester initially makes use of the drainpipe as a kind of ladder, climbing up it on the outside; this fails, and then, in the next scene, he makes a second attempt, climbing up the pipe on the inside, using it as a kind of vertical tunnel for (one supposes) a stealth approach. The two successive attempts are germane to illustrating psychological predicates.

If a speaker recalls both attempts, in the correct outside-inside order, we predict that the psychological predicate relating to the second attempt will focus on interiority, since this is the differentiating element. The immediate context is using the drainpipe to get to Tweety; and the new element is being on the inside (in contrast to outside the first time). The gesture component of this psychological predicate should therefore embody interiority and synchronize with the speech segment(s) that also convey this idea. If, however, a speaker fails to recall the outside attempt but does recall the inside attempt, or recalls the attempts in the reverse order, interiority does not contrast with exteriority, and we predict now that interiority should not be a particular feature of the psychological predicate in either speech or gesture. (No subject has ever recalled the first attempt but not the second.)[2]

---

2. I am grateful to Susan Goldin-Meadow for emphasizing the importance of elucidating these predictions. From an early date we realized that gestures for the second ascent tended to include interiority only if the speaker had already had mentioned the

Susan Duncan and Dan Loehr are currently conducting an experiment that directly tests these predictions by comparing the gestures that occur after subjects have watched the standard outside-inside order of the animated stimulus versus, with different subjects, the inside-outside order: interiority is predicted with the first group but not the second. Pending the outcome of this experiment, we can look at available narrations and still find evidence of an outside-inside focus with gestures. I will first present evidence for gesture-speech synchronization at the psychological predicate; then evidence for gesture form modulation to carry the content of the psychological predicate.

Synchrony

One speaker happened to describe the outside and inside ascents with the same verb and path particle combination, "climb up," but for the inside version shifted the timing of the gesture stroke from "climbs up" to "through" and then "inside," and formed thereby different psychological predicates. Interiority was the significant contrast only in the second (boldface shows when the gesture strokes took place).
Outside:

> and then the second part / [is he **climbs up** <u>the drain</u>]

Inside:

> <uuhh> let's see the next time / is he tries to* <uh> /tries to cliimb / [up / in / **throu**<u>gh / the</u>] [drain* / <nn> // **inside the dra**<u>inpipe</u>]

In other words, the gestures targeted the linguistic components that, together with the gesture, pulled out contextually newsworthy content; exteriority in the first instance, interiority in the second—despite having the same verb-particle

---

first, exterior ascent; Fey Parrill and Susan Duncan are now formally studying this contingency. A presentation by Duncan at the Workshop on Perceptive Animated Agents and Virtual Humans, sponsored by the National Science Foundation, April 9–10, 2004, in Del Mar, California, was the model for the logic of the following discussion.

combination ("climbs up") in both instances. The gestures also embodied significant contrasts in their forms; the "climbs up" gesture depicted upward movement without interiority, while the "through" and "inside" gestures made use of the left hand to form a hollow space through which the upward-moving right hand passed. The form aspect of the psychological predicate is registered in more detail in the following.

Form

The first two speakers below recalled only the inside attempt; interiority for them was not a significant contrast and their gestures did not contain any such content.

Inside appeared alone: in both examples, the gesture depicts ascent without any indication of interiority (just the thumb raised in the second example).

Cel. he tries **climb**ing up the rai]n barrel (Figure 4.2.1)
Den. and <um> / he tries crawling up the drainp[**ipe** /] to get Tweety (Figure 4.2.2)

Fig. 4.2.1. No interiority gesture. Hand simply rises.

Fig. 4.2.2. No interiority gesture. Right thumb (see arrow) lifts.

The next three speakers recalled both attempts in the correct order and, in each case, the gesture with the inside attempt highlighted interiority. The second and third speakers also depicted the compression a plumpish Sylvester had to undergo inside the pipe (extending the index finger, not only to point, but to depict the reduced space). None of their outside gestures had these features.

Fig. 4.2.3. Interiority gesture. This is the previously cited 'rising hollowness' gesture.

Fig. 4.2.4. Interiority gesture. The extended index finger is iconically depicting the confined space inside the pipe.

Fig. 4.2.5. Interiority gesture. Another extended index finger for the confinement inside the pipe.

Inside appeared after outside: the gesture and speech depict both ascent and interiority.

San. he goe[[ss / **up / th**][**rough** <u>the</u> pipe]] this time (Figure 4.2.3)

Viv. he <e> / tri <i>es / going [[**up**] [the in**sid**][e of **the drai**<u>npipe #</u>]] (Figure 4.2.4)

Jan. [/ this time he tr<u>ies to go</u> up **ins**<u>ide the rain gu'tter</u> /] (Figure 4.2.5)

Exception Proving the Rule

The sixth speaker is the proverbial exception that proves the rule. She remembered both attempts, in the correct order, but picked out a different significant contrast between them, a twist conceivably triggered by a lexical error she made in describing the first attempt. She there erroneously said that Sylvester's first trip up was by climbing "a ladder" and did not mention the pipe. Her gesture seemed to depict the rungs of a ladder. She did, however, mention the pipe with the second trip, so this ascent then contrasted, for her, ground elements (a pipe versus a ladder) rather than types of paths (inside versus outside). Her second ascent handshape (cupped, as if the pipe viewed from the outside) and its timing (the stroke went with "climbing") both suggest this interpretation.[3] The speaker then adopted an extended index finger form as she referenced the drainspout, echoing the other gestures above with the single finger as an image of interiority and compression.

3. I am grateful to Susan Duncan for this insight.

Fig. 4.2.6.1. Exception that proves the rule 1. Gesture with "climbing up a ladder."

Fig. 4.2.6.2. Exception that proves the rule 2. Gesture with "drainspout."

Fig. 4.2.6.3. Exception that proves the rule 3. Continuation of gesture with "drainspout."

Lau. (outside the pipe) and he trie[s / **climbing** up a la]dder # (Figure 4.2.6.1)

Lau. (inside the pipe start) he tries[s **cli**]m[[bing up the <nn> dra**inspout** /*/*]
(Figure 4.2.6.2)

Lau. (inside the pipe continued) (Figure 4.2.6.3)

Summary of Gestures and Psychological Predicates

Gestures participate in the differentiation of significant contrasts to form psychological predicates. In these examples, how interiority was built into the gesture varies, but it was present when this semantic feature was part of the contrast. In one case the space was a rising hollowness, in others it was an image of something rising upward in a confined and narrow space. A conception of interiority was absent from the two narrators (Cel., Den.) who recalled only the inside attempt. Lau., who recalled both attempts, favored a different contrast, focusing not on space but on the type of ground element that her construal of the first ascent had made the significant contrast.

These examples equally illustrate synchrony (just as the synchrony example illustrated form). Each of the interiority gestures was timed with a speech reference to interiority ("through," "inside" two times). Similarly, Lau.'s drainpipe gesture synchronized with her reference to ground in the word "drainspout."

CASE STUDY OF A GROWTH POINT

We shall see in this case study that multiple contexts can converge to form a growth point. The alignments of synchrony and form with a psychological predicate shown in the preceding section are manifested here too, but to understand how, it is necessary to consider the contexts of the GP and how the gesture embodies information from them. The narrative text is in (1) through (9) below. The case study itself directly follows the "inside" gesture by Viv. above (Figure 4.2.4).

The Scene

Sylvester has crawled into the drainpipe at the bottom. Tweety observes this, retrieves a bowling ball, and dumps it into the top of the drainpipe. The scene shifts to the side of the building, central portion of drainpipe; bulge moves down drainpipe; bulge explodes. Sylvester falls into street with bowling-ball shaped bottom; Sylvester rolls down street on bottom, feet rotating above ground; Sylvester rolls down different part of street, looks upset. Scene of empty street; scene shifts to end of street; bowling alley. Sylvester rolls into entrance of bowling alley; entrance of bowling alley without Sylvester; sounds of bowling pins crashing (see McNeill 1992, appendix, for full transcript; transcript originally created by Elena Levy).

Viv.'s Battle Plan

(1) he <e> / tri <i>es / going [[**up**] [the in**sid**][e of **the drai**npipe #]] and
1 hand: RH rises up 3 times with the first finger extended (see Figure 4.2.4 in preceding section)

(2) Tweety Bird runs and gets a bowling ba[ll and drop<u>s</u> **it do**<u>wn</u> the drainpipe #]
Symmetrical: 2 similar hands move down (see Figure 4.2.7)

(3) [<u>and /</u> as **he's** co<u>ming</u> **up**]
Asymmetrical: 2 different hand, LH holds, RH up 2 X

(4) [<u>and the</u> **bowling b**all's coming d]]
Asymmetrical: 2 different hands, RH holds, LH down (see Figure 5.4)

(5) [own <u>he</u> **sssw**a<u>llows it</u>]
Asymmetrical: 2 different hands, LH down into hollow space formed by RH

(6) [# and he comes **out the bot**<u>tom of the drai</u>]
1 hand: LH comes down

(7) [npipe and he's **got thi**<u>s big bowling ball inside h</u>]im
Symmetrical: 2 similar hands move down

(8) [and he **rolls on down**] [into **a bow**<u>ling all</u>]

Symmetrical: 2 similar hands move forward 2X
(9) [ey and then **you hear a** sstri]ke #
Symmetrical: 2 similar hands move apart

To focus on one item for analysis, consider the utterance and gesture in (2)—the words "it down" accompanied by a downward thrusting gesture, shown below.[4] My purpose will be to show how this utterance-gesture combination can be explained utilizing the GP model. I have chosen this example in part because, while "it" is the direct object of "drops" and "down" is a satellite of this verb (cf. Talmy 1975, 1985), "it" and "down" together do not comprise a grammatical unit. Nonetheless, in this example they are the inferred growth point. The challenge is to explain this GP and show why it and no other took form in the context of speaking.

First, to describe the GP itself. The gesture in (2) was made with two symmetrical hands—the palms loosely cupped and facing downward as if placed on top of a large spherical object, and the hands moving down during the linguistic segments "it do(wn)" (Figure 4.2.7). The inferred GP is this image of downward movement *plus* the linguistic content of the "it" (i.e., the bowling ball) and the path particle "down."

Fig. 4.2.7. Downward stroke with "ba[ll and drops it down the drainpipe #]."

The spoken part of the example is repeated in line (2) below (line (1) will be referred to later). The first thing to notice, as mentioned above, is that

4. This text was presented in full in *Hand and Mind* (95–104) but the bracketing there was slightly different from that shown here. Careful coding places it as here, rather than, as in the earlier work, coinciding with just the word "down." Moreover, the *Hand and Mind* coding did not reveal the holds, the possible prestroke hold at the end of "drops" and the conspicuous poststroke hold at the end of "down."

the timing of the gesture stroke (boldface) is somewhat off, if we think that gestures should line up with linguistic constituents. The stroke *excluded* the verb, "drops"; it coincided with "it down," and in this way combined two constituents, the Figure and the Satellite (using Talmy's 2000 categories), but excluded another, the Activating Process, to which the Figure is actually more tightly coupled in the sentence structure:

(1) he <e> / tri <i>es / going [[**up**] [the in**sid**][e of **the drai**<u>npipe #</u>]] Tweety Bird runs

(2) and gets a bowling ba[ll and drops **it do**<u>wn</u> the drainpipe]

This timing is not a mystery, however, if we regard gesture and speech as conveying the concept of an antagonistic force. From this vantage point, the synchronized gesture and linguistic segments agree precisely. The "it" indexes the bowling ball, the metaphoric force in question, and the "down" refers to the direction the force is taking. The verb, "drops," in contrast, refers to Tweety, the character who was the agent of the dropping or thrusting but was not the force in question.[5] In short, "drops" was outside the antagonistic force meaning and was excluded from the gesture that carried it.

The exclusion of "drops" was not random; evidence shows that it was motivated. First, the preparation phase of the "it down" gesture has two features that skip the verb. Preparation began at the first mention of the bowling ball in the preceding clause. This suggests that the bowling ball was part of the discourse focus at that moment. Second, preparation continued right *through* the verb, suggesting that the verb was irrelevant to this focus. Further, a brief prestroke hold seems to have preceded "it down" (although coding of the hold varies), which, if present, targeted "it down." Finally, a poststroke hold lasted exactly as long as it took to complete the spoken articulation of "down" and, via this hold, preserved the semantic synchrony of the gesture stroke with the articulation of the downward path in speech. So the stroke fully and exactly timed with just two words, "it down," and excluded a third, "drops." The question is: why?

The GP is both image and linguistic categorial content: an image, as it were, with a foot in the door of language. Such imagery is important, since it grounds sequential linguistic categories in an instantaneous visuospatial context. It may also provide the GP with the property of 'chunking', a hallmark of expert performance (cf. Chase & Eriksson 1981), whereby a chunk of linguistic output

---

5. More precisely, Tweety was the original antagonistic force but the caused-motion construction, "and [Tweety] drops it down," transferred the antagonistic force to the bowling ball (see below for full discussion).

(coinciding with the full gesture phrase) is organized around the presentation of the image. The downward content of the gesture is a specific case of "down," the linguistic category—a specific visualization of it—in which imagery is the material carrier of the category and possibly the unit of performance.[6]

The linguistic categorization is also crucial, since it brings the image into the system of categories of the language, which is both a system of classification and a way of patterning action. The speech and its synchronized gesture are the key to this theoretical unit.

Discovering the Context: Catchments

A GP is a psycholinguistic unit based on contrast, and this concept brings in context as a fundamental component. To explain the utterance in (2) and why it has the growth point we infer, we must consider the complete context, (1)–(9) above, and see how the parts of the utterance came together with contributions from the context. A useful approach to this analysis is by means of *catchments*— a phenomenon first noted in Kendon (1972) (although he did not use the term 'catchment'). Chapter 5 presents a more detailed discussion of the catchment.

Definition of a Catchment

A catchment is recognized when one or more gesture features occur in at least two (not necessarily consecutive) gestures. The logic is that recurrent images suggest a common discourse theme, and a discourse theme will produce gestures with recurring features. These gesture features can be detected. Then, working backwards, the recurring features offer clues to the cohesive linkages in the text with which they co-occur. A catchment is a kind of thread of

---

6. Peña et al. (2002) show experimentally that variations in the conditional proba-bilities with which sound segments follow each other create impressions of breaks in continuous speech but are incapable of inducing intuitions of 'words' ('words' were defined as having internal structure beyond discontinuity in the sound stream). They induced sensitivity to 'words' by adding short breaks (25 msecs, below the threshold of perceptibility) into the sound stream. Growth points are also units around which such segments can congeal. The important point for our purposes is that discontinuity leads to the perception of wordlike segments. Twenty-five-millisecond separations do not regularly appear in natural speech but there are abundant semantic and conceptual discontinuities, and these also could induce the perception of word breaks.

visuospatial imagery that runs through a discourse to reveal the larger discourse units that encompass the otherwise separate parts.

By discovering the catchments created by a given speaker, we can see what this speaker is combining into larger discourse units—what meanings are being regarded as similar or related and grouped together, and what meanings are being put into different catchments or are being isolated, and thus are seen by the speaker as having distinct or less related meanings. Individuals differ in how they link up the world into related and unrelated components. Catchments give us a way of detecting these individual grouping patterns, which are an aspect of one's cognitive style.

To summarize the definition of a catchment:

- A catchment is recognized from recurrences of gesture form features over a stretch of discourse. Catchments are recognized from two or more gestures (not necessarily consecutive) with partially or fully recurring features of handedness, shape, movement, space, orientation, dynamics, etc.
- A catchment is a kind of thread of consistent dynamic visuospatial imagery running through the discourse segment that provides a gesture-based window into discourse cohesion.
- The logic of the catchment is that discourse themes produce gestures with recurring features; these recurrences give rise to the catchment.
- Thus, the catchment offers clues to the cohesive linkages in the text with which it co-occurs.

Viv.'s Catchments

We can scrutinize catchments, and in this way recover the effective fields of opposition and hence the psychological predicates/GPs and their semiotic values in Viv.'s recounting of the bowling ball episode. Table 4.2.1 reveals three catchments, recognizable from hand use and handshape/hand position—right hand or left; one hand or two, and, when two hands, same or different handshape and/or hand position. Each of the gesture features embodies certain thematic content and this content is what motivates it: **C1** is about a single moving entity, and its recurring gesture feature is a single moving hand; **C2** is about the bowling ball and what it does, and its recurring feature is a rounded shape (in gesture transcription terms, '2 similar hands'); **C3** is about the relative positions of two entities in a drainpipe and its recurring feature involves two hands in the appropriate spatial configuration ('2 different hands').

Table 4.2.1. Catchment structure of Viv.'s battle plan.

Ln	Catchment	Utterance	Gesture Feature
1	C1	he tries going [up the inside of the drainpipe and]	1-hand (right)
2	C2	Tweety Bird runs and gets a bowling ba[ll and drop<u>s</u>it do<u>wn</u> the drai]npipe	2-similar hands
3	C3	[and as he's coming up]	2-different hands
4	C3	[and the bowling ball's coming d]	2-different hands
5	C3	[own he swallows it]	2-different hands
6	C1, C3	[and he comes out the bottom of the drai]	1-hand (left)
7	C2	[npipe and he's got this big bowling ball inside h]im	2-similar hands
8	C2	[and he rolls on down into a bowling all]	2-similar hands
9	C2	[ey and then you hear a stri]ke	2-similar hands

C1. The first catchment involves one-handed gestures, in items (1) and (6). These gestures accompany descriptions of Sylvester's motion, first up the pipe, then out of it with the bowling ball inside him. Thus, **C1** ties together references to Sylvester as a solo force.

C2. The second catchment involves two-handed symmetrical gestures in (2), (7), (8), and (9). These gestures group descriptions where the bowling ball is the antagonist, the dominant force. Sylvester becomes what he eats, a kind of living bowling ball, and the symmetric gestures accompany the descriptions where the bowling ball asserts its power. In (2) the bowling ball is beginning its career as antagonist. The rest of the catchment is where it has achieved its result. The two-handed symmetric gesture form highlights the shape of the bowling ball or its motion, an iconicity appropriate for its antagonist role. The antagonistic force catchment is the only one to span the entire episode description.

C3. The third catchment involves two-handed asymmetrical gestures in items (3), (4), and (5). This catchment groups items in which the bowling ball and Sylvester approach each other in the pipe. Here, in contrast to the symmetric set, Sylvester and the bowling ball are equals differing only in their spatial location and direction of motion.

With these catchments, we can analyze the real-time origins of the utterance and gesture in (2) in a way that incorporates context as a fundamental component. The occurrence of (2) in the symmetrical catchment shows that one of the factors comprising its field of oppositions at this point was the various guises in which the bowling ball appeared in the role of an antagonist. This catchment set the bowling ball apart from its role in **C3**, where the bowling ball was on a par with Sylvester. The significant contrast in (2) was the downward motion of the bowling ball. Because of the field of oppositions at this point, this downward motion had significance as an antagonistic force against Sylvester. We can write this meaning as:

Antagonistic Force: Bowling Ball Downward.

This was the context and contrast. Thus, "it down," unlikely though it may seem as a unit from a grammatical point of view, was the cognitive core of the utterance in (2)—the "it" indexing the bowling ball, and the "down" indexing the significant contrast itself in the field of oppositions.

The verb "drops," therefore, was *excluded* from this GP. As noted before, exclusion is evidenced in the fact that the stroke did not synchronize with the verb; in fact, it was withheld from the verb by continued preparation and a possible brief prestroke hold. The verb describes what Tweety did, not what the bowling ball did (it went down), and thus was not a significant contrast in the field of oppositions involving the bowling ball. The core idea at (2) was the bowling ball and its action, not Tweety and his.[7]

One Utterance, Several Contexts

That "drops" was excluded from the GP yet included in the utterance points to a second context at play in the origins of (2). The utterance, though a single grammatical construction, grew out of two distinct contexts and gained oppositional meaning from each.

The first context we have already analyzed; it was the **C2** theme, in which the bowling ball was an antagonistic force. The second context can be seen in the fact that the two-handed gesture at (2) also contrasted with **C1**—the preceding one-handed gesture in (1) depicting Sylvester as a solo force. (1) and (2) comprised a paradigm of opposed forces. This contrast led to the other parts of the utterance in (2) via a partial repetition of the utterance structure of (1), a poetic framework within which the new contrasts were formed (cf. Jakobson 1960). Contrasting verbal elements appeared in close to equivalent slots (the match is as close as possible given that the verb in (2) is transitive while that in (1) is intransitive):

7. Line (6) is simultaneously in **C1** and **C3**, a fusion that neatly captures the fact that Sylvester, by this point, has turned into a kind of bowling ball. The gesture is made with a single hand, which in **C1** was associated with the solo Sylvester in motion, but it is the *left* hand, which in **C3** was associated with the bowling ball; here the gesture belongs both to Sylvester as a solo force and to the bowling ball heading down.

(1′) | (Sylvester) | up | in "he tries going up the inside of the drainpipe"
(2′) | (Tweety) | down | in "and (Tweety) drops it down the drainpipe."

The thematic opposition can be summarized as the opposition of counterforces—Tweety-down vs. Sylvester-up. Our feeling that the paradigm is slightly ajar is due to the shift from spontaneous to caused motion with "drops." This verb does not alter the counterforces paradigm but transfers the counterforce from Tweety to the bowling ball, as required for the objective content of the episode.

The parallel antagonistic forces in (1′) and (2′) made Tweety the subject of (2′), matching Sylvester as subject of (1′). The contrast of (2′) with (1′) thus had two effects on our target utterance. It was the source of the verb, "drops," and was also why the subject was "Tweety" rather than "bowling ball." The subject slot expressed Tweety's role in the contrast and the verb shifted the downward force theme to the bowling ball. The identity of subjects, and the similar syntactic frames, expressed the antagonistic forces paradigm itself. The prestroke hold over "drops" is thus also explained: the verb, deriving from an antagonistic forces context, was propaedeutic to the GP, and the stroke was withheld until the way had been prepared for it.[8]

Let's summarize how (2) came into being:

(a) A field of oppositions in which the significance of the downward motion of the bowling ball was that of an antagonistic force—the contrast of (2) with (3), (4), (5): this gave the growth point a core meaning centered on "it down." It's noteworthy that the preparation for the gesture in (2) began in the preceding clause, concurrent with mentioning the bowling ball for the first time ("Tweety Bird runs and gets a bowling ba[ll and drops it down the drai]npipe"). That is, the new growth point embodying the idea of the bowling ball in its role as the antagonist to Sylvester began to take form as soon as the bowling ball itself entered into the discourse.

(b) A field of oppositions in which the significance was the counterforces of Sylvester-up vs. Tweety-down. This gave a sentence schema that included the words "drops," "down," "drainpipe," and the repetition of the sentence structure with Tweety in the subject slot.

---

8. The poststroke hold on the second half of "down" derives differently, as Kita (1990) observed. At one level, pre- and poststroke holds are opposites—a prestroke hold signals that the stroke is being withheld, a poststroke hold that it is being extended. In both kinds, however, the hold ensures the synchrony of the stroke with specific speech segment(s).

The choice of verb in (2) was "drops," rather than "throws," "thrusts," or some other caused-motion option for a downward trajectory from a manual launch, possibly because it, among these options, corresponds most closely to the force-dynamics of how Tweety made use of gravity to launch the bowling ball.[9] Thus, a further aspect of the context of (2) is this force-dynamics. If this is the case, we have a further argument for the analysis above in which "drops" and "it down" belong to different contexts. This comes from the handshape of the gesture in (2). The speaker made the gesture with her hands facing *down*, in a thrusting position (Figure 4.2.7). They were not a simulation of Tweety's hands when he exploited gravity to launch the bowling ball. In the cartoon stimulus, Tweety held the bowling ball from the bottom and chucked it into the pipe, allowing gravity to do the rest (Figure 4.2.8). The GP image altered this force-dynamics by making the launch into a thrust. The verb "drops," meanwhile, captured the role of gravity (hence was favored over "thrust" itself). So the two contexts—the "drops" context captured the objective content of gravity doing the work, and the opposition of forces of which Tweety was a source; a different context shaped the GP, in which the bowling ball and its direction of movement, not Tweety and his action, was the significant element. The gesture and sentence, that is, reflected the speaker's conceptualizing of the cartoon as much as the objective cartoon content. The new force-dynamics is not appropriate to Tweety, but it does fit the field of oppositions that concentrated on the bowling ball in its persona as antagonist.[10]

Metaphor in a Dialectic

In Chapter 2, I emphasized the role of conventional metaphors, such as the conduit image of a container, in explaining how an imagery-language dialectic can occur when ideas are abstract, not imageable. The cited examples were gestures featuring the Palm Up Open Hand—cultural imagery providing a way to picture abstract notions. The images are predefined in that the metaphor, the conduit image in this case, is a widely shared, recurring motif. The case

9. Pointed out by Karl-Erik McCullough.

10. Sotaro Kita has pointed out that the first-person viewpoint inherent in the gesture at (2), in which the speaker's hands depict Tweety's hands, is deducible from the agentivity tier (in Jackendoff's 1990 terminology) in the utterance. While the Sylvester-Tweety opposition is not a new contrast at this point and so cannot be a psychological predicate, the agentivity tier does carry new information in that Tweety now has 'done something'. And this fact is embodied in a first-person character viewpoint gesture.

study, however, shows something different. It exemplifies metaphoric thinking without apparent conventional packaging and suggests a wider process of metaphoricity in ordinary verbal thinking. The bowling ball was a metaphor, in the sense that it was used to present another idea. By presenting the bowling ball image in the antagonistic-forces paradigm context, the speaker induces us to see the bowling ball as an antagonistic force; this is the triadic structure of metaphor that Müller (2004a) has defined. The bowling ball moved downward, not only as a concrete depiction of a motion event, but as an image of opposed forces. The speaker was not invoking a conventionalized schema, such as the conduit; the gesture was an improvisation, created at online speed, but it had abstract content. Metaphoricity is considered again in Chapter 5, in connection with discourse.

UNPACKING

'Unpacking' is the process of articulating the implications of a core idea and using these implications as a guide to a well-formed surface structure. The ultimate sentence can be considered an action with which to present the GP. A key process is the generation of additional meanings during this unpacking process.

The question of how a GP leads to a grammatically allowable surface form can be answered in part by invoking filters or templates. The idea unit in a GP, being a point of differentiation from a background, must be realized in a surface position consistent with its communicative dynamism, but this fact does not, by itself, specify a position in a sentence framework. The concepts of 'construction grammar' (Goldberg 1995) and of 'emergent grammar' (Hopper 1998, in press) may apply here. The contextual weight generated for the initially nongrammatical pair, "it down" plus gesture, could be completed by accessing a caused-motion construction,

Subj	V	Obj	Obl
$\updownarrow$	$\updownarrow$	$\updownarrow$	$\updownarrow$
Tweety	drops	it (b-ball)	down

This construction type, learned from childhood and able to function as a unit, could ease the GP, despite its double contextual base, into a single grammatical format and guide the speaker to a well-formed output. This result is 'emergent' in the sense that the grammatical form was not part of the input (this was the GP, the nongrammatical "it down" plus gesture), yet the output was this grammatical pattern. Thus, constructions, retrievable as wholes, can provide part of the template that the speaker needs.

Activating Caused-Motion

The details of the gesture as already described suggest an answer to the following question: When was the semantic content of the construction activated? The answer is that it emerged when the speaker first mentioned the bowling ball, at the end of the preceding clause ("Tweety Bird runs and gets a bowling ba[ll," the bracket indicating the onset of gesture preparation). That is, both sets of contrasts (**C1** and **C2**) were active at this moment. Thus, the surface order of words in the speaker's speech and the order of ideas in her thinking did not coincide—she had two separate ideas (the GP and caused motion, each with its own context), and found a dialectic stopping point in the caused-motion construction that led to a speech order ("and Ø dropped it down the drainpipe") that was different from the cognitive sequence.

What is the evidence for the actual moment of emergence of the sentence's content? It comes from the fact that the gesture preparation revealed an image already shaped to embody the speaker's idea of an antagonistic force. As she first mentioned the bowling ball, her *hands turned down*, preparing to thrust the ball downward. As noted above, this caused-motion meaning implies a different force-dynamics from the actual launch, but it was a natural expression of the antagonistic force meaning. In addition, the speaker's hands were already Tweety's hands, so the agentive role of Tweety was also established. All these details are shown in Figure 4.2.8.

Gesture preparation   Gesture stroke (start)   Character's actual launch
(start)

Fig. 4.2.8. Comparison of the crucial bowling ball gesture (in two phases) to its iconogenic original in the stimulus.

Unpacking drew on multiple sources—the GP, which involved antagonistic force; the idea of caused-motion (the unpacking frame); the referential appropriateness of "drops" for describing gravity's role; and the poetic replication of the initial sentence format (1) in (2), yielding a sentence with Tweety, the agent, as the subject (cf. Furuyama 2001). The impetus for unpacking (i.e., finding a stable construction) is the inherently unstable and incomplete combination of all this information, which creates a drive to find an intuitively complete structure, or format of repose. The process in this case came to a smooth, nonproblematic conclusion. Unpacking fleshes out the material carrier of the speaker's meaning in its particular context of speaking, with added meanings generated to achieve a well-formed pattern.

The gesture phase analysis shows that the caused motion meaning, with Tweety as the agent and the bowling ball as the patient, began in the previous clause (during "ball"). Caused motion tied together the two catchments, C1 and C2. "Drops" was integrated in this caused motion construction and performed the crucial job of shifting the antagonistic force from Tweety to the bowling ball.[11]

MORALS

An utterance, even though grammatically self-contained, contains content from outside of its own borders. This other content ties the utterance to the context at the level of thinking. The incorporation of context can draw on multiple sources—in the case study, one context (C2) was the backdrop to the GP and the core meaning of a downward antagonistic force; the other context (C1) supplied the semantic framework out of which the caused-motion construction was evoked. Caused-motion, in turn, provided the template for the full utterance.

The GP model, moreover, *predicts* a context in the sense that the context is necessary for the GP to be a psychological predicate and for the construction

11. This account does not touch on lexical activation; how, given contextual inputs and the idea of causation, the brain finds the information with which to categorize the event as a form of dropping, and then reaches the pattern of articulatory instructions with which to produce the word "drops" in a running phonetic context (see, e.g., the Language Production Project under Willem Levelt, at the Max Planck Institute for Psycholinguistics, Nijmegen, the Netherlands, summarized in various annual reports from the institute).

choice to be the endpoint and resolution of the dialectic. The GP model treats context as an integral part of thinking for speaking, rather than as an external parameter (as, for example, in Levelt 1989, de Ruiter 2000). By making a prediction of the context, a GP analysis meets the Popperian standard of falsification: the analysis of a GP would be rejected should the required context not be observed. This itself refutes the assertion by de Ruiter & Wilkins (1998) that the GP is not falsifiable.

The implication of the unpacking effect is that, before a GP is unpacked, thinking is not complete. It is not that one thinks first, then finds the language to express the thought (cf. Merleau-Ponty's remark against this position, quoted in Chapter 4.1); rather, thinking, as the source of meaning, emerges throughout the process of utterance formation.

Finally, that two contexts could collaborate to form a single grammatical structure also implies that a sense of grammatical form enters into utterances in piecemeal and oblique ways that do not necessarily follow the rule-governed patterns of the utterance's formal linguistic description. The caused-motion construction disguises the actual cognitive structure of the utterance and the fact that "it down" was at the core, burying and dividing it among separate, not necessarily closely linked constituents. Such concealments are possibly frequent, so long as unpacking does not damage the growth point and cost it its core differentiation; speech breakdowns may then ensue. Analysis of grammatical structure, in short, is not a recipe for performance. Grammatical form is the point at which the process stops, not where it begins, and this could be variable, dependent upon a variety of factors, including the threshold the speaker is holding for completeness at the moment of speaking, and would generally provide an approximation rather than an algorithmic solution.

SUMMARY AND COMMENTS

The growth point concept is intended to capture the essential features of an imagery-language dialectic, including the Pontian concept of meaning 'inhabiting' words and gestures, and the H-model concept of gesture and language comprising the speaker's momentary state of cognitive being. A significant additional concept brought into the discussion is that of the inseparability of the growth point from the context of speaking. This context is modeled in the form of fields of opposition and accessed empirically via a gestural variable, the catchment. The case study illustrated such inseparability, as well as the value of looking at catchments in order to discover the sources of the core idea units of speech. A further significant concept is that of unpacking. It is with this concept that the traditional psycholinguistic interest in sentence processing is addressed. The next subchapter will consider processing further.

Q and A

The concepts we have dealt with in this chapter can be summarized in the form of a Q and A series:

Q1. What does an imagery-language dialectic accomplish?
- It brings action-imagery into contact with language.
- It grounds linguistic categorial content in a material carrier.
- It provides an imagery unit for speaking.
- It addresses the synchrony of speech and gesture as part of thought.
- It ties the current idea unit to the larger discourse.
- It motivates constructions.
- It updates the speaker's and interlocutor's state of cognitive being.

Q2. What specifically does 'instability' accomplish? Instability 'fuels' thought and language, driving them forward, but how does this occur in the model, and where?
- The image and linguistic categorial content of a growth point are unlike versions of the same underlying idea. The idea unit itself is the point of contrast in a field of oppositions; both the contrast and the field are aspects of this idea and must be considered together. In the example, it was the bowling ball heading down, and this was the point of differentiation in the context of ways of countering Sylvester. To bring gesture and linguistic content into a common framework, other meanings must appear. The other meanings, moreover, have their own contextual frameworks. In the case study, reconciliation of the dialectic came via the caused-motion construction, and this belonged to one context while the GP belonged to another. The construction provided a framework within which the bowling ball could be the bestower of the antagonistic force and as it was filled out provided an intuitively well-formed 'stop order'.
- The observed surface form of the utterance emerged in three steps in the model, not necessarily in this temporal sequence, but logically distinct:

1. The preceding references to Sylvester's ascent ("he <e> / tri <i>es / going [[**up**] [the in**sid**][e of **the drain**pipe #]]") and Tweety's reaction ("Tweety Bird runs and gets a bowling ba[ll") set up the opposed forces paradigm—Tweety-down versus Sylvester-up. The bowling ball was an element of this paradigm, but appeared as an object of Tweety's caused-motion action, not as the antagonistic force itself. This was context #1—the paradigm of opposed forces.

2. The bowling ball became a metaphor of the force against Sylvester (discovered through its catchment). This was context #2—the bowling ball as antagonistic force. It was as an antagonistic force that the bowling ball image entered the growth point. No later than this step the linguistic categories, the "it" (= the bowling ball) and "down," had to have been activated.

3. Caused-motion resolved the dialectic. The final piece of the utterance, the ground component, "the drainpipe," could also have entered via caused-motion. Caused-motion and the growth point seem to have been active concurrently, but their contexts and functions are different, implying two thought processes. In this mix, the antagonistic force meaning was primary, the caused-motion meaning was secondary.[12]

12. However, we also need to deal with the opposite hypothesis, that the speaker was primarily describing how Tweety dropped the bowling ball, then thought that the bowling ball was a symbol of an antagonistic force. In this case, caused motion would be primary, the antagonistic force secondary. Such a model, however, encounters several difficulties. First, it does not explain why the stroke excluded "drops," a word that is a central component of the caused-motion construction. Second, it must ignore the catchment evidence. The antagonistic force catchment spanned the entire episode, whereas caused motion was local. Third, Tweety, the agent of the caused motion, is in the background in both speech and gesture, at the very point where the speaker should have been focusing on him. In speech, the referring form is actually a zero; in gesture, the hands continued moving right through the verb, the reference to caused motion. Also, fourth, gesture preparation began too soon and ended too late. Initiation should have been at the end of the conjunction "and," the nearest point in speech to the zero agent, and ended just prior to "drops," the caused-motion verb. Rather than caused-motion and Tweety, the speaker apparently focused on the antagonistic force and the bowling ball.

Extensions of GP

The growth point concept can be extended to new territory without sacrificing its character. The purpose of this subchapter is, first, to catalog some of these extensions and then, in this way, demonstrate the viability of the GP beyond the framework of the discourse type (storytelling) and the language (English) where it has been illustrated so far. Among the extensions is the fact that not all gestures synchronize with co-expressive speech. The GP handles this by coordinating with Kita's information packaging hypothesis (Kita 2000). Second, the discussion has been limited to narrative discourse with no mention of affect and volition. Third, languages other than English present challenging variations of growth points and unpacking. A case of this kind is analyzed in Turkish. Fourth, a stunning discovery by Goldin-Meadow et al. (2001) is that gesture improves memory; this is given an explanation from a GP point of view. There is a fifth extension, which is to bring the GP into contact with the social fabric of interaction, but this fundamental extension receives its own subchapter (Chapter 4.4).

ASYNCHRONIES

As the case study in the previous subchapter illustrates, GPs require synchrony of co-expressive speech and gesture (specifically, the gesture stroke) so that an opposition of unlike cognitive modes will occupy the same slice of time in the speaker's cognitive experience. The co-expressive speech can be identified from catchment evidence and other clues, and this speech and the gesture stroke are usually synchronous, as has been shown in numerous examples. Nonetheless, there are cases of speech-gesture asynchrony. In these cases, which amount to not more than 10 percent of all gestures (Nobe 2000), stroke onsets precede their co-expressive speech (the reverse asynchrony—speech preceding a co-expressive gesture—is rare and will be ignored). Sotaro Kita (2000) has proposed a model—the information packaging hypothesis (IPH)—that applies to such cases of gesture-speech asynchrony.

The IPH

The IPH addresses what the GP does not, namely, what occurs when a synchronization of co-expressive speech and gesture does not occur—a contextual mismatch, a memory lapse, or some other kind of breakdown. The IPH considers speech and gesture to be independent cognitive streams, running simultaneously and interweaving in time. The concept of independent and interweaving streams gives the theory a way to deal with speech and gesture asynchronies. When a speech blockage occurs, gesture continues and is able to develop new packages of information suitable for linguistic encoding. The theory thus specifically applies to situations where speech aborts, gesture continues, and then speech resumes, utilizing a new gesture-induced information package.

A further observation in this situation is that once speech and gesture resume, a *second gesture* often takes place, and the second gesture is synchronous and co-expressive with the renewed speech; this gesture-speech combination could be a GP. The two models, IPH and GP, thus might dovetail in time as well as complement each other in function.

Kita (2000) analyzed several examples involving asynchrony, among them the following. Recounting a scene in which Sylvester catapulted himself upward by throwing a weight onto the other end of a teeter-totter device, the speaker displayed a speech lapse, a gesture without speech, and then a resumption of speech and gesture. She said:

> and he grabs the bird and then when he comes down again <um> [/ the / weight / follows him / (gesture here)

and performed the illustrated gesture during the hesitation ('/'), immediately after the phrase "follows him" (Figure 4.3.1a–b). A large downward stroke depicted the weight falling onto Sylvester (LH = the weight, RH = Sylvester):

Fig. 4.3.1 (a and b). Gesture during hesitation. Preceded 'echo' gesture in Fig. 4.3.1c–d.

This gesture was followed immediately by a second gesture, which did synchronize with co-expressive speech (viz. "he gets clobbered"). This gesture and speech are a possible GP:

<and>] / [and **he get**s clobbered by the weight]

The 'echo' gesture was a replica of the first gesture but on a micro scale (Figure 4.3.1c–d), but it was a new gesture, focusing on the climax of the arc, the moment of impact, and was co-expressive with the synchronous "he gets clobbered," which also referred to the impact.

Fig. 4.3.1 (c and d). 'Echo' gesture with co-expressive speech—climactic moment of gesture in Fig. 4.3.1a–b.

The first gesture, the weight falling, takes place in the absence of speech. It is during this gesture, according to the IPH, that the speaker works out, visually and motorically, how the weight fell on Sylvester; Kita describes this gesture sequence as follows:

> The gesture in (1.4) [the 4.3.1a–b figure here] is an elaborate expression of the spatial model of the scene. . . . No substantive speech is concurrent with this gesture, presumably because of the complexity of the spatial information that the speaker has activated. In contrast, in (1.5) [the 4.3.1c–d figure here] the speaker focuses only on the final portion of the movement that is represented in (1.4). . . . [T]he change allows the speaker to package the spatial information into a compact linguistic form. (Kita 2000, p. 173)

The catapult episode is the most complex of the entire *Canary Row* cartoon, with multiple arcs, the weight and Sylvester rising and falling in complicated sequences and opposite directions. The point of it all is the weight ultimately falling on Sylvester, so the second gesture was actually the core idea; the first and larger arc gesture was related to it but was not the core. The weight falling gesture is perhaps why there was the breakdown of speech in the first place. The field of oppositions and the psychological predicate of the GP at the time of the second gesture would have been something like:

The Weight Falls: He Gets Clobbered.

This schema makes clear in what way the long arc in Figure 4.3.1a–b was related to the GP. It embodied the *field of oppositions* of the short arc (the GP gesture). As required of a psychological predicate, the idea unit was constructed by the speaker with two elements, a point of newsworthy content *and* a context from which it was differentiated. The context is what the IPH phase of the situation worked out. Accordingly, the initial gesture was not part of the GP, but led to it, and in this way the IPH and GP combine to give a full analysis of the sequence of gestures and speech.[1]

Comparison of IPH and GP

In both IPH and GP, imagery is regarded as an integral component of language, but there are also differences:

Minimal unit issue: The GP is a minimal unit in Vygotsky's sense: a unit that retains the essential properties of the whole. Despite its use of 'packaging' the IPH does not have such units. The model envisions speech and gesture modularly, as separate, intertwining streams.

Abstract imagery issue: In the GP, imagery is categorized linguistically. It is thus never purely visuospatial. On the other hand, the IPH appears to regard gesture as visual thinking pure and simple.

Interface issue: Regarding speech and gesture as separate intertwining streams, the IPH requires an image-language interface for the exchange of information between them. The GP does not have an interface—imagery and

---

1. A second example analyzed in Kita (2000) also displayed an 'echo' with co-expressive speech, after a full-size gesture performed absent speech, and it too seems to have been reshaped to constitute a psychological predicate in the context. Other narrators also produce such examples, suggesting that the phenomenon of speechless gestures followed by speech-synchronized gestures is a not infrequent one.

language combine dialectically. An imagery-language dialectic versus an inter-face is the single difference that seems to best encapsulate the contrast between the GP and IPH views of language and thought.

UNCONTEXTUALIZING CONTEXT

The possibility of an IPH-GP synthesis assumes that the IPH is limited to ges-ture anticipation cases. The synthesis would be undermined if the IPH were extended beyond the 10 percent of such cases. Kita & Özyürek (2003) have pro-posed such an extension based on the *Speaking* model of Levelt (1989) (the in-dependent streams metaphor lends itself to this model's modularity). *Speaking* itself does not address gesture but a number of models have been put forth based on it—Krauss (Krauss et al. 2000), de Ruiter (2000), Cassell (Cassell & Prevost 1996), and now Kita and Özyürek. These extensions share the same limitation, which derives ultimately from *Speaking* itself: they do not combine imagery and language into single units (growth points), and they are unable to describe the incorporation of context into verbal thought. These limits derive from the modular architecture they share.

The 'Speaking' Model

Speaking is composed of linked modules. Each module stands in a one-to-one equivalency to some component of a classical static linguistic description.[2] The Conceptualizer creates a logical form; the Formulator creates a syntactic form; the Lexicon is a storehouse of morphemes or 'lemmas', and so on. The 'preverbal message', initiated in the Conceptualizer and the input to the For-mulator, is structured as a language-like tree with contrasts both syntagmatic (captured in the tree) and paradigmatic (contrasts of logical arguments). Con-text is problematic. Context can be represented only as a data source, like world knowledge or inputs from the physical environment, viz., it can be handled statically, but cannot be treated dynamically or embodied in the conceptual organization of the utterance, since doing so would render structures unstable and open the module to influences outside the allowed inputs from other

2. The model seems to conceive of the language problem, as quoted earlier (Müller 2004a, pp. 0.16–17), "as merely a question of how to model the facets of the linguistic system so that they are all accessed and processed in a plausible order."

modules, and hence would undermine its very modularity. This of course is the fatal conflict of modularity versus context and points to a profound inappropriateness of the modular approach in a dynamic model.

The Kita-Özyürek Modular Model

The flow chart from Kita & Özyürek (2003, fig. 7) is their extrapolation of the *Speaking* model, with two modifications (Figure 4.3.2). The modifications are the boxes on the right and left labeled, respectively, the '*Speaking* model' and the 'gesture module'.

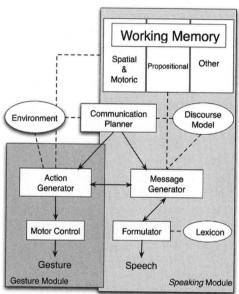

Fig. 4.3.2. Modular model of gesture performance.

Based on Kita and Özyürek (2003). Dashed lines are information sources, solid arrows are inputs. The lighter box on the right is Kita and Özyürek's speech model based on Levelt's *Speaking* (1989). The darker box on the left is their added gesture module.

The most basic division of Figure 4.3.2 is between the gesture and speech modules. Context can reach them over two routes—the Message Generator and, indirectly, the Communication Planner—but there is no way to capture the joint differentiation by speech and gesture of newsworthy content from a field of oppositions, and hence no way to provide GPs.

The unity of "it down" plus the downward thrusting image in the case study would be explained, not as an idea unit differentiated as an instance of 'ways of countering Sylvester', but as a combination of inputs, roughly as follows: an intention to speak of the bowling ball; an intention to mention Tweety; an immediately preceding mention of Sylvester. All these factors combine in the Action Generator, which is linked to the Message Generator in the speaking module. That is, a series of steps, not a minimal imagery-language dialectic unit.

How speech-gesture timing is accomplished in this system captures in a nutshell the conceptual differences between this kind of model and a dialectic. In the Kita-Özyürek model, speech-gesture timing is created externally, by sending coordinating signals between the Action Generator and the Message Generator, and between the latter and the Formulator. In a dialectic, synchrony is part of the thought itself and arises from the speaker's conceptual intentions; there are no external signals needed or desired.

One might suppose simply adding a 'GP module' to the flow chart could solve the problem. However, such a module would be redundant and would, in graph-theoretic terms, reduce to zero—the 'node' would vanish under the operation of removing redundant points from the graph, and the GP would turn out not to have been added after all.[3]

3. What would a dialectic interpretation of the 'swing' phenomenon on which Kita and Özyürek in part base their model look like? The phenomenon refers to a scene from the Sylvester and Tweety story where Sylvester, trying to reach Tweety as usual, fashions a kind of rope in the sky from which to swing between his building and the building across the street where Tweety is perched. He misses, of course, smashes into a wall, and falls to the ground. Speakers of English describing this scene use verbs like "swing" combined with gestures that follow an arc trajectory. Japanese happens not to have an intransitive verb meaning "to swing" (it has only a transitive verb meaning "to swing something"). Speakers of Japanese describing the scene often perform two gestures, one straight and a second with an arc, or sometimes one straight gesture, omitting the arc. My contention is that the explanation of this phenomenon is essentially the same from a dialectic position as it is from Kita and Özyürek's, and so the presence of either explanation does not distinguish the two positions. Kita and Özyürek explain the effect as follows. The arc gestures reflect visual recall of the cartoon scene. This information enters into the gesture module to trigger the arc gesture; the first (straight) gesture is the result of the normal utterance production process, which includes the production of a gesture to match the spoken utterance. A dialectic explanation of the same phenomenon emphasizes that Japanese speakers form a thought unit that categorizes the image as 'go', 'jump', 'fly', or 'sneak in' (the intransitive verbs that occurred). The image is shaped to fit these non-arc categorizations, just as Viv.'s image of thrusting down was shaped, in her case to fit the meaning of a causative construction. Thus, the idea unit being differentiated does not

Other Modular Models

The Krauss, Cassell, and de Ruiter models are similar but differ in where gesture hooks into *Speaking*—for Kita and Özyürek this is 'in advance' of the Message Generator (Levelt's Conceptualizer); for Krauss et al. it is the same, but this version lacks a Communication Planner; for de Ruiter it is the Conceptualizer; and for Cassell and Prevost it is the Formulator. But these differences do not alter the basic critique. In all models, modularity demands a division of gesture from language and the separation of gesture and language from context. Unlike these models, the GP can specify the relationship of the thought unit to the context. Modular models, because they cannot incorporate context, do not. For example, de Ruiter (2000) rejects 'with binoculars at' as the 'lexical' or 'speech affiliate' of a gesture of holding binoculars before the eyes that synchronized with the Dutch equivalent of that phrase:

enne,   da's dus Sylvester   die zit   [**met een verrekijker naar**]   de overkant te kijken
and eh   so that is Sylvester   who is   with binoculars at   the other side watching

De Ruiter claims that inferring the gesture's lexical affiliate based on speech-gesture synchrony entails a circular reasoning process. But it is circular only because his modular model is unable to explain how gestures incorporate context. The incorporation of context *predicts* what the field of oppositions would have to have been: a field in which looking through binoculars from a first-person perspective was the newsworthy content. If this field does not obtain, the hypothesis of an idea unit that combines 'with binoculars at' with a first-person image of holding binoculars would be falsified.

Modular Models Exemplify Vygotsky's 'Elements'

Explaining what he meant by a psychological unit, Vygotsky contrasted such a smallest unit, which retains the essential properties of a whole, to 'elements'.

---

include an arcing trajectory but does include motion of some kind. However, there is still the visual memory of the arc, and this is why a second gesture occurs. The explanations are, in other words, quite similar, but one posits an idea unit comprising two modes of cognition, in a dialectic, and the other separates them into different modules. The conclusion I take from the possibility of similar explanations based on opposed principles is that the swing phenomenon does nothing to choose between the two hypotheses.

Elements carry the reduction down to a level that enables generalizations, but loses sight of the whole:

> [I]nstead of enabling us to examine and explain specific instances and phases, and to determine concrete regularities in the course of events, this method produces generalities pertaining to all speech and all thought. It leads us moreover into serious errors by ignoring the unitary nature of the process under study. . . . Psychology, which aims at a study of complex holistic systems, must replace the method of analysis into elements with the method of analysis into units. (Vygotsky 1986, pp. 4–5)

The Kita-Özyürek and other modular models validate this insight. Modular models reduce language and imagery to a level of generality that occurs regardless of context (the Action Generator, Message Generator, Communication Planner, etc.), and the individual GP, the newsworthy content in context, vanishes.

SPEECH-GESTURE MISMATCHES

Speech-gesture mismatch is a phenomenon the IPH is well-designed to explain (cf. Goldin-Meadow 1997; the entire body of mismatch work is described in Goldin-Meadow 2003a). A mismatch occurs when speech conveys one version of a situation and gesture a different version. 'Mismatch' is to be distinguished from speech-gesture co-expressiveness. In co-expressiveness, speech and gesture jointly present the same idea unit; in a mismatch, there are two ideas that may be incompatible. The mismatch phenomenon is interpreted as a point along a developmental curve (Goldin-Meadow & Singer 2003). Early on, it appears, children have information that appears only in gesture; concurrent speech, lacking this information, presents a different, less developed version of the same event or process, and this engenders the mismatch. Speech subsequently develops a capability to convey the same version. So the mismatch phenomenon is an interesting developmental effect, whereby new developments appear first in gesture, later in spoken form, and during the interval in between, mismatches occur. At later developmental points, and also in adults (who show mismatches, of which more below), information may appear in gesture alone at some moment, but it is not confined to gesture, as it is early in development, and will be found in speech on another occasion.

Many of Goldin-Meadow's experiments are conducted with children solving an arithmetic problem such as

put the number into the blank: $5 + 4 + 3 = \underline{\quad} + 3$.

Children adopt a variety of strategies for solving such problems, not all of them successful. One incorrect strategy is to add all the numbers to the left of the equals sign and put this sum (12) in the blank. A mismatch occurs when a child states one strategy in speech and displays a different strategy in gesture. Mismatch is not tied to correct or incorrect answers but to the presence of different strategies for obtaining answers of either kind. In this example, a mismatch would be *saying* "add the 5, the 4, and the 3," while *making a gesture* with two fingers pointing to the 5 and 4 on the left side, excluding the 3.

The IPH is well-suited to explain these mismatches. In the IPH, the separate threads of gesture and speech go their own ways, and this leads to mismatching speech-gesture situations, both as a developmental phenomenon and as an adult or older-child phenomenon. The IPH predicts that, when there is a mismatch, the gesture is likely to embody the correct strategy, no matter what the child is saying at the same time. This is because gesture is the path-breaker. Speech expresses the same strategy but only after an information package has been developed in gesture.

Considering just the children who do not solve the math problems, what is fascinating is that the mismatchers, those with incompatible gestured and spoken strategies, are more likely to learn from subsequent adult instruction than matchers, children with a single wrong strategy in both speech and gesture (Church & Goldin-Meadow 1986). Also, experienced teachers, who are shown videos of matching and mismatching children, select the mismatchers as having a better grasp of the problem (without awareness that gesture was the source of their impression; Goldin-Meadow et al. 1993).

Relation to Growth Points

The implication of mismatches is that they do not form growth points. The whole thrust of the mismatch phenomenon and its effects on trainability, is that speech and gesture do *not* form a single idea unit. The child should have the feeling that things do not mesh; the disparity should puzzle her and cause the readiness to change (cf. Wagner & Goldin-Meadow, under review, who find that children expend more cognitive effort on mismatches). Indeed, the very absence of GPs with mismatches could contribute to the instability that Goldin-Meadow argues underlies the trainability of the children displaying them.

However, there is another type of mismatch that does lend itself to unified idea units and to GP formation. In this second kind of mismatch an idea unit takes form on a new level—metanarrative/metapragmatic. The following is an example:[4]

She [slugs him] or throws him out / [it doesn't work]

           1   2

1. Iconic depiction of slugging him
2. Reduced repetition of 1 (= the mismatch in this case)

The second gesture mismatches the synchronous speech on the object level (slugging), but by shifting up to the discourse level forms a coherent combination with speech. The meaning is approximately that slugging (in imagery) has the quality that it "doesn't work," and this meta-level comment plus gesture could comprise a GP that consists of an idea unit on the discourse level. Unlike the logical contradiction of the arithmetic mismatch, this mismatch forms a coherent idea unit, but one must go up a level to see it. Chapter 5 describes further how gestures form idea units on the discourse level.

Once again, the IPH and GP hypotheses can complement each other. The IPH describes classic mismatches of the kind found in the arithmetic samples, where it is impossible to form a single idea unit. The GP applies when a level shift can take place and co-expressive speech and gesture form a GP on the new level.

SELF-MIMICRY: TURKISH TEMPORAL OFFSETS

Another Seeming Asynchrony

In 1999, at the Max Planck Institute in Nijmegen, Asli Özyürek and Sotaro Kita showed me a striking example of a gesture speech-gesture temporal mismatch in the speech of a Turkish language speaker (see Özyürek 2001a, 2001b). The speaker was describing the same bowling ball scene that figured in the GP case study and produced a series of phrases, each with a gesture. However—and this was the surprise—the gestures appeared to correspond to the spoken phrases that immediately *followed* the gesture, not the phrases with which they were

---

4. Thanks to Susan Duncan.

synchronous (see Figures 4.3.3 through 4.3.5; recording, transcription, and English translation by Asli Özyürek):[5]

(1). [top bi sekil-<u>de</u>] ball in one way
   hands hopping in place. See Fig. 4.3.3a–b–c.

(2). [zipla-ya zipla-ya] while hopping
   hands hopping and moving right. See Fig. 4.3.4a–b–c–d.

(3). [yuvar-lan-a <u>yuvar-lan-a</u>] while rolling itself
   hand moves right. See Fig. 4.3.5a–b.

(4). [sokak-tan] on the street
   hands again move right without hopping = path alone

Fig. 4.3.3. (a–c). Hands hopping in place with "ball one way."

Hands hop in place = manner without path

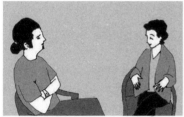

Fig. 4.3.4. (a–d). Hands hopping and moving right (= rolling) with "while hopping."

Hands hop and move to right = manner with path

Fig. 4.3.5. (a and b). Hand moves right with "while rolling itself."

Hands moves to right without hopping = path alone

5. I am grateful to Özyürek and Kita for a copy of the video from which these clips were taken.

(5). [gid-iyo] goes

> hands again move right without hopping = path alone
> "ball somehow, hopping, rolling, goes on the street"

The gesture at (1) showed hopping in place with speech that was about the bowling ball, not about motion. This was therefore already a mismatch. Then the phrase that followed at (2) ("while hopping") was co-expressive with the gesture at (1). The gesture with "while hopping" in turn showed rolling (hopping and moving to the right at the same time). This gesture was followed by its seemingly co-expressive utterance at (3), "while rolling itself." This in turn was accompanied by a gesture showing pure path, corresponding possibly to the phrase at (4), "on the street." From (4) onward, speech and gesture lined up in a familiar one-to-one way.

These temporal mismatches are not identical to the earlier "clobbers" example. Here, every gesture synchronized with some speech; there was no silence and no gesture echo. If anything, there were 'speech echoes', with the speech in each of the first three lines echoing the preceding gesture.

However, I shall argue that the *synchronous* speech and the gestures in (1) through (3) were in fact, despite appearances, co-expressive, and formed GPs. The speech-gesture offsets are due to another, newly seen process.

Analysis of the Offsets and the Synchronies[6]

The key to this analysis is the two occurrences of the adverbial "while" in (2) and (3). These adverbials do two things. First, they referentially link their speech to the gesture of the preceding phrase:

Gesture	*Speech*
1. hands hop	1. ball somehow
2. hands roll	2. while hopping
3. hands move to right	3. while rolling

Second, they add categorial content to the gestures with which they are synchronous—the rolling in (2) is 'while' there is hopping; the motion to the right in (3) is 'while' there is rolling. The co-expressivity between synchronous speech and gesture at (2) and (3) is about the *causes* of the motions displayed in

---

6. This analysis of the Turkish offsets differs significantly from one I proposed in McNeill (2000).

the gestures; this is the effect of the 'while's: hopping at (2), which is stated in speech, *causes* the rolling depicted in the simultaneous gesture; rolling at (3), in speech, *causes* the rightward motion shown in the gesture. In other words, the GPs are about causation—the speaker is trying to explain the odd sight of Sylvester's rolling on the street like a living bowling ball, which she initially flagged with "somehow," at (1), as puzzling. This second effect of "while" is therefore to establish the co-expressivity of the synchronous speech and gestures at (2)–(3). The entire sentence, as it unfolds, embodies the speaker's analysis of the causal structure concerning the way the cat ended up with a bowling ball inside him and rolling down the street.

The salience of causation, and hence a tendency to build sentences just for the purpose of exposing it, might be greater in Turkish than English. Causation is not hidden inside the verb semantics of Turkish the way it lurks within English verbs like "rolls." Croft (1999) and Goldberg (1997) have analyzed manner—the rolling itself—in English verbs as the causes of the motions the verbs imply, and the Turkish speaker seems to have performed a similar analysis intuitively. Causes in Turkish must be isolated and encoded on their own, as was the case in this example, via the instances of "while."[7]

Speech and gesture were co-expressive at (1) as well, although here the analysis differs. Statement (1) was the starting point of the entire analytic description, (1)–(5), in which the speaker was trying to work out what caused Sylvester to roll down the street. The growth point at (1) was the causal theme: The ball somehow (caused) hopping (and hopping led to rolling and the succeeding phrases and gestures). The core idea that speech and gesture jointly expressed at (1) was this puzzle the speaker was solving.

Self-Mimicking GPs

But this example also contains something never before seen. It is the echoing or 'self-mimicking' of two or three gestures by their immediately succeeding spoken phrases. My proposal is that this echoing reveals is a mechanism of *self-mimicry*, which I suggest is the source of the temporal mismatches (although they are not really 'mismatches' if this is the mechanism). Self-mimicry conceivably is a process unique to Turkish, although I suspect it is broader and could occur as a device in other languages with 'free' or 'pragmatic' word order (for example, Italian). Self-mimicry would not readily occur in English, with

7. I am grateful to Asli Özyürek for discussing this point with me.

its largely construction-based word orders. Self-mimicry is a *rhetorical* usage in which a gesture is performed and then, in a second step, is verbalized. Self-mimicry could be adaptive in 'free' word-order situations, because it bridges one GP to the next and so ensures smooth speech transitions.

Conclusion of Turkish Offsets

The important conclusions for this discussion are that there exist synchronous co-expressive speech and gestures at each step in the above sequence, and that self-mimicry is a mechanism that can determine word order when construction formulae leave this order unspecified.

✓ GESTURES IN SIGN LANGUAGE

As described briefly in Chapter 1, sign languages of the deaf are full languages that arise naturally for those who cannot use the oral-acoustic channel. Sign languages use the hands and body to create linguistically encoded messages formed out of space, shape, and motion. What could the dynamic dimension of a sign language look like? I intend to approach this question by seeking possible grounds for an imagery-language dialectic in sign language. Sign languages are comparable to spoken languages on their static dimension, and they should be similar on the dynamic dimension. If this is the case, we should find gestures co-occurring with signed utterances. That ASL and other sign languages have gestures, however, is controversial. The gist of this section is that sign language is deeply similar to speech in its underlying dynamics, it should be possible to find an imagery-language dialectic in sign language as in speech, and manual gestures involving motion, space, and form should participate in it. The difficulty is recognizing them.[8]

Some Examples

Scott Liddell has been at the forefront of articulating the hypothesis that sign usage includes gestures (Liddell 2000, 2003a,b). He describes signs (in ASL

---

8. The problem of sorting out gestures from signs is not unlike the way that prosody in speech may contain oral gestures combined with systematic aspects (cf. Okrent 2002 for discussion).

and other sign languages) that refer to transfers of real or metaphoric objects (giving, seeing, and the like) and pronouns, all of which include a deictic component. A verb like GIVE has a lexically specified start point and hand configuration, but must conclude at a locus determined by the location of the recipient of the action. So "give to a child" has a different terminus from "give to a (standing) adult." A second-person (or non-first-person) pronoun is likewise directed at its referent. The different locations could be termed categorial (e.g., a 'tall recipient morpheme' versus a 'short recipient morpheme'), but Liddell argues that the number of classes of signs required for this would be too great for such a morphological analysis to remain plausible. Hence, he argues, the deictic component is gestural.

Sarah Taub (2001) similarly describes usages of classifier signs (signs for general classes of objects, like 'a person' or 'a vehicle'), in which path and manner content combine with the classifier in an iconic fashion—e.g., a person walking up hill along a winding road: signed with an extended index finger (the classifier for a person) moving back-and-forth (the winding) and simultaneously upward (the slanted road). The classifier is a conventionalized form but the path and manner components are iconic and gestural (Taub's criterion for iconicity is that a sign is iconic insofar as it presents a structural correspondence between the signer's conception of an event—here, a person wandering up a hill—and the analysis of the event built into the *form* of the sign). This gestural approach, however, is controversial. Other linguists, foremost among them Ted Supalla, himself a native signer, have argued that the seemingly graded and iconic aspects of signs are in fact 'parameterized' or categorial. According to his position, the variations are linguistic combinations of morphological elements (Supalla has so argued since 1978; for a recent review, see Supalla 2003). To an outsider, the controversy seems overly dependent on definitions and a priori commitments, and accordingly hard to resolve. It appears that variations in signs can be viewed either as continuous and gradient (hence, gestural) or, with equal authority, as innovations on a linguistic category (hence, linguistic).[9]

9. Supalla (2003) interestingly describes his own inability to imitate gestures made by his hearing students. For him, apparently, gestures are automatically reshaped to fit ASL phonological standards.

A Possible Resolution

The dialectic hypothesis predicts that other kinds of gestures than deictic should appear in sign language performance. Susan Duncan (in press) has recorded a phenomenon in Taiwan sign language (TSL) that appears to show the co-production of signs and *iconic* gestures. The phenomenon is the deformation of canonical signs at points of newsworthy content during cartoon narrations, the same points where speaking narrators tend to perform gestures. The deformations reshape the sign to fit the immediate discourse context. Duncan proposes that sign deformation is a signal of gesture occurrence.

Figure 4.3.6 illustrates an example involving a classifier in TSL for an animate being with more than two legs. The standard form of this classifier is made with the thumb, the index finger, and the middle finger extended and spread apart, the rest of the fingers curled in, the palm down.

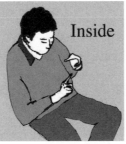

Fig. 4.3.6 (a and b). Possible gestures with the TSL sign for 'animate being with more than two legs', deformed at the same discourse junctures where gestures also occur by hearing speakers.

However, when describing Sylvester going up the pipe on the outside, the signer deformed the classifier by having the first and second fingers, instead of extending outward, 'walk up' the space above the right hand (the left hand was also curved to show the pipe but did not provide the spatial locus for the 'walking'); see Figure 4.3.6a.[10]

Describing Sylvester's second attempt, on the inside (Figure 4.3.6b), the signer used the same sign but reduced the canonical shape to just one extended first finger, which he pushed under his left hand (use of a single index finger for interiority was seen in the hearing English speaker gestures in Chapter 4.2).

10. Note that the thumb is also extended, which reinforces the conclusion that what we see here is a modified sign (extension of the thumb is part of the canonical sign form). It is not clear why the fourth finger was extended, but perhaps this was compensation for the gestural use of the first and second fingers, to maintain something of the 'extended-fingers' feel of the canonical sign.

These deformations occurred at just the discourse junctures where hearing speakers also perform gestures, and are plausibly actual gestures in TSL, co-occurring, as deformations, with conventional signs. If so, they capture the same contrast of outside-inside paths that informed the psychological predicates for English speakers (Chapter 4.2).

The Gradients Question

For Liddell, one of the hallmarks of a gesture is that it should be 'graded' and not normalized to categories. Not every speech-synchronized gesture is graded. Partitioning space into right and left for two characters in a narration, for example, does not imply any sort of graded significance. But if something is graded, it is potentially gestural. Very little experimentation has addressed the gradient issue. Emmorey & Herzig (2003) have conducted perhaps the first experiment explicitly designed to address it. They presented fluent signers with a range of signs that, in small steps, differed in the locus of a classifier element contained in the sign (a tapered-O, signaling the location of a small object, like a gnat). Emmorey and Herzig found that signers who saw these signs in a video understood the variations in a continuous way—that is, saw the location of the classifier *iconically*, as a gradient signal, rather than as a categorial one. Such results seem to support Liddell's interpretation. Supalla (2003), however, citing the same study, regards it as supporting his claim for categorial normalization: so the controversy continues. Ambiguous results are perhaps not surprising, because the stimulus presentation was lacking in contextual framing. Decoupling the sign from any kind of field of oppositions leaves room for intuitions of form but little space for the differentiation of new content (through which signs could tap the dynamic dimension).

Homesigns

The great majority of children who are born deaf have hearing parents, and the parents sometimes elect to raise their children 'orally'. As a consequence, the children are effectively deprived of linguistic input during the early stages of language acquisition. The situation in effect is the ancient Herodotus experiment actually carried out. The children, unlike those imagined by Herodotus, devise miniature gesture languages of a kind referred to as 'homesign', making up their own manual-spatial linguistic codes. Homesigns are of particular interest for the light they shed on the human capacity for language. The home-sign solutions by different children, despite isolation and living in different cultures and times, show remarkable similarities, and it is this resemblance that makes homesign so evocative of a deeply entrenched human language capacity.

Susan Goldin-Meadow has devoted many years to collecting and studying homesign systems, first in a group of children living in Philadelphia, then with others in Chicago, and more recently with children in a non-English-speaking environment in Taiwan. Though adults appear to comprehend homesign ut-terances, they typically do not adopt the children's homesigns in their own gestures. This absence is important, because it shows that the parents are not the source of the homesign regularities displayed by the children. Goldin-Meadow has published her findings in full detail in a book, *The Resilience of Language* (2003b), with a title that captures her central thesis: the qualities that appear in homesign, invented again and again, are the 'resilient' qualities of human language that can appear even in the absence of linguistic input.

It seems plausible to interpret homesign as the creation of a *static* dimen-sion, a miniature Saussurian langue (but with an unusual split of the social facts: the children produce it, parents and sibs understand it but don't pro-duce it themselves, and so no one both produces and understands it).[11] A question therefore arises not unlike that in ASL: What are the gestures when space and movement are dominated by sign production? The answer is similar also. Goldin-Meadow illustrated one deaf child's use of space that is strikingly similar to what Liddell has described for ASL. The child performed a twist-ing movement (= a 'verb' meaning to remove something by twisting) in the direction of a jam jar, whose lid she was requesting the addressee, an adult inter-locutor, to remove (Goldin-Meadow 2003b, Fig. 12, panel B, p. 111). As in ASL, the location of the recipient blended with the sign for the action. It is unknown whether deaf children also create homesign deformations, like the TSL defor-mations seen earlier (Figure 4.3.6). This too would suggest the co-occurrence of gesture and sign. However, none of the examples in Goldin-Meadow suggest such deformations (though perhaps they haven't been sought).

11. Although Goldin-Meadow has recorded instances where one of the children uses his homesigns to 'talk' to himself while looking for an object.

Why Homesigns Are Considered Static

Despite the asymmetric division of production and comprehension noted above, homesigns have the property of 'shareability' (Freyd 1983). The very fact that signs must be shared, albeit asymmetrically, moves them toward static forms that recur in different contexts.

Two reasons for saying that homesign, as described, does not reveal the dynamic dimension of language can be mentioned, anticipating the discussion in Chapter 6. A developmental signature of the dialectic is an abrupt increase in gesture output; this seems to occur between ages three and four, after an earlier stage in which gesture is at a low frequency. The upsurge suggests that gestures have become integrated into the child's linguistic output. In contrast, homesigns are always at a high frequency.

The 'decomposition effect' is another dialectic signature. Decomposition means the avoidance of path and manner in the same gesture, even though path/manner combinations occur at younger ages; decomposition also appears between three and four. It suggests that gestures are becoming integrated with speech analytically, path and manner being handled separately as opposed to participating globally, without individuation, as at younger ages. Susan Goldin-Meadow tells me that homesign children do not show decomposition at any age, again suggesting that homesigns are on a different track.

THE 'INCREASED MEMORY WITH GESTURE' EFFECT

theater

Goldin-Meadow et al. (2001) published a sensational result: memory for inci-   ✓✓
dental information *improves if you perform gestures*. The gestures are appropriate to speech, not to the incidental information; yet the incidental information is remembered better. The experiment was as follows. The subject, a child or an adult, solved math problems (an equivalence problem for children, finding factors for adults), and then explained the solution to the experimenter. While giving this explanation, he or she was also told to retain in memory a set of letters or names the experimenter provided; the extra items had no connection with the problem or the explanation. When no gestures were made, subjects recalled fewer of the letters or names. This was true if the subjects were told not to gesture by the experimenter and also true if a subject, on her own, although allowed to gesture, did not. In both nongesture cases, memory was

poorer, and by the same amount. Clearly, therefore, any extra effort to obey the instruction not to gesture cannot explain the decrement. Thus, one infers that making gestures increases the capacity of memory, and/or not making them decreases it. What could explain this surprising result?

Why would a gesture improve memory for irrelevant information? One possible factor is that a material carrier effect enhances whatever state of being exists, a state that could broadly include memory both for the problem to be solved and for anything else taking place concurrently. A general enhancement would be consistent with the H-model.

From a GP perspective, we can nominate three specific mechanisms whereby gesturing enhances memory and/or not gesturing decreases it.

- First, many of the gestures in the experiment were deictic and functioned to organize the problem spatially. With gestures occurring, the problem was treated as an extended spatial object. Absent a gesture, this spatial structure would have less substance.
- Second, because of the imagery in GPs, thinking could align with the spatial layout of the problem when gestures occur, but was less able to when absent.
- Third, speech rhythms align with gestures and spatial content when gestures occur, but absent a gesture would be less coordinated with the spatial layout of the problem.

These mechanisms are not mutually exclusive: gesture can materialize the spatial structure of the problem, lead to GPs (idea units) mapping this structure and produce a corresponding rhythmic speech flow. All can affect memory. Spatial structure is a mnemonic, especially when externalized. The linkage of memory to spatial structure was known in ancient times. Roman orators made use of the layout of space around them to recall the points of a speech—point 1 is on top of an urn, point 2 at the foot of the statue, point 3 on the tip of the emperor's nose, and so forth (Yates 1966); this technique was called the 'method of loci' (Gregory 1987, pp. 493–494). The Goldin-Meadow et al. experiment may have tapped the same mechanism.

THE LAST 'WHY'

Obviously, we should expect quite different growth points depending on the propositional content of the story being recounted. However, we should also expect different growth points depending on the speaker's emotions and interests. Vygotsky, at the conclusion of *Thought and Language* (1986), writes:

> Thought is not begotten by thought; it is engendered by motivation, i.e., by our desires and needs, our interests and emotions. Behind every thought there is an affective-volitional tendency, which holds the answer to the last "why" in the analysis of thinking. (252)

The growth point would also be dependent on the affective context at the moment of speaking. A speaker who sees irony sees different oppositions and points of departure than a speaker who sees honest effort. Anger, fear, amusement, interest—these are different fields and foster different potential oppositions within them. 'The next thing' in a story is defined by the actual events of the story and the speaker's memory for them, but the context in which these events are opposed is self-created. This is where the affective-volitional tendencies of the speaker can enter in, since the growth point is differentiated from a set of oppositions. We should accordingly *expect* different growth points and utterances depending on affect.

Here is one illustration of an 'affective tendency'. Tweety's dropping of the bowling ball can be recast in an ironic mood. This actually appears in some narratives. Although the propositional content is the same, the significant oppositions are not the interiority of the path but the convenient fact, arranged by the animators, that the top of the pipe is right next to Tweety's window, not at the roof of the building. An ironic point of view has consequences for what is seen as significant, and this translates into different kinds of growth points. The growth point might be not "up" + an image of the interior, but "contrived by the filmmaker" + the image of the top of the pipe. The sentence that unpacks this GP would be not "up through the pipe" but something like "of course there's a drainpipe right next to Tweety," all this arising from the same memory trace of the cartoon but interacting with an ironic mood that induces a different set of oppositions. The important point is that *all* utterances would be formed in this way, not just ironic ones, so an affective tendency *is*, as Vygotsky states, an ultimate 'why' of language and thought (and, we add, gesture).

If this way to include affective tendencies is clear, at least in principle, there is still the question of how to include volition. It is clear that Viv.'s battle plan was guided by overarching 'volitional tendencies'—her memory for the episode, her goal of explaining the course of events and its several climaxes (becoming a living bowling ball, rolling, entering the bowling alley, and knocking over the pins), a commitment to sequentiality, and probably others. The set of oppositions that gave the case study growth point significance presupposed several of these themes. Yet how to represent them is anything but clear. Consistent with the theory, we should like to trace their effects on the field of oppositions, and from these effects see how volition shaped the GP or focal idea unit; this remains a remote goal. The overarching catchment, C2, suggests some of this tendency was carried in imagery of the bowling ball as an antagonistic force, but this is only a part of a complete account. Not only is volition the 'last why' but also is another extension of the GP (yet to be achieved).[12]

12. Arriving too late for mention other than via this note, Adam Kendon's *Gesture: Visible Action as Utterance* (Cambridge University Press, 2005) and the present book could well have been presented as companions. Kendon admirably provides quantities of detail with which to contextualize gestures from a rich assortment of Neapolitan and English materials. From these details, encompassing form and context and including the social interactive situations in which the examples appeared, it is often possible to infer growth points. I observe ample confirmation of the principle of an imagery-language dialectic that incorporates the context of speaking. In the Neapolitan examples especially, we can also see the potential for new insights into how conventionalized forms (which these gestures display in abundance) blend with and steer an imagery-language dialectic.

Social-Interactive Context

Thus far my illustrations of an imagery-language dialectic and the attendant discourse and semantic context have come from narrative discourse. In this subchapter, I explicate the social framework of gesture production. I intend the chapter to be an illustration, in clarified form, of a process that I believe exists in all gesture performance. A social framework is felt not only in the form of specialized social regulators and the gravitational pull of the social other (cf. Özyürek 2002), but in *all* gestures and the growth points formed out of them. Even a seemingly monologic narration is social; one person does most of the talking but the performance is strongly geared to the listener, and this applies to the gestures as well (cf. Özyürek 2000). The social framework exhibited by conversational gestures is not a performance of a distinct type but is a process present in all gesture performance. (Cf. the simplistic distinction of the controversy over speaker-benefit versus listener-benefit in Chapter 2.)

THE MR. A–MR. B 'MORAL DILEMMA'[1]

The example to be analyzed comes from a conversation recorded in the early 1970s by Starkey Duncan as part of a larger investigation of face-to-face interaction (see Duncan & Fiske 1977 for the full study). The participants were previously unacquainted male graduate students at the University of Chicago. Mr. A was a law student; Mr. B a social work student. A and B were introduced,

---

1. An earlier version of this section appeared in McNeill (2003).

Table 4.4.1. Selection from a conversation between two male students.

Mr. A	Mr. B
Q$_{A6}$ how do you like Chicago compared to	
Q$_{A7}$ did you [go to school thére] or uh	
points to shared space	
	R$_{B7.1}$ I did go to school [there]
	points to shared space
	R$_{B7.2}$ [I went to school hére]
	points to left
	R$_{B7.3}$ [álso]
	circles to left
uh-huh	
	R$_{B7.4}$ [I]
	points to shared space
	R$_{B7.5}$ [/ um]
	points to left
	R$_{B7.6}$ so I [came back]
	points to shared space
oh, uh-huh	
	R$_{B7.7}$ [kind of /]
	points to right
Q$_{A8}$ an' [you wént to undergraduate hére or .... (A's gesture hold) ....]	
points to shared space	
	R$_{B8}$ [in Chicágo] át, uh, Loyola
	points to shared space
óh óh óh óh óh I'm an óld Jésuit boy mysélf //	
unfórtunately	

placed in front of a video camera, and told simply to "have a conversation." As would be expected in such a situation, the participants, seeking topics about which they could talk, started with their respective academic biographies. Each already knew that the other was a graduate student at the University of Chicago and knew the specific school within the university to which the other was attached, but did not know anything else about the other's history. This unknown history created the situation we shall examine.

Table 4.4.1 gives the snippet of the Mr. A–Mr. B conversation on which we will be focusing. It picks up at the end of what has been Mr. A's already, by then, extended effort to uncover Mr. B's academic history, something about which Mr. B was oddly unforthcoming. Mr. A had asked earlier, "Where did you come from before?" and Mr. B had offered, "Mm, Iowa. I lived in Iowa." This led Mr. A down the garden path, however, because Mr. B proved reluctant to take

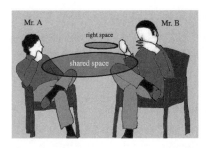

Fig. 4.4.1. Spatial arrangement of the Mr. A and Mr. B during the conversation.

up Iowa as a topic, but the Iowa theme is relevant in that it led directly to the exchanges in Table 4.4.1. After Iowa petered out, Mr. A resumed his quest (Q means a question, R means a reply, A or B means the speaker, and the number of the question or reply is the ordinal position of the item in the snippet; notation as in Silverstein 1997). (See Figure 4.4.1 for the spatial arrangement of Mr. A and Mr. B.)

Michael Silverstein's Analysis of the Text

Silverstein (1997) identifies "stretches of interactionally-effected denotational text." These are runs of local cohesion indexed via references to past or present locations. In Q_{A7} Mr. A formulates his probe about Mr. B's 'then$_B$' with "go to school". His goal is to elicit information about Mr. B's relationship to 'there$_B$'. The most recent denotational frame was that of cities and states in Iowa and this would be the default frame for the emphasized "thére" of Q_{A7}. Yet, ambiguity remains since the form "thére" can substitute for either "in Iowa" or "at Iowa" (and which, "in" or "at", is left unsaid). In other words, it could equally designate '^{S}there$_B$' or '^{U}there$_B$'. (C means City, S State, and U University).

Mr. B does nothing to disambiguate the frame in R$_{B7.1}$, where he repeats the precise formulation of Mr. A's Q$_{A7}$, using the same predicating phrase "go to school there." Mr. B, however, continues to clarify the temporal order of the paradigm that he has set up, but still not the institutional affiliation: He has gone to school "here$_B$," he says in R$_{B7.2}$, as well as "there$_B$" in R$_{B7.1}$.

This sequence still contains multiple ambiguities of deictic reference between "in" and "at," but the most important of these for the remainder of the snippet is which "Chicago" Mr. B is speaking of: "the University of" ("at") or "the city of" ("in")? Mr. A pursues the topic once again and asks in Q$_{A8}$ if Mr. B had been an undergraduate at the University of Chicago ("an' you wént to undergraduate hére or"), using a noninverted, confirmatory question that preserves the form of RB7.1, "go to school."[2] Even this formulation by Mr. A is not without "denotational-textual wiggle-room," as Silverstein described it. It would have been possible for Mr. B to have replied as though Mr. A had been asking if he had been an undergraduate "^Chére," that is, in the city of Chicago, simply by saying "yes," for example.

Yet "for reasons unknown," Mr. B chooses to reveal that "most important of emblems of identity in professional- and upper-class America, the 'old school tie'" (Silverstein 1997, p. 293) and supplies the long-sought information in RB8 ("in Chicágo át, uh, Loyola")—although apparently with reluctance.

As it turned out, Mr. A also "went to undergraduate" at a Jesuit institution, as revealed in A's last line of Table 4.4.1. The conversation thereupon took off and Mr. A's hard-won discovery led to many nonproblematic exchanges on the theme of Jesuit higher education and its advantages.

Analysis of the Gesture Space

Not included in Silverstein's analysis of the A-B text is the creative use by both speakers of the gesture space via pointing. Understanding the metaphoric uses of this space will lead to an explanation of Mr. B's unexpected capitulation in RB8. In general, the patterns of pointing were:

- Mr. A points only into the shared or landmark space.
- Mr. B points into this space and also points to the left and, crucially, once to the right.

'Right' and 'left' are labeled from Mr. B's point of view.

The shared space acquired meaning as the discourse topic. This meaning, its shifting values, and the contrasts of other gestures in it, are the subjects of the analysis to follow. The shared space initially had the meaning of Mr. B's academic past in Iowa, "Iowa-then." As noted previously, this reference is ambiguous between the state of Iowa and the University of Iowa and was never spelled out. The meaning at RB7.1, when Mr. B pointed to the shared

2. "[Mr. A] seems to blend two simultaneous informational quests in his utterance, which makes for a rather strange discontinuous colloquial phrase with focal stress, "wént . . . here" superimposed upon the . . . repetition of [an] earlier construction. . . . The different focalization of these two blended constructions leaves no doubt to us analysts which is the more important piece of information being asked for; it is the undergraduate institution with which Mr. B's identity can be affiliated" (Silverstein 1997, p. 293).

space and said, "I did go to school [there]," thus could have been either the state or the University of Iowa.

A corresponding ambiguity exists during RB7.2–3 when Mr. B continued, "[I went to school hére] [álso]," and pointed two times to the left, that is, away from the shared space. As with the verbal deixis, "hére," this left space could have meant either the city of Chicago or the University of Chicago, and following Silverstein, is designated "$^{C/U}$Chicago-then."

The meaning of the deictic field changed for Mr. B at RB7.6, when he said "so I [came back]" and pointed to the shared space that previously had meant "Iowa-then" (the status of the shared space at RB7.4–5 is unclear). This meaning shift could simply have hinged on temporal updating. Mr. B wanted to move the topic into the present and contrasted "now" to the "then" that had been the left space at RB7.2–3. This put "now" into the shared space, and "Chicago" came along with it. However, once imported, "Chicago" too became part of the shared space. Thus, at RB7.6, the shared space meant "Chicago-now," and this became Mr. B's new thematic reference point. But which "Chicago"—the city or the university?

I argue that, at this moment, if not sooner (for we can't be sure about RB7.4–5), the shared space meant for Mr. B the *city*. The crucial indication is that Mr. B pointed to the *right* at RB7.7 and hedged the reference to coming back with "[kind of /]." He was evidently saying that he had come back to Chicago, but hadn't come back to *Chicago*, and placed this Chicago$_1$ versus Chicago$_2$ opposition on a new shared versus right space axis (Figure 4.4.2).

Fig. 4.4.2. Mr. B's gesture to the right side of space as he said the hedge "kind of."

I claim that the shared and right spaces cannot have the same meaning; that one is the city and the other is the university (or at least is *not*-the-city), although we cannot say from the spatial contrast itself which space has which meaning. Subsequent pointing, however, soon makes clear what B had been thinking.

Mr. A now asks his fatal question (QA8): "an' [you wént to undergraduate hére or]" and points again to the shared space with an extended hold that is maintained during Mr. B's response. Mr. A's use is unambiguous: The space means for him the university (see note 2). Mr. B's response at RB8 also points to this space while saying, crucially, "[in Chicágo] át, uh, Loyola"—the unexpected capitulation after a career of evasion.

The preposition "in" shows that Mr. B was indicating the city as opposed to the university. Thus the shared topic space for Mr. B at this point meant the city, not the university. This in turn suggests that the *right* space at RB7.7 meant the university and not the city.

This meaning allocation, moreover, would explain the hedge "kind of." What Mr. B meant when he said "so I came back kind of," was that he had returned to one kind of Chicago (the city), but it was not the Chicago that might have been supposed in this conversation—the university where Mr. B and Mr. A were students and where the conversation was taking place (or alternatively, the "kind of" hedge flagged *not*-the-city).

That Mr. B hedged and introduced a new spatial contrast also suggests that he was aware of the ${}^{C/U}$Chicago' ambiguity. Had he been thinking only of his own meaning of '^{C}Chicago' for the shared space, there would have been no motivation for introducing a new space for '^{U}Chicago' (or '*not* ^{C}Chicago') and the hedge. In other words, Mr. B, without realizing it, tipped so to speak his hand that his persistent '${}^{C/U}$Chicago' ambiguity had been intentional.

That Mr. A and Mr. B had conflicting meanings for the shared topic space and that Mr. B was aware of this also explains why Mr. B gave up his resistance at this very moment. This is the puzzle that remains after Silverstein's analysis. As noted earlier, Mr. B easily could have continued dodging Mr. A by perpetuating the ambiguity, had he wished, merely by answering QA8 with "yes" or some equivalent means of assent.

However, the shared space and "here" meant the city for Mr. B whereas they meant the university for Mr. A. This contradiction confronted Mr. B with an interactional problem on a new level: the need to cease being merely evasive and to start lying; apparently Mr. B did not make this choice.

Mr. B could not avoid his moral dilemma by not pointing: Mr. A had already pointed into the shared space with the unambiguous meaning of '^{U}Chicago' and Mr. B had previously pointed to it with the opposite meaning

Table 4.4.2. Meanings attributed to the right, center, and left spaces by Messrs. A and B.

	Right	Shared	Left
Q$_{A7}$ did you go to . . .		$^{S/U}$Iowa-then	
R$_{B7.1}$ I did go to . . .		$^{S/U}$Iowa-then	
R$_{B7.2}$ I went here			$^{C/U}$Chicago-then
R$_{B7.3}$ also			$^{C/U}$Chicago-then
R$_{B7.4}$ I		??	
R$_{B7.5}$ /um			??
R$_{B7.6}$ so I came back		^{C}Chicago-now	
R$_{B7.7}$ kind of	^{U}Chicago-now		
Q$_{A8}$ you went to undergraduate here		^{U}Chicago-now (held through the following)	
R$_{B8}$ in Chicago at Loyola		^{C}Chicago-now	

of '^{C}Chicago'; moreover, Mr. A was *continuing* to point at the shared space with the contradictory meaning; Mr. B's confrontation with morality was inescapable.

That Mr. A maintained his pointing gesture during the entirety of Mr. B's response suggests that for Mr. A, also, there was a sense that the central gesture space had become a field of confrontation.

Thus, the role of pointing into the gesture space was an active one in this stretch of conversation. Pointing contributed to the dynamics of the conversation and included such interpersonal factors as evasion, probing, and confession. Table 4.4.2 summarizes the meanings given to the right, shared, and left spaces in the snippet.

Analysis of B's Growth Point at RB8

Although Mr. B's "[in Chicágo] át, uh, Loyola" displays minimal linguistic structure, it is interesting as a microcosm of the conditions under which utterances form in general.

The concept of a GP elucidates Mr. B's thinking at the critical juncture when he confronted the crisis of lying or telling the truth. Under the prevailing imperative to orient himself to the proffered topic of his personal biography (itself a product of the pointing procedure), Mr. B's thinking was dominated by the distinction between ^{C}Chicago and ^{U}Chicago on which his biography turned, and his apparent wish to blanket this distinction under the ambiguous word "Chicago."

In the case of RB8, the field of opposition, as Mr. B construed it, was something like To Lie about Loyola versus To Tell the Truth about Loyola. Mr. B's chosen contrast in this field was the To Tell the Truth pole. That is, Mr. B's meaning at this point was not just the denotational content of "in Chicago, at Loyola," but also the moral content of coming out with the truth when the alternative was lying. It was a product of his current field of oppositions. This hidden content was, I believe, the core of his meaning at this moment, and the various parts of this core materialized in one or both of the modalities, speech and gesture (in other words, I claim, his utterance could not have significantly deviated from this form); to wit:

- Mr. B's contradiction with Mr. A materialized via pointing at the space that Mr. A had designated as ^{U}Chicago' but meaning by this space ^{C}Chicago'.
- The "in" lexical choice brought out ^{C}Chicago, which is the "Truth" alternative.
- The "in"–"at" succession arose from the $^{C/U}$Chicago' ambiguity that Mr. B had been perpetuating. Having separated the city meaning with "in," Mr. B went on to lay out the university component with "at."
- The stress pattern, "in Chicágo—át," displays precisely this contrast within a consistent rhythmic and vocalic pattern (i.e., "ín Chicago—át," or "in Chicágo—at Loyóla," which are the two other possible combinations, twist the rhythm and the poetics, and lose the contrast that splits out ^{U}Chicago as something distinct from ^{C}Chicago).
- The "át," in turn, led to "Loyola" but with hesitancy as if completion of the city-university paradigm had taken on a life of its own and was unfolding somewhat against the will of the speaker, or at least with lingering uncertainty.

The conditions leading to RB8 included: (a) Mr. A and Mr. B's joint orientation to the shared gesture space, (b) Mr. B's awareness of his contradiction with Mr. A over the meaning of the shared space, and (c) the role of this contradiction in creating the moral dilemma that Mr. B ultimately confronted. The contradiction with Mr. A was one pole of the utterance and the resulting moral dilemma for Mr. B was the other. The contradiction was highlighted by Mr. A's protracted pointing to the shared space while Mr. B invoked the ^{C}Chicago' meaning. Together, these poles were the direct determinants of the form of the utterance that we observe. The GP thus incorporated information about the contradiction with Mr. A and Mr. B's awareness of it, plus Mr. B's sense that he was confronting a moral dilemma and his decision to resolve it. Mr. B's unpacking of the GP into "[in Chicágo] át, uh, Loyola" grew out of the contrasts built into it, despite Mr. B's squeamishness over the final revelation. Thus, according to this model, this simple utterance was a product of Mr. B's individual thinking at a particular moment in a specific pragmatic-discourse context, and encompassed interpersonal, moral, discourse, and historical-biographical dimensions.

(RE)SHAPING THE GESTURE SPACE

A demonstration of the inter/intrasubjective interface is the reshaping of the gesture space when the social arrangement changes. Asli Özyürek (2002) experimented with changing the number of addressees that narrators of the animated cartoon faced, and observed systematic changes in the shape of the gesture space as a result. With a single addressee, the space was cigar-shaped between the speaker and the listener. The evidence for this was that gestures depicting Sylvester moving into or out of a story event entered or exited the gesture space laterally, a direction equally 'out' or 'in' for both participants. But when two speakers were angled in front of the speaker, the gesture space became circular, and gestures sought a path equally 'into' and 'out of' for all three participants; 'out of' was often to the rear, for example, over the speaker's shoulder. The same event was therefore depicted gesturally in opposite ways depending on the social context. Viewed in GP terms, the imagery-language dialectic would be shaped by the number and location of the addressees. Even though the speaker creates the space, the space is jointly defined by speaker and listener.

SHARING GESTURES

In this section we examine the phenomenon of gestural sharing. In the H-model, communication is joint inhabitance of the same state of cognitive being. If one person assimilates another person's gesture or speech, the material carriers of being, this inhabits some aspect of this other person's verbal thinking. The joint inhabitance includes gesture sharing and this appears in two broad forms—*mimicry* and *appropriation*.

Mimicry

Irene Kimbara (2002) has studied gestural mimicry; the examples below are from her research. Mimicry is a process of 'interpersonal synchrony', as Kimbara terms it, which creates a sense of solidarity and is prominent when the interlocutors are personally close.

Figures 4.4.3 and 4.4.4 present such a case. Two friends are having a conversation. The example begins in 4.4.3a with a gesture by the friend on the right. She is describing the kind of chaotic scene that develops on Tokyo subway platforms during rush hour where multiple lines of waiting passengers take form but disintegrate when the train arrives, the neat lines merging into a mob. Figure 4.4.3a depicts the lines; Figure 4.4.3b is their thickness and leftward direction. The listener is commencing her gesture preparation during 4.4.3b as well, and Figure 4.4.4a–b is her mimicry. The imagery is the same: the same

Fig. 4.4.3 (a and b). Speaker on right: describing the line as 'irregular'; her gesture depicts lines of waiting passengers; the separation of her hands may depict the density of the crowding. Speaker on left: in (b), hands entering the gesture space and preparing to perform gesture in Fig. 4.4.4. From Kimbara (2002).

Fig. 4.4.4 (a and b). Continuous with Fig. 4.4.3. Speaker on left mimics right speaker's two-lines gesture as she emphatically agrees ('yes, yes, yes, yes'), including absolute direction (in both figures, the hands are moving toward camera). Meanwhile, in (b), right speaker is preparing her next gesture. From Kimbara (2002).

two lines, the same thickness and (even the same absolute) direction. From a GP viewpoint, the second speaker's idea unit included imagery from the first speaker's GP.

Appropriation: Embodiment in Two Bodies

Mimicry can also appear with previously unacquainted participants. Figure 4.4.5 is drawn from an experiment devised by Nobuhiro Furuyama (2000), in which one person is teaching someone else how to perform a manipulation (the learner is on the left). The learner is shown mimicking the teacher's gesture, and the mimicry, again, has social-interactive content. Mimicry occurred without speech by the learner, but her gesture synchronized with the *tutor's* speech. As the tutor said, "[pull down] the corner," the learner performed the gesture during the bracketed portion. The learner thus appropriated the other's *speech* by combining it with her *gesture*, and in this way inhabited the speech of another, with the help of the gesture, as if they were jointly creating a single GP.

Fig. 4.4.5. Mimicry by a learner (left). **Fig. 4.4.6.** Appropriation by a learner (left).

Furuyama observed a second kind of appropriation. In this situation the learner appropriates the tutor's *gesture* by combining it with her *speech*. Again, there is inhabitance, this time of gesture, and again a kind of joint GP. In Figure 4.4.6, the learner is using the tutor's gesture to clarify how to fold a paper at one particularly confusing step in making an origami box. She says, "[you bend this down?]," and during the bracketed speech moves her hand downward and away from his (the illustration shows the start of her gesture). As Furuyama observes, the tutor had turned in his chair so that the same left-right gesture space was before him and the learner, a maneuver that might have invited the learner to enter his gesture space. It is striking that in gesture appropriation the taboo that normally prohibits strangers from coming into physical contact was overridden. (The tutor and learner were previously unacquainted).

INTERNALIZATION

The dilemma that Mr. B confronted occurred at the interface of mind and social context. The most visible manifestation of this interface occurred at RB8 when both Mr. B and Mr. A were simultaneously pointing at the shared space but had opposite meanings. *Inter*psychically, it was a tussle over what the space meant. *Intra*psychically, there was the further meaning of Mr. B's dilemma, to lie or tell the truth. On the intra-plane, the tussle was part of Mr. B's personal mental life and was subjected to autochthonous forces (his wish to camouflage his past, his rejection of lying), while on the inter-plane it was subject to the social forces of the interaction between Mr. A and Mr. B (politeness especially; cf. Brown & Levinson 1987). The point is, both planes were effective forces in Mr. B's mind at this moment, as evidenced in the precise form of his utterance at RB8 and its detailed reflection of the dilemma and the social demands of the interaction. Moreover, the very construction of the meaning—his Chicago past—as a deictic field with entities, an origo and a perspective is a model of significant relationships translated from the inter to the intra-plane. The GP as a unit of thinking is the point where these various factors come together. At the moment of capitulation his GP (awareness of his contradiction with Mr. A., the moral dilemma of whether to lie or come clean) is intrapsychic in the Vygotskian social-mental dichotomy (Vygotsky 1986). Internalization refers to movement of significances from the interpsychic plane to the intrapsychic. While the GP itself is intra-, it ties together forces on thought and action that scatter over both the interpsychic and intrapsychic planes. Vygotsky said that everything appears in development twice, first on the social plane, then on the individual.[3] The same logic and direction of influence applies to the GP. Vygotsky also saw the necessity of a unit that encompasses this transformation, invoking the concepts of psychological predicates and inner speech to express

3. An assertion occasionally subjected to an 'intraectomy'—only the interpsychic side is considered, the mental plane becoming nothing more than a passive sketchpad of the social plane, despite the logic of internalization. Vygotsky becomes a kind of sociologist, rather than the semiotician of mind he truly appears to have been.

this unity in the minds of socially embedded individuals. The growth point concept is meant to be heir to these insights.

SUMMARY

While the social context has been presented here in its own subchapter, I wish to emphasize the continuity of this chapter with the earlier presentation of the dynamic dimension of language. The embeddedness of thinking and speaking in a social framework is the dynamic counterpart of the Saussurian static view of language as a social fact. Embeddedness of the social fact will be taken up again in the last chapter as part of the 'ultimate explanation' for the imagery-language dialectic in the evolution of language.

CHAPTER 5

Discourse

INTRODUCTION

Discourse elements have been invoked repeatedly in previous chapters. This chapter focuses specifically on discourse itself, providing mainly an empirical characterization of how gestures embody discourse information. The topics are catchments and the layering in gestures of discourse information. Gesture catchments can create common ground elements between interlocutors (cf. Clark 1992); the antagonistic force catchment in the Chapter 4.2 case study, for example, created a theme of the episode that the listener could share. The living space example to be described below likewise can be seen in this light. The speaker shifts topics in a way readily followed by the listener (and observer), which suggests successful updating of common ground. Since gestures are the chief vehicles of these shifts, they also imply the active role gestures can play in creating, shifting and updating common ground between interlocutors. For a comprehensive review of the nonverbal aspects of discourse and other pragmatic functions in language, see Payrató (2003).

THE CATCHMENT CONCEPT

Introduction

A catchment is a gestural discourse segment. It is recognized when gesture features recur over multiple gestures; the recurring features can reveal a segment that coheres through a shared image. The catchment is a kind of thread of visuospatial imagery running through a discourse, to reveal the larger discourse units. We saw catchments in the case study of Chapter 4.2. I present here another extended example and provide an analysis of how catchments correlate with prosody and discourse purposes.

Living Space Example[1]

The speaker was describing her house and had reached, in her description, the kitchen at the back of the house and was about to explain that a spiral staircase goes up from the kitchen to the floor above. But, at this moment, she realized that she had not yet told her listener that the house in fact had a second story, and aborted the description and ongoing gesture in midstream. Figure 5.1 is the full transcript. (The usual gesture transcription conventions apply. Numbers at the head of and above each line of text are referred to in the appendix.) Using hand deployments as the criterion, four catchments appear in this selection, and they are numbered below each line of the text. Gestures are also numbered below a line of text when it has more than one gesture. For ease of reading, the gesture movements themselves are not included, but the significance of each gesture, as determined by coders in close consultation with the speaker, is given in angled brackets.

Here are the four catchments:

C1 consists of 'RH' (right hand) gestures elevated above the right knee; all are associated with the kitchen at the back of the house.

C2 consists of two-handed symmetrical gestures; all are associated with the theme of the front doors of the house.

C3 consists of 'LH' (left hand) gestures made with the arm extended and lifted up; all are associated with the front staircase and second floor.

C4 consists of right hand gestures where the hand rises and turns in a spiral motion; all are associated with the back staircase.

Each catchment is distinctive in form, location, and/or movement, and has nonconsecutive occurrences. The **C2** catchment links back to an earlier description of the front doors of the house (not shown in Figure 5.1). The centerpiece

---

1. This example was described in McNeill et al. (2001). It is revisited in the appendix, as part of a presentation of new automated methods of analysis developed in collaboration with our engineer colleague, Francis Quek.

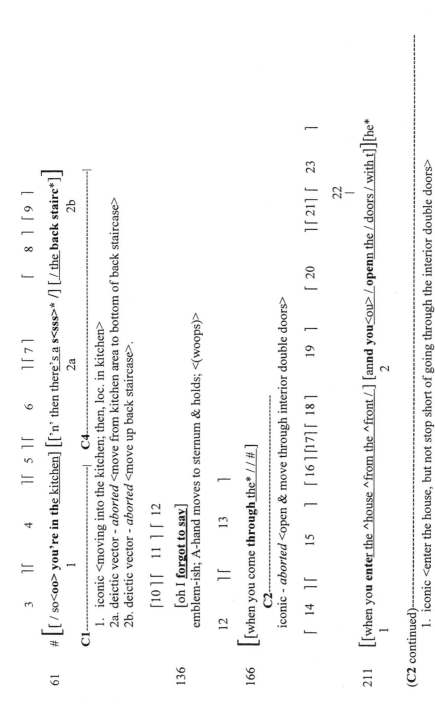

61 # [[/ so<oo> you're in the kitchen] [['n' then there's a s<sss>* /] [/ the back stairc*]
                3   ] [4   ][5][6] [7]   [8] [9]

C1 ‑‑‑‑‑‑‑‑‑‑‑‑‑‑‑‑‑‑| C4 ‑‑‑‑‑‑‑‑‑‑‑
      1   2a   2b

1. iconic <moving into the kitchen; then, loc. in kitchen>
2a. deictic vector ‑ *aborted* <move from kitchen area to bottom of back staircase>
2b. deictic vector ‑ *aborted* <move up back staircase> .

136   [10][11] [12
     [oh I **forgot to say**]
    emblem‑ish; A‑hand moves to sternum & holds; <(woops)>
    12   ][13   ]

166 [[when you come through the* // #]
    C2 ‑‑‑‑‑‑‑‑‑‑‑‑‑‑‑‑‑
    iconic ‑ *aborted* <open & move through interior double doors>
    [14][15] [16][17][18]   19] [20] [21][23   ]
    1. iconic <enter the house, but not stop short of going through the interior double doors>
    2. iconic ‑ *repeat & complete* <open & move through interior double doors>

211 [[when you **enter** the ^house ^from the ^front /] [**annd you**<ou> / **openn the** / doors / with t]][he*
    1   2   22

(**C2** continued)‑‑‑

BEGIN INSERTED REFERENCE TO FRONT STAIRCASE TO SECOND FLOOR

Fig. 5.1. Selection of a living space description with gesture coding. Frame numbers and F_0 numbers (above each line) correspond to Figs. A.4 and A.5.

[24]   [25][26] [27]   [28]

391 / /⊿/ [/ /<u̲u̲m̲m̲> / %smack /⌣] [/ the glas][s inn them #] [[[LH / there's a*/
     /⌣] [/ /<u̲u̲m̲m̲> /zxm %smack /⌣] [/ the glas][RH s in them # / there's a*] /
       1   2   3   4   —C3——

(C2 continued)
1. iconic <the two windows in the interior double doors>
2. iconic/localizer w/lexical search agitation <the two panes of glass in the interior double doors>
3. iconic/localizer w/lexical search agitation - *repeat* <the two panes of glass in the interior double doors>
4. iconic/localizer <the two panes of glass in the interior double doors> NB: RH holds the location & orientation of <door> for a bit during the start up of the subsequent <staircase> gesture.

[29][30] [31][32] [33] [34] 35] [36] [37]

481 the **front staircase**] [runs / **right up there**/o][n* on your **left**]
       1   2   3

(C3 continued)
1. iconic <move up staircase at left>
2. iconic *sl. modified repeat* <move up staircase at left>
3. iconic *sl. modified repeat* <move up staircase at left>

[38][39][40] 41]   [42]   [43] [44] [45] [46]   [47]

601 [so you can go **straight up**]][[**stair**][s to the se][econd **floo**][r from there] [LH / if [**you**] **wann**t]
       1   2   3   4   5   6

(C3 continued)
1. iconic - *repeat* <move up staircase at left>
2. iconic/localizer <at the top of the stairs / 2nd floor>
3. iconic/localizer - *enhanced repeat* <at the top of the stairs / 2nd floor>
4. iconic/localizer - *repeat* <at the top of the stairs / 2nd floor>
5. iconic/localizer - *repeat* <at the top of the stairs / 2nd floor>

Fig. 5.1. *(continued)*

6. iconic/localizer w/superimposed emblem - *repeat* <at the top of the stairs / 2nd floor + (flip)>

721
$\quad$ [48][49] [50][51][52]

[LH # / **but if** you come around through the kitchen] into the back
$\quad$ 1

[[RH # / but if **you come around through** the ki][tchen **into** the bac][k
$\quad$ 2 $\qquad$ 3

LH (C3 continued)-----------------------------------

RH C1-----------------------------------|

1. iconic/localizer <level of 2nd floor>
2. iconic <move toward back of the house on the 1st floor>
3. deictic vector <move through kitchen to bottom of back stairs>

END INSERTED REFERENCE TO FRONT STAIRCASE TO SECOND FLOOR

791
$\quad$ [53] [54][55][56][57][58][59][60][61][62]

there's a back staircase that winds around like this / # and puts you up on the second floor /
$\quad$ 1

there's a back s^sta][[ircase that **winds around like this /**]] [# and puts you up on the second floor /] [# and **putss you up on the second floor /**
$\quad$ 2 $\qquad$ 3 $\qquad$ 4

LH (C3 continued)-----------------------------------

LH C3-------------------------------------2DHS **C3+C4**------|

(1. iconic/localizer <level of 2nd floor>)
2. deictic vector - modified repeat <spiral movement up back staircase>
3. deictic vector - *modified repeat* <spiral movement up back staircase>
4. iconic/localizer <level & flat surface of 2nd floor>

Fig. 5.1. (*continued*)

of the discourse is the back staircase (**C4**) and its location at the back of the house, where it connects the kitchen to the second floor. The first mention of the back staircase is immediately aborted ("oh I forgot to say") and is replaced by **C2** and then **C3**. **C3** (the left hand catchment) is held as the kitchen **C1** and back staircase **C4** catchments resume. Based on the fact that it is motionless **C3** appears to be hierarchically dominated by the active catchments, **C1/C4**. The catchments are illustrated in Figures 5.2.1–5.

Fig. 5.2.1. C1 KITCHEN gesture with "so you're in the kitchen." Photo corresponds approximately to frame #61 in Figs. A.4 and A.5.

Fig. 5.2.2. C2 FRONT DOORS gesture with "when you enter the house." Photo corresponds approximately to frame #223 in Figs. A.4 and A.5.

Fig. 5.2.3. C3 FRONT STAIRCASE/SECOND FLOOR gesture with "to the second floor." Photo corresponds approximately to frame #635 in Figs. A.4 and A.5.

Fig. 5.2.4. C4 BACK STAIRCASE gesture with "there's a back staircase that winds around like this." Photo corresponds approximately to frame #781 in Figs. A.4 and A.5.

Fig. 5.2.5. C3 + C4 BACK STAIRCASE + SECOND FLOOR gesture with "and puts you up on the second floor." Photo corresponds approximately to frame #871 in Figs. A.4 and A.5.

Table 5.1. ToBI profiles of the four catchments.

Catchments	Number of Low Tone Boundaries	Number of High Tone Boundaries
C4 RH rises and twists \<back stairs\>	3	1
C1 RH above knee \<kitchen\> \<connect\>	3	–
C3 LH rises up and forward \<front stairs\> \<2nd floor\>	2	5
C2 BHs spread apart in front of chest \<front doors\>	1	6

Correlations of Catchments with Prosody and Discourse Purposes

In our earlier work with this example (McNeill et al. 2001), we correlated the four catchments with other discourse measures—prosody, as indexed with the ToBI (Tone Break Index) coding method (Beckman & Hirschberg 1994; also see description at http://www1.cs.columbia.edu/~jjv/tobitut.html),[2] and a hierarchy of the judged purposes of each intonation unit (for intonation units, cf. Chafe 1994). The purpose hierarchy was recovered following the guidelines described by Nakatani et al. (1995).

These descriptive orders—one of sound, the other of intention—correlated with gestural catchments with remarkable tightness. Prosody is of course also a material carrier, thus we have a correlation between two material carriers: gesture and an aspect of speech. Discourse purposes are likewise related to GPs, since, for coding purposes, we ask why this information was being highlighted, which is to ask about the basis of psychological predicates. Thus, correlations among catchments, purposes, and prosody are predicted. The correlation with prosody is shown in Table 5.1.

The table suggests that each catchment had its own distinctive boundary tone. The C1 (kitchen) and C4 (back staircase) catchments, which join together at the end of the discourse, were both Low. C2 (front doors) and C3 (front staircase), which were part of the discourse repair, were preponderantly High. Catchments, which are motivated by visuospatial imagery, thus exhibit distinct prosodic features. The discourse dominance of C1 and C4 is shown in their Low boundary tones, indicating declarative finality. C2 and C3, by the same token, showed their embedded status with High tones, indicating a continuation of the discourse. Thus, these aspects of prosody are predictable from gesture catchments.

2. ToBI coding conducted by Karl-Erik McCullough.

The correlation of catchments with the other discourse measure, purposes, is seen in the following—a list that shows the hierarchy of discourse purposes, recovered by the Nakatani et al. query procedure.[3] Catchments are indicated by their numbers, and the decimal numbers refer to levels in the hierarchy.

WHY? To locate the back staircase (1.1) **C1**
    # [so <oo> **you're in the** kitchen]
WHY? Ways of getting to the second floor (1) **C4**
    ['n' then there's a s <sss>*]
    [the back stairc*]
WHY? To note the existence of the first staircase (1.1.1)
    [I forgot to say]
WHY? To restart the tour (1.1.1.1) **C2**
    [when you come **through** the*]
    [when yo**u enter** the house from the front]
    [an**nd you** <ou> **open**n the doors with t][he*]
    [<uumm> %smack/]
    [/ the glas][s inn them #]
WHY? To explain first staircase and second floor (1.1.1) **C3**
    [there's a*
    the front staircase] [runs
    right up there
    o][n* on yo**ur left**]
    [so you can go **straight up**][**stair**]
    [s to the **se**][ec**ond floo**][r from **the**re]
    [if **you wann**t]
WHY? To locate the back staircase (1.1) **C1**
    [but if you come around through the ki]
    [tch**en into t**he bac][k
WHY? Ways of getting to the second floor (1) **C4**
    there's a back s sta]
    [ircase that winds around like this]
    WHY? To connect to the second floor (1.2) **C4 + C3**
    [and putss you up on the second floor]

---

3. The purpose hierarchy was recovered in consultation with the speaker.

The purpose hierarchy and the catchment structure correspond closely—in fact, 100 percent! Each catchment has its own purpose level or levels, not shared by the other catchments. At this degree of delicacy, there is a perfect mapping of the discourse structure onto gesture, and it seems correct to conclude that the speaker created discourse segments on the basis of consistent WHY-purposes.

Within each purpose, the gesture answers the WHY? question. Gestures are accurately accounted for as presenting information that is relevant to purposes. This points to their GP status—answers are newsworthy content, given the purpose. For example, the answer to purpose 1.1 is 'in the kitchen', and a gesture that conveyed this content was performed (the hand held in the space identified as the kitchen; see Figure 5.2.1). This image, classified as the 'kitchen', is plausibly the GP. This correlation suggests that the GPs were formed around the differentiation of information from the catchment that underlay the purposes identified with the WHY? procedure.

DISCOURSE LEVELS

In addition to catchments, gestures materialize the discourse structure through 'layering'. Layering takes multiple forms. Basically, the term means that single gestures convey content on the discourse and narrative levels simultaneously. I offer here several examples of this process.

Single Complex Gestures (in a Series of Such)

One of the cartoon narrators, Cel., carries through a series of GPs that incorporate iconic imagery and motion event content and simultaneously index the discourse on metanarrative and paranarrative (MN and PN) levels, terms suggested by Bill Eilfort and used in Cassell & McNeill (1991) and McNeill (1992).

We can identify three levels of discourse running in parallel, each with its own characteristic form or forms of gestural imagery:

Paranarrative (PN): The narrator steps out of her role as storyteller and speaks for herself, addressing the listener. The PN level is interpersonal. Pointing in the direction of the listener is a characteristic gesture at this level.

Metanarrative (MN): The narrator speaks within her role as official storyteller and makes a reference to the structure of the narration qua narration. The MN level is intertextual. Metaphoric gestures tend to occur at this level.

Narrative (N): The narrator speaks within the storyteller role and refers to an event from the story. The N level is intratextual and it alone is subject to the sequentiality constraint—that the order of mention on the N level is understood as corresponding to the time line of events of the story (see Labov & Waletsky 1967). Iconic gestures are dominant here.

The Cel. example demonstrates three points: (a) cohesion exists on each of these levels, not just one; (b) each level is materialized on its own; and (c) the material carriers on different levels can coalesce into complex gestures that have cohesive linkages on different levels simultaneously. The ability to index multiple cohesive linkages is obviously a powerful feature of discourse organization. That this ability inhabits imagery is the theme introduced by this example (see Figures 5.3.1–6).

At the MN level, the content is Tweety's inaccessibility and Sylvester's attempts to overcome it. The MN level provides the overarching source of cohesion. We see a catchment consisting of the two hands in a grip (roughly, the A-handshape) and arranged one above the other in the upper left periphery (see Figures 5.3.1 through 5.3.6). This pose appears at the end of each of the seven gestures in the example, and ties the gestures together into a single exposition on the theme of inaccessibility; it does this by iconically modeling the first character's location in an upper-story window of a high-rise, beyond the reach of the other character on the street below (the upper hand is Tweety, the lower hand Sylvester).

The individual GPs arrive at the catchment pose in their different ways, and the differences embody images unique to each specific motion event. Each GP is simultaneously cohesive with the others on the MN level and is an individualized idea unit on the N level.

There are, in addition, mergers of MN and N. The mergers are marked 'MN, N' in the following. They directly reveal the two levels on which Cel. was thinking. The MN level was her overall frame, as embodied in the two-hand catchment, and the N was an actual event from the story inserted into it.

The immediately preceding context:

PN and <um>/ let's see I think the <f*> the last way he [decides] the*]]⁴

---

4. Transcription by Susan Duncan. As in earlier transcriptions, a gesture phrase (hands in motion) is indicated with square brackets (double brackets when one gesture phrase occurs inside another); a gesture stroke with boldface; a hold with underlining; a beat with a caret; accent with larger font; a speech interruption with an asterisk; a hesitation with a slash; and a nonspeech sound in angle brackets. Time code is in minutes:seconds:frames (thirty per second).

PN I'd say [there's like] / [four] [or five] [different] [attempts]] to get to Tweety Bird

MN, N # the last] one he tries is to walk **acro<u>ss</u>***] #

START OF INACCESSIBILITY (TWO-HANDED ASYMMETRY, LEFT HAND = TWEETY, RIGHT HAND = SYLVESTER: METAPHOR OF TWEETY'S INACCESSIBILITY)

MN part of the problem] is that [Tweety Bird's ings*
MN inaccessible because he can't really just go in the front door of this hotel...
2:29:29

Fig. 5.3.1. Simultaneous thematic and depictive gesture: initiation of inaccessibility metaphor.

(Listener: Oh, because of the grandmother?)
PN Right, because of the grandmother.]
(Listener: Okay.)

MN,N [[so he has to **cl<u>im</u>b**]
2:35:19

Fig. 5.3.2. Iconic depiction within inaccessibility metaphor.

MN,N [in the **w<u>in</u>**<u>dow some</u>how #]]
2:36:03
(right hand fingers extend)

Fig. 5.3.3. Further iconic depiction within inaccessibility metaphor.

MN [so he's devised several different ways of*
2:37:06

Fig. 5.3.4. New metaphor within inaccessibility metaphor.

N of g][**etting int**o the win]dow
2:39:08

Fig. 5.3.5. New iconic depiction within inaccessibility metaphor.

N <um> / tryi[ng to swing **across** by a rope #]
2:43:04

Fig. 5.3.6. New iconic depiction within inaccessibility metaphor.

MN finally the last one he [decides to tr]y
N is [to ^walk ^[**across**]
Total duration = 18.4 secs.

Model of Cel.'s Discourse

A GP explanation of the above example is that Cel. had had the focal idea of 'inaccessibility' in mind throughout on the MN level and had embodied this in the image of the two entities, one above the other. Each GP occurs within this overarching material carrier. However, the effect of a focus on the MN level is to *disconnect* the embedded N level from the sequentiality constraint, in that it normally applies at the N level alone. Cel. apparently was responding to this disconnect, in that the order in which she mentions motion events within the MN level was uncorrelated with the order of episodes in the cartoon story itself. With embedding, an N-level event is effectively a summary not felt to contribute to the story line itself. It is accordingly free, in the speaker's mind, of any constraint to present the story line sequence.

At other points in her description, content was at the PN level, and the GPs here were embedded too, with a similar effect of disconnection from the story line.

Linguistic Indexes of the Three Levels

Cel. differentiated the three levels verbally as well:

>*MN*: In addition to metaphoric gestures, the chief linguistic indexes are discourse markers (*so, somehow*).

>*N*: In addition to iconic gestures, the linguistic markers are motion event verbs and, perhaps special to this level, embedded clauses with progressive aspect that carry story line content (*getting into the window, climbing up the rain barrel, trying to swing across by a rope*). The progressive aspect implies a story line locus.

>*PN*: In addition to pointing at the interlocutor, the linguistic indexes are first-person pronouns and actual conversational interaction with the interlocutor.

Some of her linguistic indexes, which can be components of GPs, are summarized in Table 5.2. The indexes seem motivated by various factors and are not a random selection. PN markers arise out of interactions with the interlocutor. MN markers include discourse markers, which are inherently 'meta-', and (more unexpectedly) main clauses; a main clause carries MN content while its embedded clause has the N content. Finally, the N markers consist of these same embedded subordinate clauses.

Cel.'s 'rule' for complex sentences, if such it is, seems to have been itself iconic: Her main clause carried the dominant discourse frame, the MN level, while her subordinate clause took the nondominant frame, the N level (it's not hard to imagine a sentence where the N level is in the main clause and MN

Table 5.2. Cel.'s linguistic indexes at the paranarrative (PN), metanarrative (MN), and narrative (N) levels.

PN Level[1]		MN Level		N Level
First-Person Pronoun, assent	Occurrence in Conversation	Addition of Discourse Marker	Main Clause	Subordinate Clause
Right	(Listener: Oh, the grandmother?) right, the grandmother (Listener: OK)	so he has to climb	so he's devised several different ways of	getting into the window
I'd say		in the window somehow		climbing up the rain barrel
		so he's devised		trying to swing across by a rope

[1] Criteria for PN: (a) first-person pronoun (sg. or pl.) and/or (b) part of a conversational exchange. If PN appears anywhere, the entire segment is classified as PN.

in the subordinate—"he tries X while he waits," for instance, though Cel. did not create any sentences of this kind in her description).

Layering in an Academic Lecture

We have observed layering in the Cel. example, but layering can go much farther and reach positively baroque levels in academic lectures. Karl-Erik McCullough (in preparation) has analyzed such a lecture, delivered at the 1986 Linguistic Institute of the Linguistic Society of America, in which the lecturer was explaining the then-new theory that he and a colleague had developed. According to McCullough, gestural layering creates a snapshot of the theory itself:

Thus we see that the emergent gestural model has *location* representing a foundation of language activities, a linguistic theory that is a set of constraints, a central processing box, and a control structure above it; *motion* or directionality plus *iterativity* represents production/perception processes, the multiplicity of tasks and activities, and interaction between the processor and the controller. Unidirectional motion represents unification, the flow between processor and specific language activities, and, perhaps, directed knowledge access. Locations are overlaid, with the process representation operating both within the foundational activities and the central processing layer. *Hand orientation* captures both the coherence of the overall gestural expression (palm orientation to center) with respect to the theory architecture and the distinction between the constraints of the linguistic theory (palm oriented away from center) and the actual processes of language use (palm to center).

Layering with Two Hands

Susan Duncan has compared the functional roles of the hands when both hands are creating a single gesture but have a separate form and motion. In this 'two-handed asymmetry' situation, the subordinate hand tends to be used for discourse content and the dominant hand for object content, or one hand (either dominant or subordinate) enters hold mode and then carries discourse content.

In other words, two-handed asymmetrical gestures can simultaneously carry semantic and discourse content, with the distinction between the active and inactive hand separating the two layers of information (ASL employs a similar device; cf. Liddell 2003a). The accompanying drawing illustrates this two-handed asymmetrical layering (Figure 5.4): the right hand holds and so becomes a background reference point for the left hand as the speaker said, "$_{LH}$and the **bowling b**all's coming do] [wn." The right hand was Sylvester, carried over from a previous gesture in which the right hand was the active component with "an[$_{RH}$nd // a**s he's** coming] [up." Then the right hand stopped its motion and the left hand, the bowling ball, moved downward from above (the arrow). The hands alternated this way through several rounds. The actual

Fig. 5.4. One hand with depictive content (left hand moving downward); while the other (right hand held) maintains discourse content.

animation involved a series of camera angle shifts between the bowling ball (a downward moving bulge) and Sylvester (just blank drainpipe but where the viewer assumes he is), so the gesture holds reproduce this cinematic alternation, and achieve something like the same dramatic effect of building-up, through a series of stopped motions, to a denouement (which is that Sylvester swallows the bowling ball).

Ishino (2001b) has observed in a Japanese language discourse sample left hand gestures expressing content of which the speaker had direct knowledge, while right hand gestures indicated hearsay information not directly apprehended. The left hand, in other words, functioned as an evidential marker, with gestures forming a catchment manifesting this significance on the discourse level.

SUMMARY: MATERIAL CARRIERS OF DISCOURSE

Discourse, the overarching structure beyond the individual sentence, must attain cohesion; cohesion is by definition a multiutterance property. Without the ability for the parts to cohere, a discourse cannot exist. And we see that discourse, no less than the individual utterance, is also inseparable from imagery. Discourse, like individual idea units, is materialized in action and has imagery content. We have seen that the catchment is the chief material carrier at this level, but that gesture stratification into meta-, para-, and object-level layers, both within a gesture and across gestures, is also source of cohesion.

CHAPTER 6

Children and Whorf

The acquisition of language by children and the hypothesis that language has an influence on thought (the Whorfian hypothesis) are not typically linked, but they share an underlying concept. In both domains, language has the potential to affect cognition. The Whorfian hypothesis, in one of its classic statements, claims for example that "[c]oncepts of 'time' and 'matter'... depend upon the nature of the language or languages through the use of which they have been developed" (Whorf 1956, p. 158). Given the Whorfian hypothesis, a developmental hypothesis is almost entailed—only through language acquisition could such concepts as time and matter come to depend on the categories of the language. This chapter begins with children and ends with the (classically, adult) Whorfian hypothesis, although I quickly shift to the more dynamic version of linguistic determinism that Dan Slobin has called 'thinking for speaking'.

CHILDREN

Introduction

The acquisition hypothesis of this chapter is that an imagery-language dialectic undergoes a developmental process of its own; this process in turn shapes thinking in new ways. Support for this hypothesis will center on two signature phenomena that appear around three or four years of age and signal a dialectic: what I will call the 'gesture explosion' and the 'decomposition effect'. The dialectic itself may be triggered by other developments, in particular the reconfiguration of the self as a self-aware agent (Hurley 1998) that is manifested in other ways as well, such as the classic development of a 'theory of mind', at the same time. Finally, the advent of a dialectic and of growth points changes the way that children construct and relate to context. The chapter considers these points in turn. By virtue of the linkage of the dialectic to the shaping of thought, we also predict that the linguistic determination of thought on the dynamic dimension begins only with the emergence of the two hallmarks.

An approach to children's language on the dynamic dimension, however, must cope with an extreme paucity of evidence. After decades of child language study, almost nothing exists with which to sketch this side of development. The tradition has focused on the static dimension almost exclusively. As a result, very little is known of what comprises children's real-time thinking at different stages; how and when speech is shaped by context; if thinking for speaking changes; when an imagery-language dialectic emerges; and, after it emerges, if it develops still further. This chapter addresses these questions from the vantage point of the dialectic mechanism we have been discussing, by tracing, insofar as possible, the development of a language-gesture system.

First Stages: Advancing Toward a Dialectic

Children's first gestures consist of pointing and appear a month or two before the first birthday. Indexicality seems to be the thinking mode—connecting oneself to interesting events and objects. Next to appear are gesture 'names', which dominate during the single-word period and include both indexicality and a range of semantic relationships that continue to emerge during the second year (Greenfield & Smith 1976). An example is placing a cup to the mouth, not to drink, but to label the action of drinking (summary from Bates & Dick 2002). At this stage, there is not a consistent speech-gesture temporal relationship. Speech may not be present, and, if present, it may precede or follow the gesture but rarely synchronizes with it (Butcher & Goldin-Meadow 2000, Goldin-Meadow & Butcher 2003; also see Capirici et al. 1996). Because of the lack of synchrony, the child does not harbor unlike cognitive modes at the same moment, and an imagery-language dialectic is probably impossible; the 'essence' of language at this stage is single, not double.

Speech and gesture begin to synchronize with each other only near the end of the single-word period. Goldin-Meadow and Butcher classified the semantic relationships between speech and gesture in these combinations, and found that speech-gesture combinations foreshadowed the child's initial word-word combinations, which appeared a few weeks later with the same semantic relationships. A child who pointed at an object and said "go" would, a couple of weeks later, produce word-word combinations with "go" plus object names. The early gesture-word combinations cover a range of semantic relations: "open" + points a drawer, "out" + holds up toy bag, "hot" + points at furnace, "no" + points at box, "monster" + two vertical palms spread apart (= big) (Goldin-Meadow & Butcher 2003, Table 3). Barbara Kelly (2003) has discovered an earlier step in the development of speech-gesture synchrony, in which the first pairings of the modalities involve gestures and speech that denote the same elements; it is only slightly later that different speech and gesture elements synchronize to form semantic units, as described by Goldin-Meadow and Butcher. If such combinations are truly redundant they do not imply a dialectic either. Thus, the full story of the second year of development may be, first, speech and gesture occurring in rough vicinity of each other but not yet synchronized; then the synchrony of redundant speech and gesture; next the synchrony of different speech and gesture in discernible semantic relations; and last the same relations in word-word combinations. In none of this would the 'double essence' of language be found.[1]

Are these first gesture-word combinations the pioneering steps of an imagery-language dialectic? I think not. The speech-gesture combinations seem complementary as opposed to co-expressive. Complementarity implies they offer not two modes of thinking for one meaning, but different meanings each in a different mode.

In the adult example I have cited several times, the gesture embodied an image of upward moving hollowness, while speech conveyed "up through." The combination presented the *same idea in two modes.* Is a two-year-old's saying "open" and pointing at the object to be opened also a single idea in two modes? The answer is not obvious. We must not impose uncritically what to us look like distinct idea units—one an action, the other the object of the action.

1. Recent research by Özçalıskan & Goldin-Meadow (2004) has carried this type of investigation past the second birthday. Again, semantic relationships appear first in gesture and again, a month or two later, for the first time in speech (relationships such as direct objects, locative verbs, double predicates, etc.). The gestures in question occur initially without accompanying speech and it is not clear if they continue to occur once the semantic relationship has made the transition to speech.

Perhaps the action and the object are synthesized into a single idea unit of an as-yet-undescribed kind, perhaps action based. In this case, the speech-gesture combination could be the two-year-old's counterpart of upward hollowness + "up through." But on the face of it, children's speech and gesture convey separate idea units; their juxtaposition is syntagmatic, albeit synchronous, a combination of different semantic objects. While it is conceivable that children at this stage have other gesture-speech combinations with co-expressivity, these combinations, if they exist, have yet to be described. So, while we leave open the possibility that the first gesture-speech combinations fulfill the conditions of a dialectic, this currently seems unlikely. More likely is that speech and gesture are complementary, not co-expressive; that co-expressivity is yet to come, and that some further developments are required for an imagery-language dialectic to appear. I will later suggest what some of these developments might be (see section on sources of decomposition, below).

The Start of an Imagery-Language Dialectic: Gesture Explosion, Meaning Decomposition

The Gesture Explosion

What happens after age two is unclear. All that is currently known is that, compared with older children, two-year-olds produce few gestures immediately after they have begun to combine words into linguistic units. Gesture output, however, abruptly increases—ascending to near adult levels—between three and four years. I propose that this upsurge is one signature of a dialectic. The upsurge suggests that gestures are, more than before, becoming integrated into the child's linguistic output. The explosion relates to a dialectic in two ways. First, an abundance of gesture makes a dialectic more accessible; there are more gesture-speech co-occurrences in which it can develop. Second, a dialectic itself can cause the upsurge, since an imagery-language dialectic requires, for the first time, that gestures be part of speaking.

The accompanying graph shows the output of gestures across a range of ages from a sample of monolingual Mandarin-speaking children. Similar graphs can be drawn for children acquiring other languages. Two curves are shown: one is the number of gestures per clause in a sample of narrative speech, the other is the number of episodes recalled from the animated stimulus. Comparing the two curves establishes that the sudden upsurge of gesture is not due

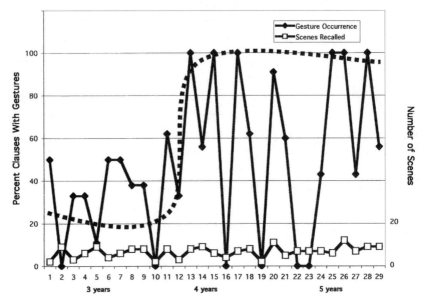

Fig. 6.1. Gesture explosion in a sample of twenty-nine Mandarin-speaking children of ages from three to five. Each child is shown individually in age order (dotted curve: the approximate smoothed version). The occurrence of gestures (the percentage of clauses with gestures) abruptly more than doubles at c. four years. An obvious explanation would be that memory for the cartoon improved at that point, but this is not the case (the number of recalled scenes is constant). Data from Susan Duncan.

to improved recall—the number of remembered episodes curve remains essentially flat while gesture surges.

What we observe is, therefore, a *gesture* explosion (see Figure 6.1).

The Decomposition Effect

'Decomposition' refers to a *reduction* of motion event complexity in gestures after an earlier stage where they seemingly have full complexity. Decomposition is the second signature of a dialectic. Decomposition also appears suddenly, and at the same age, around three or four. It suggests that meanings within gestures are becoming *analytically* integrated with speech: the path and manner components of motion events come to be handled separately, as they also are in linguistic representations (cf. "he climbs [manner and the fact of motion] up [path]").

Episodes in the animated cartoon are often comprised of motion events in which path and manner components are simultaneously present. Sylvester rolling down a street with the bowling ball inside him is a motion event incorporating both path (along the street) and manner (rolling). Adults, when they describe such motion events, typically produce gestures showing only path (for example, the hand moving down) or gestures showing in a single gesture both manner and path (for example, the hand rotating as it goes down for rolling). Manner without path, however, rarely occurs. Children, like adults, have path-only gestures but, unlike adults, they also have large numbers of pure manner gestures and few path + manner gestures.

In other words, they 'decompose' the motion event to pure manner or pure path, and tend not to have gestures that combine the semantic components.

Decomposition, while seemingly regressive, is actually a step forward. The youngest child from whom we have obtained any kind of recognizable narration of the animated stimulus was a two-and-a-half-year-old English-speaking child. The accompanying illustration (Figure 6.2) shows her version of Sylvester rolling down the street with the bowling ball inside him (she reasons that it is under him).

Fig. 6.2. No decomposition below age three. English speaking two-and-a-half-year-old with path and manner in one gesture. The hand simultaneously swept to the right, moved up and down, and opened and closed.

The important observation is that she does *not* show the decomposition effect. In a single gesture, the child combines path (her sweeping arc to the right) and manner (in two forms—an undulating trajectory and an opening and closing of her hand as it sweeps right, suggested by the up-and-down arrow).

Is this an adultlike combined manner-path gesture? I believe it is not. An alternative possible interpretation is suggested by Werner & Kaplan (1963), who described a nonrepresentational mode of cognition in young children, a mode that could also be the basis of this gesture. Werner and Kaplan said that the symbolic actions of young children (in this case, the gesture) have "the character of 'sharing' experiences *with* the Other rather than of 'communicating' messages *to* the Other" (1963, p. 42). Sharing with, as opposed to communicating and representing to, could be what we see in the two-and-a-half-year-old's gesture. The double indication of manner is suggestive of sharing, since this redundancy would not be a relevant force, as it might have been in a communicative representation of this event, if the child were merely trying to re-create an interesting spectacle for her mother.

One of the first attempts by children to shape their gestures for combination with language could be the phenomenon of path and manner decomposition. The mechanism causing this could be that the decomposition effect creates in gesture what Karmiloff-Smith (1979) has suggested for speech: When children begin to see elements of meaning in a form, they tend to pull these elements out in their representations to get a 'better grip' on them. Bowerman (1982) added that the elements children select tend to be those with 'recurrent organizational significance' in the language. Manner and path would be such elements, and their reduction in gesture to a single component could be this kind of hyperanalytic response. Because in speech there is a distinction between path and manner, there would be pressure, arising from a dialectic process, for an analytic separation of path and manner. Going too far, this leads to the decomposition effect.

Three illustrations show the decomposition effect in English (age 4, Figure 6.3), Mandarin (age 3;11, Figure 6.4), and Spanish (age 3;1, Figure 6.5).

Fig. 6.3. English-speaking four-year-old with decomposition to manner alone. The child is describing Tweety escaping from his cage. The stimulus event combined a highly circular path with flying. The child reduces it to pure manner—flapping wings, suggested by the two arrows—without path, which was conspicuous in the stimulus and had been emphasized by the adult interlocutor (not shown, but who demonstrated Tweety's flight in a simultaneous path-manner gesture). The embodiment of the bird, in other words, was reduced to pure manner, path excised.

Fig. 6.4. Mandarin-speaking 3;11-year-old with decomposition to manner—clambering without upward motion. The child is describing Sylvester's clambering up the pipe on the inside. The hands depict manner without upward path (while he says, "ta* [# ta **zhei- # yang-zi*** /] he* ('# he this- # way* /'). Direction is shown through his upward-oriented body and arms. Direction is one aspect of path, although there is no upward motion in this case. Example from S. Duncan.

Fig. 6.5. Spanish-speaking 3;1-year-old with decomposition to manner—clambering without upward motion. The child is likewise describing Sylvester as he climbs up the pipe on the inside. His mother had asked, "y lo agarró?" ('and did he grab him?') and the child answered, "no # /se subió en el tubo [**y le corrió**]" ('no # he went up the tube and he ran'), with the gesture illustrated—both hands clambering without path.

In languages as different as English, Mandarin, and Spanish, children beyond three years decompose motion events that are fused in the stimulus, and are fused again by adult speakers of the same languages (see 'Whorf' section below).

Perspective

We gain added insight into the decomposition effect and how it forms a step in the child's emerging imagery-language dialectic when we consider gestural viewpoint: the first-person or character viewpoint (CVPT) and the third-person or observer viewpoint (OVPT). Table 6.1 shows the viewpoints of path decomposed, manner decomposed, and fused path + manner gestures for three age groups; all are English speakers.

Table 6.1. Gestural viewpoints of English speakers at three ages. Note: All figures are percentages. M = manner; P = path.

	VIEWPOINT	M + P Combined	M Decomposed	P Decomposed
Adults	CVPT	0	5	0
N = 28	OVPT	34	0	51
	Dual VPTs	0	0	11
7–11 years	CVPT	3	25	17
N = 25	OVPT	4	12	31
	Dual VPTs	0	0	9
3–6 years	CVPT	5	24	2
N = 47	OVPT	9	10	47
	Dual VPTs	0	0	4

For adults, we see that most gestures are OVPT (observer viewpoint), both those that fuse manner and path and those with path alone. Few gestures in either viewpoint occur with manner alone.

For children, both older and younger, we see something quite different. Not only do we see the decomposition effect, *but manner and path are sequestered into different viewpoints.* Path tends to be OVPT and manner CVPT. This sequestering enforces the path-manner decomposition: if one gesture cannot have both viewpoints, it is impossible to combine the motion event components.[2]

The decomposition effect and this viewpoint sequestering are very long lasting; children up to twelve years old still show them. Longevity implies that the final break from decomposition depends on some kind of late-to-emerge development that enables the child (at last) to conceptualize manner in the OVPT. Until this development, whatever it may be, the difference in perspective locks in path-manner decomposition.

Imitation

The decomposition of manner and its sequestering in CVPT is revealed in another way by imitation. Children do not imitate model gestures with manner in OVPT, even when the model is directly in front of them and the imitation is concurrent. They change the model to fit their own decompositional

2. As Table 6.1 shows, dual-viewpoint gestures are rare for children.

semantics, putting manner into the CVPT and omitting path. In Figure 6.6, a four-year-old is imitating an adult model. The adult depicts manner (running) plus path in OVPT, his hand moving forward, fingers wiggling. The child watches intently; nonetheless, she transforms the gesture into manner with no path, in CVPT (in the gesture, she is Sylvester, her arms moving as if running).

Fig. 6.6. Decomposition to manner alone in imitation of model with combined path and manner.

Sources of Decomposition

Why does decomposition set in at the age it does, why is it tied to perspective the way it is, and why does it last so long?

Symbolic Distance

If the English speaking 2;6-year-old's simultaneous manner and path gesture was re-creating an experience, it would have been what Werner & Kaplan (1963) termed presymbolic, lacking 'symbolic distance'—the separation of symbols from the child's own immediate experience.

The distancing principle explains why children adopt the particular associations we see between manner and CVPT, and path and OVPT. According to Werner and Kaplan, symbolic distance has three aspects. The first is social sharing, the second is placing objects at a psychological distance, and the third is differentiating signifiers from signifieds. The explanation is that the child's steps into distancing would be the smallest on each of these aspects in her initial forays. Steps minimal in this way would lead to manner-CVPT and path-OVPT combinations and the decomposition effect.

The *differentiation of path would be smallest in the OVPT*. This is because path in the OVPT matches most closely the perceptions of the child, is in the same perspective as for caregivers, and is separable as a viewable object of contemplation. Equivalently, *differentiation of manner is smallest in the CVPT*. This is because manner is enhanced in enactment or pantomime, is consequently more sharable in CVPT, and a manner enactment, being one's own performance, would be totally available as an object of contemplation. Only the differentiation of signifiers would seem to be sharper for manner in OVPT (and in Table 5.6.1 the sequestering effect is in fact weaker for manner than path).

Considering the preponderance of properties, the favored combinations could arise as products of selecting those representations where the gesture's symbolic distance is minimal. However, not all occurrences of manner decomposition occur with CVPT perspectives. Figure 6.7 shows two gestures by an English-speaking three-year-old again describing the bowling ball and its aftermath. The child is saying, "the wolf [the cat] got twirled down," and matched the manner of "twirls" with the purely manner gesture shown Figure 6.7a, and then the path content of "down" with the purely path gesture in Figure 6.7b; both gestures are in the OVPT, and thus both decompositions took place within a single perspective. The passive form, "got twirled," could have been a factor in bringing out the OVPT with manner.[3]

Fig. 6.7. (a) Manner decomposition in OVPT. (b) Path decomposition in OVPT. The first gesture, in (a), is OVPT, despite manner, and is co-expressive with the narrative distance of the passive construction in the accompanying speech.

3. The passive encodes narrative distance. Narrative distance, which is not symbolic distance (see below), helps explain how this child combined manner with OVPT. CVPT, narratively, is inherently 'closer' to the event being described, in the sense that the

Self-Aware Agent

Ultimately, the mechanism underlying the decomposition effect could be a developing sense of the self as an independent agent. Awareness of the self opens the way to distinguish self as an observer (i.e., OVPT) and self as a character (i.e., CVPT), and thus to the decomposition effect. Susan Hurley (1998) has written of the link between perspective and self-awareness: "[H]aving a unified perspective involves keeping track of the relationships of interdependence between what is perceived and what is done, and hence awareness of your own agency" (p. 141).

The age at which the dialectic signatures occur—the gesture exposition and decomposition effect—is also when children develop a 'theory of mind'. This theory, as it is whimsically termed, is awareness that perspectives exist other than one's own. In the classic experiment (e.g., Wimmer & Perner 1983), a child is told a story in which a puppet sees some candy being put in yellow box on the right. The puppet then leaves the scene and the experimenter, in full view of the child, removes the candy and hides it in a red box on the left. The puppet returns and the child is asked to say which box the puppet will approach for the candy. Pre-theory-of-mind children tend to say the new red box on the left, the one they know it is in. Theory-of-mind children say the original yellow box on the right, not the one they know it is in but where the puppet last 'saw' it. To say the old yellow box the child must differentiate her own viewpoint from the puppet's. Thus, the theory-of-mind task includes components that also figure in semantic decomposition and points to the fundamental role in the child's development of perspective and a sense of the self as an agent. These widespread developments seem to occur at the critical ages of three to four years.

Bekkering, Wohlschläger & Merideth (2000) have linked decomposition to the development of goal-directed actions. Goals in their view are organized

---

speaker becomes a character in it. Referring to this as a lack of *narrative* distance is to use the term "distance" in a way distinct from the reference in this chapter to a developing sense of *symbolic* distance in CVPT or OVPT. With symbolic distance, a CVPT gesture is felt not to be one's own action but a communication of an action "*to the Other.*" In the CVPT, a gesture can have minimal narrative distance, in that the speaker enters into the event, but still possess symbolic distance, in that the child regards it as a symbolic presentation. In the example, with the passive, the cat is regarded as at a distance, narratively, and the OVPT gesture brings out this same narrative effect.

hierarchically, and when mental resources are limited actions are simplified to conform only to the most dominant of the goals. Taking this view, we can interpret the CVPT hierarchy as dominated by manner and the OVPT hierarchy by path; but either hierarchy can include the motion event component of the other when mental resources are not pressed. This could explain the nonzero incidence of the 'wrong' viewpoint-motion event combinations in Table 6.1; they occurred, hypothetically, when the child was less pressed and able to dig down into a given hierarchy. Further, Decety & Sommerville (2003) have identified specific brain regions in adults that are active in distinguishing self-actions from other-actions (the right hemisphere, inferior parietal lobe, at the junction with the temporal cortex, and the right prefrontal cortex). It is not known (but would be important to discover) if these regions are partly under development and/or undergoing some form of consolidation during the critical three- to four-years age range when motion event decomposition is emerging.

Discourse

A final factor that could lead to decomposition is a child's growing capacity to perceive, comprehend, and control discourse via imagery and perspective. Adopting a consistent perspective enables a child to link events that are seen in that perspective. Discourse perspective could thus cement in decomposition if children, when they begin to decompose motion events analytically, seize upon viewpoint as a way to tie references together—references to (say) Sylvester in CVPT and the bowling ball in OVPT. This would be a discourse process carried out with co-perspective rather than co-reference. As a source of cohesion it is limited in that only two patterns are available, but these two might suffice for the levels of complexity with which children at this age deal.

An Immense 'U-Curve'?

Implicit in the decomposition effect is a colossal developmental 'U-curve'. U-curves are seen in many aspects of children's mental development (cf. Strauss & Stavy 1982), and are generally considered to arise when in the course of development an old function is reconstituted to take new form. Such also may be the process with motion event decomposition. The 'U' in the case of the decomposition effect is remarkably broad: from age three, roughly, to past twelve (the oldest children we have tested, twelve-year-olds, still display the effect). It is unclear why motion event decomposition should persist so long. It lasts through major developmental changes (this long period runs from preoperational, through operational, to formal operational intelligence in the Piagetian analysis; cf. Inhelder & Piaget 1958). To overcome it, the child has to see the two motion event components, path and manner, from a single viewpoint, and this could be the reconstituted form. But it is not clear what such a reconstitution of viewpoint itself comprises. Whatever the ultimate explanation, it appears that a key development is expansion of the scope covered by third-person OVPTs—this perspective somehow becomes compatible with manner; alternatively, manner becomes dissociated from first-person, CVPT reenactments and thus becomes, for the first time, available under OVPT.

Dawn of Dialectic

The development of an imagery-language dialectic age three or four could have widespread effects:

- The child can begin to fashion his/her own contexts such that the motion event component—manner or path—is contextually contrastive, not simply an index to a referent in the story.
- Having a yoked viewpoint can add discourse cohesion. For example, a CVPT can carry through to other growth points, as in this example from a 4;1 year-old:

[[he **rolled in**] [**to the** /]] [/ **place** //] [// // b**ooo**mm]
    manner   manner   manner   path

Each gesture (three manners and one path, all showing decomposition) seems an appropriate albeit short-range catchment. Manner, first separated from path in the motion event decomposition, is carried through the whole utterance via gestures and then onomatopoeia. The discourse theme was Sylvester's *manner* of motion.

- The dialectic could also have an effect on the static dimension, bringing out aspects of syntax that have discourse functionality[4] and explaining how

---

4. Such as the use of embedded clauses for background content. Such functions could foster access to mechanisms of linguistic recursion in general.

children's utterances pass from a predominantly referential mode to a mode in which they are also shaped by discourse.[5]

The basic claim is that the course of cognitive development takes a new turn as an imagery-language dialectic and growth points become available. The experience of motion is universal, but children start to understand it in a new light. It becomes hyper-analyzed and placed into perspectives that children cannot easily alter. Ultimately, this conception must be overcome and the components be put back together under a single perspective, but this step may require attaining a wholly new stage of development and be delayed for many years. The process of overcoming it is where the dialectic begins to guide thinking into grooves that can be traced to "the nature of the language or languages through the use of which they have been developed," in the language of the Whorfian hypothesis, quoted at the beginning of the chapter.

Summary

The onset of an imagery-language dialectic is by no means a single step. Prior to the decomposition effect the gestures of children have a relationship to language different from the gestures coming later—they are sparse, seem not to function as symbols, do not have consistent perspectives, and do not show motion event decomposition or segregation of perspective. The pacesetter of development may be awareness of the self as an agent, as this can create a distinction between the CVPT and OVPT, from which, in turn, path-manner separation descends, and with this the beginning of an imagery-language dialectic. Such a reconfiguration begins at about the same age as the gesture explosion and motion event decomposition, and leads to other developments, including the child's intuition of 'other minds'. Once path and manner have been tied to different perspectives, decomposition is locked in and persists, creating a colossal U-curve.

5. For example, the following from a 3;11 year-old incorporates a background index to 'the house' that implies awareness of the context of speaking: "it made Sylvester cat # goo d<u>own</u>] [**out**] of the thing / I mean that # house thing that was right there / the cat / slid on the road a[nd then # **slid**<u>ed off</u> the ro][**ad right on** to the /] side[walk ///]."

'WHORF'

Just as the development of growth points is presumed to alter children's imagery, growth points also alter imagery, and this is expected for all speakers, including adults. The term 'Whorf', in quotes, is used emblematically in the title of this discussion for a range of ideas having to do with the influence of language on thought. The Whorfian hypothesis proper addresses language as a static object. It describes 'habitual thought' (a static mode of cognition identified by Whorf) and how it is shaped through linguistic analogies (see Whorf 1956; Lucy 1992a,b).

The corresponding dynamic hypothesis is 'thinking for speaking', described by Dan Slobin as follows: "'Thinking for speaking' involves picking those characteristics that (a) fit some conceptualization of the event, and (b) are readily encodable in the language" (Slobin 1987, p. 435). In terms of growth points, the thinking for speaking hypothesis is that, during speech, GPs may differ across languages in predictable ways. It might be better to call this version of the hypothesis thinking *while* speaking. A major insight into the dynamic hypothesis, however it is named, comes from the distinction between 'satellite-framed' versus 'verb-framed' languages identified by Leonard Talmy (1975, 1985, 2000), a distinction referring to how languages package motion event information, including path and manner—the motion event components traced in the "Children" section of this chapter.

S-Type and V-Type Languages

Spanish and English share features with all Indo-European languages, but differ in a crucial way that has implications for thinking for speaking. Motion events are analyzable into multiple semantic components (Talmy, 1975, 1985, 2000)—in addition to the bare fact of motion, there is path, figure (the moving object), ground (the landmark with respect to which motion is located), manner (how the motion is carried out), cause, and others. Consider a simple example—in the bowling ball episode, Sylvester rolls down an inclined street with the bowling ball inside him. The *figure* is Sylvester and/or the ball; *path* is the downward direction of motion; *manner* is the way in which the motion is performed (rolling); *ground* is the street; *setting* is the overall scenario of the motion event including but not limited to the landmark; and *cause* is the cause of motion (unspecified in this example, but in some analyses, the rolling causes the motion; Croft 1999). Underlying all these components is the basic *fact of motion*—the idea that something is moving.

Languages differ in their highlighting tendencies, depending on how verbs package semantic information. English follows a *satellite-framed* or 'S-type' semantics (Slobin 1996).[6] German and Mandarin are also S-type. In S-type languages, a verb packages the fact of motion with information about *manner*. "Rolls" is an example, and the verb describes, in one package, that something is in motion and how it is moving—motion by rolling. The path component, in contrast, is outside the verb. From "rolls" alone, we have no inkling of the direction of motion; for that we add one or more satellites: "rolls out/in/down/up/through."

A complex curvilinear path in an S-type description tends to be resolved into a series of straight segments or paths. E.g., "and it goes <u>down</u> but it rolls him <u>out</u> <u>down</u> the rainspout <u>out</u> <u>into</u> the sidewalk <u>into</u> a bowling alley" (a recorded example)—one verb and six satellites (underlined) or segments of path. It is also typical of these languages to emphasize ground—each path segment tends to have its own locus with respect to a ground element, as in this example: the sidewalk, rainspout, and bowling alley.

The other broad category of language is the *verb-framed* or 'V-type', of which Spanish, French, Turkish, ASL, and Japanese are examples. In such languages, a verb packages the fact of motion with *path* (the direction of motion)—"ascend" or "descends," "exits" or "enters," etc.—and it is manner that is conveyed outside the verb (or omitted altogether).

Unlike an S-type language, a complex curvilinear path can be described holistically with a single verb—"descends," for example, for the same curvilinear path that was broken into six segments in the English example. V-type languages tend to highlight a whole mise en scène rather than an isloable landmark or ground (e.g., a collection of descriptions like "there are tall buildings and a slanted street with some signs around, and he ascends climbing," in contrast to "he climbs up the drainpipe," where upward path is localized to the ground, the drainpipe). This is termed the setting by Slobin.

English, of course, also has V-type verbs (the very ones I have been citing: ascend, descend, enter, exit, etc.). These verbs historically entered English from Latin, which is V-type, and as verbs retain a V-type semantics that does

6. Slobin (2004) emphasizes that this is more a continuum than a dichotomy.

not fully integrate into the native English S-type system. Such a verb already contains path and to combine it with a native satellite seems redundant ("exits out the room").

Implications for Growth Points

Gestures also differ between S-type and V-type, implying the possibility of different GPs and imagery-language dialectics in languages of the two kinds (cf. McNeill & Duncan 2000). The evidence for such differences is described in the following.

Effects on Path

The following comparisons are of English and Spanish speakers describing the same bowling ball episode, and in each language speakers seem to create different visuospatial imagery.

English. The example above of a speaker describing the aftermath of the bowling ball event divided the event into six path segments, each with its own path gesture:

(1) and it goes <u>down</u>
(2) but it rolls him <u>out</u>
(3) <u>down</u> the rain spout
(4) <u>out</u>
(5) <u>into</u> the sidewalk
(6) <u>into</u> a bowling alley and he knocks over all the pins.

The match between speech and gesture is nearly complete. The speaker's visuospatial cognition—in gesture—consists of a half dozen straight line segments, not the single curved path that Sylvester actually followed (Figure 6.8.1–6).[7]

---

7. It is of interest that the cartoon stimulus, designed and conceptualized by animators from an S-type linguistic culture (viz., Hollywood), has a satellite-framed-like division in its scene shifts, new camera angles, etc. Such a division of the cartoon into path segments makes the V-type representation imposed by Spanish speakers all the more remarkable.

Fig. 6.8.1. [/ and it **goes** down] PATH 1   **Fig. 6.8.2.** but [[it **roll**][s him **out***]] PATH 2

Fig. 6.8.3. [[down **the** //] PATH 3   **Fig. 6.8.4.** [/ **rain**spo]] PATH 4

Fig. 6.8.5. [ut/ out i] PATH 5   **Fig. 6.8.6.** alk/ into a] [bowling **alley** PATH 6

Spanish. Spanish speakers, in contrast, represent this scene without significant segmentation. Their gestures are single, unbroken curvilinear trajectories. In speech, the entire path may be covered by a single verb. The following description is by a monolingual speaker, recorded in Guadalajara:[8]

[ent**onces SSS**]
then he-falls ONOM
'then SSSS he falls'.

The accompanying gesture traces a single, unbroken arcing trajectory down and to the side (Figure 6.9). What had been segmented in English becomes in

8. Recordings by Karl-Erik McCullough and Lisa Miotto.

Spanish one curvaceous gesture that re-creates Sylvester's path. In speech, the speaker made use of onomatopoeia, which is a frequent verb substitute in our Spanish-language narrative materials.

Fig. 6.9. Spanish speaker's single continuous arc for Sylvester's circuitous trip down the pipe, along the street and into the bowling alley (scan images from left to right). Elapsed time is about 1 sec. This illustrates Spanish-style visuospatial cognition of a curved trajectory as a single, unsegmented path.

To quantify this possible cross-linguistic difference, Table 6.2 shows the number of path segments that occur in Spanish and English gestures for the path running from the encounter with the bowling ball inside the pipe to the denouement in the bowling alley. English speakers break this trajectory into 43 percent more segments than Spanish speakers: 3.3 in English, and 2.3 in Spanish. Extremes, moreover, favor English. Five English speakers divided the trajectory into six or more segments, compared to only one Spanish speaker. Thus Spanish speakers, even when they divide paths into segments, have fewer and broader segments.

Table 6.2. Segmentation of paths by
English- and Spanish-speaking adults.

	Number of gestures	
Segments	English	Spanish
0	0	1
1	3	5
2	7	6
3	3	4
4	2	1
5	1	0
≥ 6	5	1
Total	21	18

Effects on Manner

Fogs in Spanish, Modulations in English

Manner fogs. Slobin has observed many times in Spanish speech and writing that manner is cumbersome to include, and consequently speakers and writers tend to avoid it if they can (Slobin 1996). However, manner does not necessarily disappear thereby from consciousness. The result is often a 'manner fog'—a scene description that has multiple manner occurrences in gesture but lacks manner in speech. An example is the following, a description of Sylvester climbing the pipe on the inside:

e entonces busca la ma[nera **(silent pause)[9]**]
'and so he looks for the way'
Gesture depicts the shape of the pipe: **ground.**
[de **entra**][r // **se met**][**e por el**]
'to enter REFL goes-into through the'

9. Kendon (personal communication) observes that when a gesture occurs during a speech pause, listeners tend to look at it, and this may be a way of calling attention to the gesture. However, such a device does not appear to have been in use here (speech amplitude during the pause trailed off, for example, rather than ceasing abruptly, suggesting not deployment of a conscious device but rather an involuntary delay in forming the upcoming idea unit).

Both hands rock and rise simultaneously: **manner** + **path** *combined (left hand only through "mete")*

[de**sague**//] [// si?]

'drainpipe . . . yes?'

Right hand circles in arc: **manner** + **ground** *(shape of pipe).*

[de**sague entra** /]

'drainpipe, enters'

Both hands briefly in palm-down position (clambering paws) and then rise with chop-like motion: **manner** + **path** *combined.*

Gestural manner was in the second, third, and fourth lines, despite the total absence of spoken manner references. Thus, while manner may seem absent when speech alone is considered, it can be present, even abundant, in visuospatial thinking.

Manner modulation. In English, in a sense, the opposite process takes place. Whereas a manner fog adds manner when it is lacking from speech, modulation adjusts manner that is obligatory in speech. Modulation solves a problem created by English verbs, that they often package manner with motion and are accordingly manner verbs as well as verbs of motion, even when a speaker intends to convey only the fact of motion. A gesture, however, can include manner or not, and can accordingly modulate the manner component of verbs in exact accord with intentions. The following examples, from different English speakers, show manner modulation—respectively, reinforcement of manner and removal of manner:

Speaker A (reinforces manner)

but [it **roll**]s him out down the

Both hands sweep to right and rotate as they go, conveying both path and manner.

The gesture contains manner and synchronizes with the manner verb, "rolls." The context highlighted manner as the point of differentiation. The content and co-occurrence highlight manner and suggest that it was part of the psychological predicate.

Speaker B (removes manner)

and he rolls [/ **down the** drai]nspout

Left hand plunges straight down, conveying path only.

This gesture, despite the presence of the same verb, "rolls," skips the verb and presents no manner content of its own. It shows path alone, and co-occurs with the satellite, "down." Both the timing and the shape of the gesture suggest that manner was not a major element of the speaker's intent and that "rolls," while referentially accurate, was de-emphasized and functioned as a verb of motion only, with the manner content modulated (the speaker could as well have said "goes down," but this would have meant editing out the true reference to rolling).

Chinese: Effects on Semantic Grouping

Chinese motion event gestures often resemble those in English, as would be expected from their shared typology as S-type languages. However, there are also differences. Chinese speakers perform a kind of gesture that appears, so far as we are aware, only in that language. It is as if, in English, we said "a stick" and, simultaneously, performed a gesture showing how to give a blow. While such a combination is obviously possible for an English speaker (for this writer, for example), it does not occur often, and when it does occur the attested instances are treated as errors by their speakers. However, they take place with Mandarin speakers, and seem to do so with some frequency (Susan Duncan, once she noticed this pattern in our Chinese language videos, spotted similar combinations in common use by speakers in Taiwan). The GPs formed in this way might have meta-level significances—somewhat like topics formed jointly of speech and gesture (where neither speech nor gesture, considered alone, would be the topic).

The hallmark of this Chinese pattern is that a gesture occurs earlier in the temporal sequence of speech than we would find in English or Spanish. An example is the following:

lao tai-tai [na -ge   da **bang hao**]-xiang gei   ta da-xia
old lady hold CLASSIFIER   big stick seem CAUSE   him hit-down$_{\text{verb-satellite}}$
'The old lady apparently knocked him down with a big stick'

The gesture (a downward blow) that accompanied the spoken reference to the stick ("da bang" 'big stick') was expressively the same as the verb and satellite, "da-xia" 'hit-down'. However, the speaker's hand promptly relaxed, long before this verb phrase was reached in speech.

Chinese is what Li and Thompson (1976, 1981) termed a 'topic prominent' language.[10] English and Spanish, in contrast, are 'subject prominent'. Utterances in the latter languages are founded on subject-predicate relations. In line with this typological distinction, we find cases like the above, in which gesture provides one element and speech another element, and they jointly create something like a topic frame. This may be again, therefore, the impact of language on thinking for speaking.

In English, too, gestures occasionally occur that depict an event yet to appear in speech (referring here to time lapses far longer than the previously discussed fraction-of-a-second gesture anticipations). Such precocious imagery is handled by the speaker as an error, requiring a repair. In the following, a gesture shows the result of an action; it occurred with speech describing its cause. This is a semantically appropriate pairing not unlike the Chinese example, but it involved separating the gesture from the predicate describing the same event. It was repaired first by holding it until the predicate arrived, and then repeating it in enlarged form.

[so it **hits** <u>him on</u> **the hea**]
[<u>d and he winds up</u> **rolling down the stre**]et

The two gestures in the first clause depicted Sylvester moving down the street, an event described only in the following clause. The difference between Chinese and English in this situation is apparent in the second line, the point at which the target predication emerged in speech. Unlike the Chinese speaker, whose hands were at rest by now, this English speaker held the gesture (underlined text) and then repeated it in a larger, more definite way when the possible GP occurred (cf. 'gesture echoes' in Chapter 4.3).

The subsequent enhanced repeat indicates the relevance of the gesture to the predicate. In other words, the speaker retained the imagery from the first clause for the GP of the second. She did not, as the Chinese speaker did, use it as a self-contained framing unit when it first appeared.

10. Chafe (1976) stated the intended sense of topicalization: "What the topics appear to do is limit the applicability of the main predication to a certain restricted domain . . . the topic sets a spatial, temporal, or individual framework within which the main predication holds" (p. 50).

Summary: Visuospatial Cognition Differs Across Languages

From the gesture evidence, we infer the following differences in visuospatial cognition across the languages surveyed:

(a) Gestural paths tend to be broken into straight line segments in English and be preserved as curvilinear wholes in Spanish. Chinese also tends to break paths into straight line segments.

(b) Gestural manner tends to expand the encoding resources of Spanish and to modulate them in English (the relationship in Chinese is not known).

(c) Gestures can combine with linguistic segments to create discourse topics: this occurs in Chinese, but not in English or presumably Spanish.

MOTION EVENT DECOMPOSITION: ADAPTIVE?

Japanese and Turkish are two languages in which a kind of 'decomposition' takes place as a pattern of adult gesture performance (Kita & Özyürek 2003). I use quotes because I am not suggesting that this adult decomposition is the same as children's. On the contrary, I propose to describe it, where it appears, as a yet another case of language having a shaping influence on cognition.

I discussed the Kita-Özyürek paper in Chapter 4.3 in connection with their modularity theory. Here, I focus on their empirical results. Kita & Özyürek compared narrations of the Tweety and Sylvester cartoon by speakers of English, Japanese, and Turkish. In the latter two languages, both V-type, they observed a much greater tendency to 'decompose' motion events—that is, to perform gestures with only manner (no path) or only path (no manner). Whereas their adult English speakers showed such single-component motion event gestures 10 percent of the time (not too far from the 5 percent decomposition of manner alone by English speaking adults cited earlier), Turkish speakers did so about 40 percent of the time and Japanese speakers did up to 50 percent of the time. Kita and Özyürek interpret the cross-linguistic difference as revealing a "crucial difference among the three languages . . . [namely] that Japanese and Turkish require a more complex expression for Manner and Trajectory than English" (Kita & Özyürek 2003, p. 26). What would cause this pattern in the two V-type languages? They suggest, and I agree, that the force separating path and manner is the same V-type semantics that we have already considered.

The key to the effect I wish to emphasize is *verb scope*—the range of sentence constituents a verb is able to influence or cover semantically and structurally. In English, verbs have a scope that extends over any number of path particles, each with its own surface phrase, so long as it is not interrupted by another verb. V-type languages, on the other hand, have intrinsically limited scope where manner is involved. The English language example cited earlier in this chapter has five particles within the scope of "rolls": "but it rolls him out down the rain spout out into the sidewalk into a bowling alley and he knocks over all the pins." The most remote, "into a bowling alley," is five phrases away, and this is not the limit.[11] If verbs have a scope that extends up to the next verb, the theoretically unlimited scope of English manner verbs can be seen as a by-product of the fact that path is encoded in particles. The addition of manner in a language of the V-type, in contrast, entails another verb, and hence the scope of any single verb is limited by the deployment of manner (Aske 1989).

To account for Kita and Özyürek's cross-linguistic gesture results, then, I suggest that each semantic package built around a verb tends to have a different gesture. This would tend to pull path and manner gestures apart in Japanese and Turkish, since each manner component requires its own verb. It should do the same in Spanish, but Spanish speakers can and often do omit manner in the spoken formulation (which might be an interesting difference to explore within the V-type class). For English, this analysis predicts that speakers will tend to tie manner in gestures to path, but that path can also separate itself from manner and occur alone, and indeed Kita and Özyürek found more path-alone than manner-alone gestures for their English speakers (with still more path-alone gestures for Japanese and Turkish speakers, a difference that is not directly relevant to this prediction).

HOW LANGUAGE CHANGES VISUOSPATIAL THINKING: WHORF MEETS CHILD

It seems clear from the evidence described in this chapter that languages can shape the visuospatial cognition of their speakers *as they are speaking*. Japanese,

---

11. Kita and Özyürek suggest that motion event packages in English are 'more compact' than in the two V-framed languages, but this proposition seems in conflict with this lengthy stream of path particles within the scope of a single verb.

Turkish, English, Spanish, and Chinese speakers, as they produce speech, seem to visualize motion in contrasting ways traceable to the specific features of their languages. The GP theory explains these effects as a dialectic of imagery and language within GPs, leading to adjustments of imagery to mesh with language. Children also undergo cognitive adjustments as they develop an imagery-language dialectic, something commencing apparently about age three or four. Cross-linguistic differences in thinking for speaking may appear even later. We have not seen variations across languages at the beginning stages. The controlling factors at the beginning of this development (an emerging sense of self and perspective) appear to be shared, at least across the three linguistic-cultural groups we have compared (North American English, Mexican Spanish, Taiwanese Mandarin).

Such effects of language on thought illustrate the so-called 'weak' Whorfian hypothesis (as opposed to the 'strong' hypothesis). The strong hypothesis proposes that the effects of language on thought are stable and do not require the production of speech to activate them. Lucy (1992b), for example, showed differential attention to changes in object numerosity in pictured scenes between English and Mayan Yucatec speakers, as a function of where in the two languages the line is drawn between objects that lexical items treat as having forms built in versus those denoted as substances without specific forms. English thinks of corn as formless, for example, but thinks of implements like shovels as having a form that is built in. This form/formless difference affects how one counts objects, because counting is an operation that refers to forms. Hence, we say, in English, "two shovels" but must specify a form for corn—"two kernels of corn" and the like. In Yucatec, a shovel is of the formless type, and to say the equivalent of "two shovels" one must say two long 'pieces' of metal and wood substance, or somesuch. In responding to pictured scenes, while not speaking or counting, Lucy observed that Yucatec speakers were less likely than English speakers to notice a change in the number of shovels (just as English speakers were unlikely to notice a change in the amount of corn). This is a 'strong' effect in that it seems to reveal a habitual thought, or dispositional difference between speakers of the two languages in how to divide things in the world.

I will conclude this chapter by relating the 'strong'/'weak' Whorfian contrast to the two dimensions of language. A question to address is, in general, what is most visible on each dimension? The 'strong' Whorfian effects inhabit the static dimension. 'Habitual thought', by definition, is something that exists without context and is listable in the same way that linguistic forms are listable on the static dimension. 'Thinking for (and thinking *while*) speaking', on the other hand, occurs on the dynamic dimension. It is part of the dialectic. The difference between the strong and weak versions, therefore, is really a difference of the dimension on which the effect of language on cognition appears. I prefer to use the less tendentious terms 'static' and 'dynamic', over the traditional 'strong' and 'weak', since the latter were coined under the spell of the Saussurian synchronic tradition and carry this historical coloration with it. To me at least, there is little doubt that language has impact on thought on both dimensions, though I confess to believing that the effects look actually stronger, in the sense of being easier to find, on the dynamic dimension (so paradoxically, the 'weak' version is the stronger).

PART 3

Brain and Origins

CHAPTER 7

Neurogesture

INTRODUCTION

Little is known about how gesture is organized in the brain. Nonetheless, by invoking the principle that thinking for speaking is dynamically organized in a dialectic of imagery and language, we can predict some features of the 'neurogestural' system. This system should engage the same brain circuits as language, in part. And conversely, if we discover something about brain action with gesture, we should be able to add this discovery to our picture of what the brain is doing when it handles language. I do not present myself as a neuroscientist, but I hope to bring basic information about the brain into contact with ✓ what has not been considered in this area previously—the insight that gesture is actually part of language and must be considered along with it. I believe the perspective of an imagery-language dialectic can lead to new understandings of some familiar facts.

In this discussion, I will be looking at data from speakers with brain injuries, including two of the aphasias, anterior (Broca's aphasia) and posterior (Wernicke's aphasia). Figure 7.1 illustrates the approximate locations of these areas. I will also discuss data from patients with right hemisphere injury; and finally I will consider data from split-brain speakers, that is, speakers who have undergone an operation in which all communication between the right and left hemispheres has been interrupted, while leaving the hemispheres intact. I relate these topics to the hypothesis that the neurogestural system converges on Broca's area, where speech and gesture are orchestrated as motor actions.

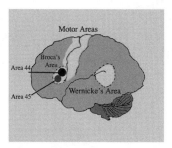

Fig. 7.1. Annotated brain (viewed from the left side).

Broca's area is more than a 'speech center'. It is *the area of the brain orchestrating actions under some significance*—that is, it is the area of the brain that assembles sequences of movements and/or complexes of moving parts into performance packages unified by goals, meanings, and adaptability. We have seen that performance units in the case of human language are also unified by imagery—a primary organizational factor—and Broca's area may be where actions (articulatory, manual) are organized around gesture images (visuospatial-actional). An orchestration specialty is suggested by brain imaging results. For example, Nishitani & Hari (2000) observed that activation of this region preceded activity in the motor area by some 250 msecs, and seemed have the function of organizing the mirror neuron system, located in areas 44 and 45 by Rizzolatti & Arbib (1998; there is further discussion of mirror neurons in Chapter 8). Broca's area also mediates higher-order control of fore-limb movement,[1] and, in this, resembles the neuronal mechanisms subserving speech (Binkofski et al. 2000). Bonda et al. (1994) also found that Broca's area became active during arm and hand movements. Even more germane, Decety et al. (1994) found Broca's activity during *mental imagery* of grasping. Horwitz et al. (2003) report that a region in Broca's area (area 44) is activated by "generation of complex articulatory movements of oral/laryngeal or limb musculature." Ferrari et al. (2003) observe activation in the F5 region of the monkey brain, which is the presumed homolog of Broca's area, by communicative face gestures.[2]

1. Broca's area sends axons to the primary motor cortex but not to the spinal cord (Ana Solodkin, personal communication).

2. Thanks to Ana Solodkin, Department of Neurology of the University of Chicago, and Tae Kunisawa, Department of Linguistics of the University of New Mexico, for bringing several of these references to my attention.

Distinguishing Kinds of Orchestration

In goal-directed actions, the action's significance is carrying out the action itself, and achieving its intended effects. In speech and gesture, however, actions (manual as well as oral-laryngeal) have a significance other than the actions of the moving parts themselves or their endstates. While Broca's area is not necessarily the source of intention and meaning, as noted above it orchestrates movements under them. In the monkey brain, area F5 appears to be adapted for the orchestration of action as well (Rizzolatti & Arbib 1998, Cantalupo & Hopkins 2001), but lacks Broca's area's ability to apply significances other than that of the action itself. If Broca's area of the human brain evolved out this homologous F5 area, part of what was new, and had to have evolved, is the ability to draw on significances other than actions themselves to orchestrate movements.[3]

Sketch of a Brain Model

In the model that I am proposing, the neurogesture system involves both the right and left sides of the brain in a choreographed operation with the following parts: The left posterior temporal speech region of Wernicke's area supplies categorial content, not only for comprehension but for the creative production of verbal thought; this content becomes available to the right hemisphere, which seems particularly adept at creating imagery to capture discourse content (McNeill & Pedelty 1995). The right hemisphere could also play a role in the creation of growth points. This is plausible since GPs depend on the differentiation of newsworthy content from context and require the simultaneous presence of linguistic categorial content and imagery, both of which

---

3. A favorite sport among primatologists is to take statements like this, in which some feature of behavior is proclaimed to be 'unique to humans', and find another primate species capable of doing the same or something similar. I will anticipate this response by citing the chimp Beleka (due to William Hopkins, who described Beleka at the conference on Evolution, Cognition and Development, the University of Chicago, 2002). As described in Chapter 8, Beleka organizes gestures that accompany vocalizations to mean, roughly, "hey look!" (at a banana, say). Her gestures and vocalizations appear to be orchestrated actions with meanings other than action itself, and might be considered a precursor on which the evolution to be proposed in the next chapter could have been built if such coordination was present in the last common chimp-human ancestor.

seem to be available in the right hemisphere. The frontal cortex also might play a role in constructing fields of oppositions and psychological predicates, and supply these contrasts to the right hemisphere, there to be embodied in GPs. Everything (right hemisphere, left posterior hemisphere, frontal cortex) converges on the left anterior hemisphere, specifically Broca's area, and the circuits specialized there for action orchestration. Broca's area may also be the location of two other aspects of the imagery-language dialectic (at least, such would be convenient)—the generation of further meanings via constructions and their semantic frames, and intuitions of formal completeness to provide dialectic 'stop orders'.[4] All of these areas are 'language centers' of the brain. I will return to this model at the end of the chapter.

The brain model also explains why the language centers of the brain have classically been regarded as limited to two patches—Wernicke's and Broca's areas. If the model is on the right track, contextual background information must be present to activate the broad spectrum of brain regions that the model describes. Single words and decontextualized stimuli of the kinds employed in most neuropsychological tests would not engage the full system; they would be limited to activating only a small part of it.

BROCA'S APHASIA

Consideration of data from the tragic natural experiment of brain injury can be informative for modeling the localizations of functions in the brain. We begin with a discussion of Broca's aphasia. Broca's aphasia is characterized by a severe impairment of speech output—often termed agrammatism—together with inaccurate phonetic and lexical activations, including difficulty articulating stop consonants (which require precise control of motor sequences; Lieberman 2002). Patients demonstrating this array of symptoms generally share an injury in the posterior region of the left inferior frontal gyrus, Broca's area (Horwitz et al. 2003), as well as subcortical injuries, which may be necessary as causal factors (Lieberman 2002). An example from Gardner (1974) illustrates

---

4. Or more than convenient. A recent study (Ben-Shachar et al. 2003) shows an fMRI response in Broca's area for grammaticality judgments. Grammaticality judgments, obviously, depend on linguistic intuitions. The same study found verb complexity registering in the left posterior superior temporal sulcus area. In the brain model, the left posterior area provides the categorial content of growth points.

the kind of speech: "Yes, sure. Me go, er, uh P.T. nine o'cot, speech...two times...read...wr...ripe, er, rike, er, write...practice...getting better" (1974, pp. 60–61). While extremely fragmented, the speech is not meaningless. Nearly all the elements comprise possible points of differentiation from context, a context that we can register and interpret.

The point I wish to emphasize is that Broca's speech appears to more or less completely preserve growth points and catchments. GPs and catchments entail an intact contextual framework. What disappears or is impaired is the ability to orchestrate motor actions under meanings.[5] There is severe impairment of the patient's access to constructions and their associated semantic frames, but since the process is dynamic, agrammatism can become grammatical, given sufficient support from imagery. I will show below an example of an agrammatic speaker who, over a two-minute period, with catchment support, constructed a two-clause sentence with embedding; at that point one could say that he was not 'agrammatic'.

Broca's Agrammatic Speech Retains Growth Points and Catchments

I describe here two cases of severe Broca's agrammatic aphasia from Pedelty (1987). The first case demonstrates the presence of growth points. The second shows recurring catchment imagery.

The Growth Point

The speaker had viewed the animated stimulus (the bowling ball scene). Speech is similar to that in the Gardner example. Clearly, she was able to remember many details of the scene: "cat – bird? –'nd cat – and uh – the uh – she (unintell.) – 'partment an' t* - that (?) – [eh ///] – old uh – [mied //] – uh – woman – and uh – [she] – like – er ap – [they ap – #] – cat [/] – [an' uh bird /] – [is //] – I uh – [ch- cheows] – [an' down t' t' down]." Gestures occurred at several points, indicated with square brackets, and they appear to convey newsworthy content. The gestures with "she" and "they ap-," for example, depicted a flat surface in the upper space, apparently the window sill of Granny's apartment, where

---

5. Apraxia is an impairment of actions in which the action itself is the significance (e.g., pretending to comb your hair). Apraxia is sometimes an accompaniment of Broca's aphasia but it is not always present and is distinct from speech impairment.

Fig. 7.2. Gestures by an agrammatic speaker timed with "an' down t' t' down."

Tweety was perched. Figure 7.2 shows two successive gestures synchronous with "an' down t' t' down," depicting the bowling ball's downward path. Plausibly, this combination of imagery and linguistic categorization was a GP. As Susan Duncan has pointed out in connection with this example, the gesture occurred at the same discourse juncture where gestures from normal speakers also occur, implying that for the patient, as for normals, a psychological predicate was being differentiated from a field of oppositions. Using the schema employed in Chapter 4.2, the GP had something like the following content:

What The Bird Did: Bowling Ball Down

To judge from such cases (and others in Pedelty's data), Broca's aphasia spares:

- GPs,
- the capacity to construct context, and
- the differentiation of psychological predicates.

But it impairs the ability to access constructions and to orchestrate sequences of speech and gesture movements under some significance. The next aphasic case suggests that while Broca's aphasia greatly impedes access to constructions, catchment imagery can assist the patient to overcome this obstacle in part.

The Catchment

The speaker was recounting an episode in which Sylvester is being pursued along overhead wires by a trolley. The speaker refers to the trolley as the 'el', which is the local way of referring to Chicago's elevated train system. The

Fig. 7.3. Catchment from an agrammatic speaker made by repeated gesture points into the upper space. Speech advanced from single elements ("el") in the first slide, to phrases ("on the tracks"), to a single clause ("he saw an el train") to, finally, in the last slide and without a gesture, a sentence with an embedded clause ("he saw the el train comin'"). The duration of the catchment and the time it took to reach the final construction was two minutes seventeen seconds.

important feature of the example is his repeated indicating of the upper gesture space—first raising his left arm at the elbow, then lifting his arm overhead (Figure 7.3). This recurrent indexing is a source of gestural cohesion. Verbally, speech was initially limited to just 'el' (with and without an article). It then expanded to "on the tracks" (which, like the trolley wires, are overhead in an elevated train system). A full sentence with a single clause then emerged ("he saw the el train"), and finally, dramatically, considering the depth of his initial agrammatism, a full sentence with two verbs and clauses ("he saw the el train comin'"). The example illustrates a catchment (the overhead wires/tracks) and a step-by-step accessing of a construction under its spell.

Summary of Broca's Aphasia

The effect of injury to Broca's area lies especially in the interruption of the orchestration of articulatory and gestural movements. Both speech and gesture emerge as if not orchestrated. What remains is strikingly similar in speech and gesture. It is this residue, the same in both modalities, that above all points to a specialized function in this brain region for motor orchestration under some significance. According to the model, both articulatory and manual gestures would be organized there. The neural streams underlying GPs and catchments originate outside Broca's area and converge onto it. The area is possibly also the locus of unpacking. Injury seems to make constructions for unpacking highly inaccessible, but repeated catchment imagery, especially on a large scale, is able to reawaken them. Such recovery, albeit temporary and slow to act, demonstrates that discourse relations are retained in this form of aphasia and can be used to compensate for the absence of orchestration.

WERNICKE'S APHASIA

Within traditional models of the brain, Wernicke's area supplies linguistic categorial content. It is known to be essential for speech comprehension, which is severely disrupted after injury to the posterior speech area (Gardner 1974). However, it also might play a role in speech production. Wernicke's aphasia, in a sense, is the inverse of Broca's. While fluent, speech is semantically and pragmatically empty or (perhaps more accurately) unconstrained. Although not part of the orchestration process in Broca's area, Wernicke's area may be part of something deeper, taking part in the genesis of verbal thought itself. After injury, gestures, likewise, are garbled and lack intelligible pragmatic or semantic content. Such gesture-speech parallels suggest that Wernicke's area plays some essential role in generating the categorial content of GPs. Wernicke's area could also help shape GP imagery and ensure that it takes on langue-relevant forms. All of these considerations suggest that the posterior left hemisphere sends categorial information to the right hemisphere, where imagery, discourse, and categorial content can be distilled into GPs. The distinctive speech of Wernicke's aphasia would then be explained as arising from an inadequate kind of categorial content and an insufficiently adapted mode of imagery. A GP takes form but it is deformed. It nonetheless converges in the normal way on Broca's area, there to be unpacked and orchestrated into vocal and manual actions, which run off fluently. The product is the mode of fluent yet unconstrained speech that is typical of the Wernicke's aphasic.

The examples in Figure 7.4 are again from Pedelty's data. The speaker was describing an event from the animated cartoon in which Sylvester got "to it," the "it" initially being the location of the other character, Tweety (the references beyond this are difficult to decipher). The first "to it" was accompanied by a gesture in which the left hand moved laterally and contacted the open upright palm of the right hand. Gesture and speech were possibly co-expressive in this first occurrence. However, they began to recur without traceable meaning. While recurrence is essential for a catchment and might aid a Broca's aphasic, as we saw earlier, these recurrences were a kind of *anti-catchment*—recurring imagery that added to a *lack* of coherence. The illustrations show three widely spaced appearances of the gesture and "to-it."

Fig. 7.4. Wernicke aphasic recurring imagery with the phrase "to-it." Each panel shows a separate speech-gesture combination, without meaningful context. The panels represent temporally widely separated points.

The following transcript, by Laura Pedelty, gives a sense of this patient's speech. The lack of pragmatic and semantic control is readily seen. Other classic features associated with Wenicke's aphasia are present as well, such as distortions of word forms (paraphasias) and 'clangs', or unbridled phonetic primings such as "a little tooki tooki goin' to-it to him," for example.

a little tooki tooki goin to-it to him
looki' on a little little tooki goin' to him
it's a not digga not næhe weduh
like he'll get me mema run to-it they had to is
then he put it sutthing to it takun a jo to-it
that's nobody to-it
I mean pawdi di get to-it she got
got got glasses she could look to-it
to set something to in to-it to a to a got in to-it
to a duck to-it
hit on hit him on nice to him

then she just sent to 'im
to ah my knowledge anyway
she trie to get the little little ah ak it t- t- tush t- t- take it
the part of the gun ta- take a part of a gun she's tryin' a take up a he got into a puky
she was trying to be that she was going to take
to make d- her take the part of the little ton't little the gar gen to-it little little little little like puss to-it
that's all I tooki
an' run someplace
she dropped hi baggage up
she 'member that she was to-it
nothin' but a byum that's all
'n I lef' the whole damn the whole damn
side look bloorep 'n to-it I use to
look I look at it way day way took
I look to-it
ju' a little ol' toy
with tappn'
why he ed take the part of 'im
an' they give 'im away to 'im
they gvme him an' they they find out who it was
it was a no no 'n that was
bammed up
an'
that was all to-it

Summary of Posterior Left Hemisphere

As inferred from the effect of injuries, Wernicke's area could generate the categorial content of GPs; in turn, this content gives the imagery content of the GP a shape that accords with the linguistic meanings. Damage in Wernicke's area accordingly interferes with the content of the GP, as we see in the transcript and Figure 7.4. The repetitiveness in the 'to-it' example, whereby an initially meaningful speech-gesture combination (as it appears) became detached from context and sense, ensures that all ensuing GPs would be drained of content (since among other things they cannot vary their linguistic categorial parts).

RIGHT HEMISPHERE IMAGERY
AND FIELDS OF OPPOSITION

The right hemisphere is often called 'nonlinguistic'. This label is appropriate in one sense—the right hemisphere appears to have limited access to the static dimension of language. But the dynamic dimension of language—imagery, context, relevance—depends crucially on it. As suggested in the Wernicke discussion, the right hemisphere may be the brain region involved in the creation of growth points. In contrast to Wernicke's aphasia, where the GP itself breaks down, right hemisphere damage affects the contextual background of the GP, the catchments and fields of oppositions, and hence the differentiation of psychological predicates. All of this is demonstrated in the cases below, recorded in collaboration with Laura Pedelty (see McNeill & Pedelty 1995, for an early summary).

Right Hemisphere: The Amount of Imagery

One effect of right hemisphere damage is to reduce the sheer output of gesture (Table 7.1). In turn, reduced output implies depletion of imagery. The table

Table 7.1. Gesture output after injury to the right hemisphere.

	Right Hemisphere						
	59.Mpr	51.Mhd	78.Fbf	74.Fmb	62.Fge	45.Mkj	52.Msj
Clause count	59	117	213	146	90	139	61
Word count	496	936	1183	1094	631	1134	461
Number of gestures	3	118	7	43	40	202	5
Time (min.)	4.6	5.9	7.3	6.6	3.4	9.2	4.5
G/clause	0.05	1.01	0.03	0.29	0.44	1.45	0.08
G/min	0.65	20.00	0.96	6.52	11.76	21.96	1.11

	Normal Control		
	C	D	J
Clause count	98	81	110
Word count	707	515	745
Number of gestures	112	69	128
Time (min.)	7.1	5.9	7.3
G/clause	1.14	0.85	1.16
G/min	15.77	11.69	17.53

Table 7.2. Narrative sequence of right hemisphere injured speaker. S = Sylvester;
TB = Tweety Bird.

S paces back and forth Climbs up outside of pipe	Start drainpipe scene
Chases TB in apartment S looks under Granny's skirt, rug	Middle of organ grinder scene (inside apartment)
(long pause)	
S finds TB in cage (something) TB outside	End drainpipe scene
Organ grinder attended by monkey	Start organ grinder scene
TB tempts monkey	Reference error
S punches monkey S dons monkey clothes	More start of organ grinder scene
Goes back into hotel Tries to trick Granny	Middle of organ grinder scene (inside apartment)

summarizes the gesture output of seven right hemisphere injured patients and three normal controls.[6] Injury has no impact on speech, as measured in the number of clauses and number of words, or the length of time taken to recount the stimulus; if anything, RHD speakers are higher on these measures. While not reflected in the table, there was no apparent aprosodia (flat, affectless voice). However, gesture output is cut in half—half as many gestures overall, half as many gestures per grammatical clause, and half as many gestures per unit of time. Gesture imagery thus seems to be a specific target of right hemisphere damage.

Right Hemisphere: Cohesion

It is well-known that right hemisphere injury interrupts the cohesion and logical coherence of discourse (Gardner et al. 1983). This breakdown is seen in the verbal descriptions such patients produce. Table 7.2 shows the sequence of events in one patient's cartoon description (the table indicates his ordering of events, not his actual words). The narrative clearly exhibits a breakdown of cohesion/coherence. It begins with one event (ascending the drainpipe) and then immediately, without indicating the transition, jumps to the middle of

6. Data tabulated by Martha Tyrone, Inge-Marie Eigsti, and Laura Pedelty.

a different event (involving an organ grinder and a monkey disguise). It then shifts back to the end of the drainpipe event, then it moves back to the start of the organ grinder-monkey event; and finally returns to the organ grinder-monkey event, in the middle.[7]

The patient seems unaware, in other words, of the logical and temporal flow in the story. Susan Duncan, who has studied this case, points out that the speaker recalls events from the animated cartoon in a more or less random order. His narrative strategy was to follow stepwise associations, with each successive association triggering a further step. We shall encounter a similar incremental style in a split-brain patient (patient LB). Reliance on association might be the left hemisphere's modus operandi in both cases.

Right Hemisphere: Memory

Another reflection of the inability to apprehend the structure of discourse is memory fragmentation; not merely forgetting details, but a form of forgetting that derives from diminished contextual grasp or cohesion. Table 7.3 shows the sequential recall for three of the episodes that make up our standard cartoon stimulus by three of the right hemisphere damaged patients also represented in the earlier table, and the three normal controls. Two patients (74.Fmb and 78.Fbf) show extremes of fragmentation; a third (59.Mpr) presents a pattern not different from that of the normal speakers (though with less recall overall). Variation among speakers is not unknown, of course, including brain damaged patients. The controls show variation as well, but all maintain cohesion in memory.

To read the chart, one tracks successive cartoon events down the page. When a subject produced any identifiable reference to an event, an 'X' was entered at the appropriate row (annotated with '(p)' if recall was prompted; with '*' if it was inaccurate in some respect). To illustrate, 74.Fmb recalled (with prompting) that Sylvester looked through binoculars, and then that he was thrown out of a building. The pattern exhibits a breakdown of discourse cohesion—the

---

7. Pedelty's description of the patient is as follows. "**45.Mkj** is a 45 year-old right-handed man, a computer scientist with a college education who sustained a stroke involving both divisions of the right middle cerebral artery three months prior to testing. At the time of testing, he had a flaccid left hemiplegia with sparing of proximal leg muscles, and decreased sensation on the left hemicorpus. He had a crescentic peripheral left visual field deficit, with unreliable extinction to double simultaneous stimulation. He tended to prefer to orient to the right sensory hemispace but attended to the full environment."

Table 7.3. Memory fragmentation after right hemisphere injury.

	RHD Subjects			Normal Subjects		
Cartoon events: grouped by episode S = Sylvester, TB = Tweety, G = Granny	74.Fmb	78.Fbf	59.Mpr	Subject C	Subject D	Subject J
A. Birdwatchers' Society sign				X	X*	X
S looks through binoculars	X(p)	X(p)	X	X	X	X
Broken Arms Hotel sign appears			X	X	X	X
TB is on window ledge			X	X	X	X
S & TB look at each other						X
S puts down binoculars & leaves						
S runs across street into hotel						X
Hotel & "No cats or dogs allowed" signs						
S is thrown out & lands in trash	X					X
B. TB swings in cage & sings						X*
S climbs drainpipe, outside	X*	X			X	X
S goes inside						
S is thrown out; G appears w/umbrella	X*	X			X	X
C. S paces beside building						
S goes up inside drainpipe	X	X	X	X	X	X
TB looks down & sees S				X		X
TB drops bowling ball into pipe	X		X(p)	X	X	X
B-ball goes down pipe & collides with S		X*	X	X	X	X
S falls out of pipe w/b-ball in tummy				X	X	X
S rolls down street	X	X*		X	X	X
S rolls into bowling alley					X	X
Sound of pins falling					X	X

X = mentioned; X* = mentioned incorrectly; X(p) = mentioned after being prompted

intervening events linking the first and second events are absent. Even more dramatically, 78.Fbf recalled first the binoculars and then that Sylvester was shown entering and climbing up the drainpipe on the inside. The events are in different episodes but the patient juxtaposed them to create a faux scene.

Normal recall is, of course, also incomplete but it maintains internal cohesion. Subject C recalls the least of the normal speakers, even neglecting the punch line of the first episode (given in the last row), but her recall preserved internal coherence as seen in the unbroken line of Xs.

Compared to normal speakers, right hemisphere–damaged speakers have fewer and shorter sequences of cohesive description, more isolated event

Table 7.4. Summary statistics (based on Table 7.3)

Measure	RHD Subjects			Normal Subjects			Comments
	74.Fmb	78.Fbf	59.Mpr	C	D	J	
Runs of Xs (number of connected items/ number of runs)	0/0	0/0	5/2	10/2	10/2	16/3	Fewer runs with RHD
Single Xs (number of isolated items)	7	6	1	0	3	2	More isolates with RHD
Total Xs (total recall)	7	6	6	10	13	18	Lower total recall with RHD
% total Xs in runs (percent of total in connected runs)	0%	0%	83%	100%	77%	89%	Lower %s in RHD (zero for two, normal for one)
Av. number Xs in run (length of each run)	0	0	2.5	5	5	5.3	Shorter runs in RHD (including 59.Mpr)

descriptions, a lower proportion of sequentially recalled events, and a lower overall recall of events (see Table 7.4). Patients 74.Fmb and 78.Fbf have no sequences of recalled events at all. This is in contrast to the three normal speakers, whose narrations consist almost exclusively of sequentially recalled events (100 percent in the case of C).

Right Hemisphere: Unstable Growth Points

Given the central role of imagery in the formation of growth points, right hemisphere injury could (a) disrupt GP functioning by disturbing the visuospatial component of the GP. It could also (b) lead to instability of the imagery-language dialectic, making catchments difficult to achieve.

A phenomenon supporting both hypotheses is that, in some right hemisphere patients, *seeing one's own gesture* causes a simultaneous change of linguistic categorization. This illustrates an instability and fragility of the language-gesture combination and a lack of discourse cohesion. In the following, there is a lexical change after the subject observes her own hopping gesture:

I just saw the* # the cat running ar* run* white and
black cat [# **running here or there. t* hop to** here*] here, there, everywhere.
      a   b   c

Hand hops forward 4X:

a = onset of first hopping gesture

b = between second and third hopping gestures, and the approximate point
when her hand entered her field of vision

c = fourth hopping gesture

The speaker was describing Sylvester's running, and began with this verb, but, for reasons unknown, her hand was undulating as it moved forward.[8] As she caught sight of her own motion, she changed the verb to "hopping." Kinetic experience also may have been a factor, but it was not sufficient since the change occurred only when the hopping hand moved into her field of vision.

The example illustrates an imagery-language *looseness* and release from on-going cohesive constraints that seems to be a result of right hemisphere damage. The imagery with "running" was not constrained by the linguistic category 'to run', in contrast to normal gesture imagery that is strongly adapted to the immediate linguistic environment. It also illustrates, however, that speech and gesture are still tightly bound after right hemisphere damage, in that speech shifted when the undulating gesture came into view.

Summary of Right Hemisphere

To create a negative image of what is removed or diminished after right hemisphere injury, the right hemisphere is sensitive to the synchronization of co-expressive speech and gesture, and it shapes imagery to fit linguistic content. The right hemisphere could thus be important for the creation of GPs. It also organizes cohesive discourse and maintains memory with internal coherence. Injury interferes with all these processes. In terms of the brain model, the result of right hemisphere injury would be an unstable, poorly situated GP unit. Such a GP would converge on Broca's area, and fluent speech would result, but with defects of the kinds we have seen.

THE PREFRONTAL AREAS

This section will necessarily be brief, because I have no direct observations of frontal functions or disruptions after injury. However, Terrence Deacon has

---

8. She was not explicitly describing the bowling ball scene, where hopping is a reasonable image, although a segue into this episode is not impossible, given the extensive memory fragmentation by this speaker (74Fmb).

written at length in *The Symbolic Species* (Deacon 1997) about the expansion of this part of the brain over evolutionary time and its intimate connection with symbol formation and use, including language. Deacon summarizes the functions of the prefrontal cortex in the following terms. These functions are the kinds that could make the frontal areas the locus of fields of opposition and the differentiation of psychological predicates (the findings refer to animal models, and imply a functionality that would accordingly be regarded as preadaptations for language):

1. Damage to this area in monkeys causes them to look for a prize where they had first seen it, despite having watched it being hidden someplace else. They seem unable to hold the two places—the old and new—in mind and reject one. The intact frontal cortex, conversely, handles these kinds of arrayed alternatives and has the ability to suppress and select within them. The human frontal cortex could have inherited such an ability. This very ability was singled out as critical for the onset of the imagery-language dialectic in children (Chapter 6).

2. In general, animals with prefrontal lesions are unable to divorce information from the specific contexts in which they encountered it. The prefrontal area might be part of the ability to form new contrasts.

3. The most difficult task by animals with damage to the frontal cortex is the transfer of an inverse pattern of associations. Again, the prefrontal area seems essential for creating new relations that require negating something already learned.

4. All prefrontal deficits impair holding information while not acting on it. This statement captures an essential feature of creating a field of oppositions—the information in a field of oppositions is not to be acted upon but is to be opposed to, in part; and the whole defines a set of meanings.

5. All prefrontal deficits impair shifting between opposites—a relationship of negation. The operation of a forming a contrast in differentiating a psychological predicate from a field of oppositions could be linked to this prefrontal function.

THE SPLIT BRAIN

The surgical procedure of commisurotomy (the complete separation of the two hemispheres at the corpus callosum) has been performed in selected cases of intractable epilepsy, where further seizures would have led to dangerous brain injury. Such cases have fascinated neuropsychologists for generations. The patients seem to have two sensibilities inside one skull, each half brain with its own powers, personality, and limitations. I became curious to know what the gestures of these patients would be like and finally had an opportunity to test two patients, LB and NG (for a general description of the split-brain patient, see Gazzaniga 1970, and for a history of how they have been studied, Gazzaniga 1995). Colwyn Trevarthen, at the University of Edinburgh, introduced me to Dalia Zaidel, a psychologist at UCLA, who was studying and looking after the patients. Dalia generously agreed to videotape them retelling our standard animated stimulus.

There should be obstacles as a result of the split-brain procedure for organizing linguistic output in terms of the expected coordination of the two hemispheres. Straightforward organization of linguistic actions should not be possible. In fact, LB and NG appear to follow distinct strategies designed to solve the two-hemisphere problem (see McNeill 1992). LB seems to rely heavily on his left hemisphere, even for the production of gestures, and makes little use of his right hemisphere. NG, in contrast, seems 'bicameral', her left hemisphere controlling speech and her right hemisphere her gestures (she was strongly right handed, but a bicameral division of function is possible since each hemisphere has motor links to both sides of the body). Accomplishing this feat implies that NG was communicating to herself *externally*—her left hemisphere watching her right hemisphere's gestures and her right hemisphere listening to her left hemisphere's speech. As a result, although her gestures were often synchronized with speech, they also could get out of temporal alignment. The most telling asynchrony is when speech precedes co-expressive gesture, a direction almost never seen in normal speech-gesture timing, but not uncommon in NG's performance.

LB had few gestures. Most were beats or simple conduit-like metaphors, performed in the lower center gesture space, near his lap. This absence of iconicity is consistent with a left-hemisphere origin of his gestures. He could make bimanual gestures, almost always two similar hands of the Palm Up or Palm Down Open Hand (PUOH or PDOH) type, with corresponding metaphoric significances. Again, this could be managed from the left hemisphere via bimanual motor control. His narrative style was listlike, a recitation of steps from the cartoon, sometimes accompanied by counting on his fingers, which also is consistent with a preponderantly left-hemisphere organization. This decontextualized style and minimal gesturing may be what the left hemisphere is capable of on its own. His approach was not unlike that of the right-hemisphere patient described earlier, who also displayed a listlike form of recitation (LB's recall, however, was better, and far more sequential). Such similarity is explained if neither speaker was using his right hemisphere to any degree, albeit for different reasons.

In contrast, NG remembered less, but had gestures of greater iconicity. Her gestures look to me repetitive and stylized, although this impression is difficult to verify. Still, her narration, while poorer than LB's in the amount recalled, was more influenced by a sense of the story line.

LB and NG therefore jointly illustrate one of the main conclusions of this chapter—the right hemisphere (available to NG, apparently minimally used by LB) is necessary for situating speech in context and imbuing imagery with linguistically categorized significance; the left hemisphere (relied on by LB, available to NG) orchestrates well-formed speech output but otherwise has minimal ability to apprehend and establish discourse cohesion.

A Right Hemisphere Coup?

In some examples, LB demonstrated a trade-off between speaking and iconicity. He sometimes performed elaborate iconic gestures; the trade-off was that speech then stopped completely. Perhaps we observe here a kind of coup d'état by the right hemisphere. The right brain takes control and speech—the left brain Broca's area specialty—simply stops for the duration. Lausberg et al. (2003) suggest that the isolated left hemisphere simply ignores experiences arising from the right hemisphere (also Zaidel 1978). An example is in the accompanying illustrations. Figure 7.5 shows a typical LB gesture with accompanying speech; he was saying, in his list-like way, "he was thrown out once." With normal speakers this event is a discourse climax and would typically be registered in an iconic gesture. For LB it was merely the next item to be counted off on the fingers (he uses his left hand as the abacus—the illustration shows his hand just after the final finger moved outward: it is not Palm Up Open Hand). Figure 7.6 is a far more iconic gesture depicting Sylvester catapulting himself upward by pitching a weight onto a teeter-totter device. LB was saying, "he had a plan," then all speech stopped while the entire illustrated gesture took place (the elapsed time more than a second), and then resumed with "to get up," completing the clause—as if the left hemisphere had switched off while the right hemisphere switched on. This coup could have been induced by the

Fig. 7.5. LB counting off episodes as he says "he was thrown out once."

Fig. 7.6. LB's iconic depiction of Sylvester throwing a weight and launching himself; performed totally without speech.

complexity of encoding this complex event, LB's difficulty with the linguistic formulation creating an opening for the right hemisphere's adventure.

SUMMARY: ANOTHER LOOK AT THE BRAIN MODEL

This chapter can be summed up by returning to and updating the brain model sketched at the beginning.

Language created a restructuring of the brain; this claim has been made by many others before (e.g, Condillac in the eighteenth century, Hewes 1973, Deacon 1997). We can specify some aspects of this restructuring as follows:[9]

1. The brain must be able to combine motor systems—manual and vocal/oral—in a systematic, *meaning-controlled* way (cf. Kelso 1995).
2. There must be a convergence of two cognitive modes—visuospatial and linguistic—and a locus where they converge in a final motor sequence.

9. The list is limited to cortical areas. However, Lieberman (2002) argues persuasively that subcortical areas equally—and integrally—are parts of the brain circuits that underlie language. In particular, the basal ganglia appear to be involved in cognitive sequencing, which suggests a role in the orchestration of action.

Broca's area is a logical candidate for this place. It has the further advantage of orchestrating actions that can be realized both manually and within the oral-vocal tract.[10]

3. More than Broca's and Wernicke's areas underlie language—there is also the right hemisphere and interactions between the right and left hemispheres, as well as possibly the frontal cortex.[11]

4. Wernicke's area serves more than comprehension—it also provides categorization, might initiate imagery, and might also shape it.

5. Imagery arises in the right hemisphere and needs Wernicke-originated categorizations to form GPs. Categorial content triggers and/or shapes the imagery in the right hemisphere.

6. The GP is unpacked in Broca's area. GPs may take form in the right hemisphere, but they are dependent on multiple areas across the brain (frontal, posterior left, as well as right and anterior left).[12]

7. The frontal area of the brain establishes fields of oppositions and differentiates psychological predicates. This functionality implies access to the context of thinking and speaking in the right and left hemispheres by the frontal area and feedback from the frontal area to these other brain areas.

8. Catchments and GPs specifically are shaped under multiple influences— from Wernicke's area, the right hemisphere, and the frontal area—and take form in the right hemisphere.

Throughout the model, the claim is that information from the posterior left hemisphere, the right hemisphere, and the prefrontal cortex converge and

10. MacNeilage (1998) relates speech to cyclical open-close patterns of the mandible and proposes that speech could have evolved out of ingestive motor control.

11. A germane result is Federmeier & Kutas (1999), who found through evoked potential recordings different information strategies in the right and left sides of the brain—the left they characterized as 'integrative', the right as 'predictive'. These terms relate very well to the hypothesized roles of the right and left hemispheres in the generation of GPs and unpacking. Also, Kelly et al. (2004) observe evoked response effects (N400) in the right brain when subjects observe speech-gesture mismatches.

12. In addition, the cerebellum would be involved in the initiation and timing of gesture phases relative to speech effort (cf. Spencer et al. 2003). However, this area is not necessarily a site specifically influenced by the evolution of language ability.

synthesize in the frontal left hemisphere motor areas of the brain—Broca's area and the adjacent premotor areas.[13]

Broca's area in all this is the unique point of (a) convergence and (b) orchestration of manual and vocal actions guided by GPs and semantically framed language forms. The evolutionary model to be presented in Chapter 8 is specifically aimed at explaining orchestration in this brain area and how it could have been co-opted by language and thought.

13. This circuit could be composed of many smaller circuits—"localized operations [that] in themselves do not constitute an observable behavior . . . [but] form part of the neural 'computations' that, linked together in complex neural circuits, are manifested in behaviors" (Lieberman 2002, p. 39).

CHAPTER 8

The Thought-Language-Hand Link and Language Origins

INTRODUCTION

This final chapter is framed by the following broad question: *Why* is imagery part of language? That it is so has been a leading theme of this book. I shall develop a hypothesis at the end of the chapter: that the evolution of language crucially depended at one point on gestures and imagery. Without gestures, according to the hypothesis, some of the brain circuits required for language (Broca's area, including mirror neurons, and possibly others) could not have evolved in the way they have in the human brain, whereby thought and language orchestrates them directly via a thought-language-hand (and vocal) link. This hypothesis entails that the integration of gesture with language is an essential part of the machinery that was selected in evolution. It further entails that gesture is not a behavioral fossil, not an 'attachment' to language or an 'enhancement', but is an indispensable part of our ongoing current system of language and was selected with speech in the evolution of this system.

THE THOUGHT-LANGUAGE-HAND LINK

An implication of the GP hypothesis is that gestures, as part of the process of speaking, are generated as an integral component. Without imagery, there could not be speech; gestures embody these images. Thus, if we can examine a speaker whose physical condition would prevent normal motion, we should still see gestures. Although action and gesture cannot be dissociated in normal speakers, a speaker whose physical condition prevents the normal occurrence of instrumental actions, but who is not paralyzed and whose cognitive and linguistic faculties are normal, should still produce appropriately formed speech-synchronized gestures. This is because gestures arise from the processes of thinking and speaking and can arise separately (in part) from the brain systems controlling instrumental actions.

The man referred to as IW is such a speaker. His case shows a dissociation of gesture from instrumental action. He cannot perform instrumental actions unless he has visual control, yet he is able to perform gestures under no-vision conditions, and this dissociation of gesture and action suggests the existence in the human brain of a dedicated thought-language-hand link, separate in part from action. Such a dedicated link, used for language, could have arisen as part of the origin of language.

Relationship to the Brain Model

Broca's area is the most likely place for such a dedicated thought-language-hand link. The brain model described in Chapter 7 focuses brain processes underlying GPs and unpacking on the left anterior speech area (areas 44 and 45, or Broca's area). It is here that inputs from the right hemisphere, the frontal areas, and the posterior regions of the left hemisphere are held to converge. It is also the part of the brain that appears to be specialized for the orchestration of movements under some significance, as described in Chapter 7.

IW CASE: NEUROPATHY[1]

IW suffered a sudden loss, at age nineteen, of all sense of touch and proprioception (movement and position sense) below the neck, due to an infection of unknown etiology. The immediate cause of damage is thought to have been an auto-destructive immune reaction. The damage was to the sensory fibers and was proportional to the extent of myelination, more damage with more myelination. The slow-conducting, unmyelinated sensory nerves concerned with pain, temperature, and such ill-defined modalities as muscle fatigue were unaffected. Likewise the motor nerve fibers were left intact. But IW's

---

1. The study of IW is ongoing and is being carried out with Jonathan Cole and Shaun Gallagher. I am drawing on Cole (1995) for this background sketch of IW's neuropathy. I am greatly indebted to IW himself for his willingness to devote time, effort, and travel over long distances to the project of studying his gestures and language.

fast-conducting, mylenated proprioception and spatial position sense fibers were totally destroyed. Although not paralyzed, IW lost all motor control that depends on feedback and was unable to walk, write, or feed himself. Speech and all cognitive functions were completely unaffected. The medical providers at the time gave him the grim prognosis that he would be wheelchair bound for the rest of his life. But after some thirty years of effort IW has taught himself to move again using cognition and vision in place of proprioception and the spatial position sense. He has been so successful that to a causal observer, nothing in his movements appears out of the ordinary. He moves his arms and hands accurately and with speed, is able to stand up, walk, and sit down with balance and fluidity, and can track his shifting center of gravity as he leans over to pick something up. His effort and motivation are succinctly captured by the title of Jonathan Cole's 1995 book, *Pride and a Daily Marathon*. To imagine what deafferentation might be like, try this experiment devised by Shaun Gallagher:

- sit at a table with your hands placed underneath it, out of view.
- make a fist and then extend your index finger.
- curl it back into the fist and then extend it again.
- move one hand below the other.

The mechanisms that allow you to tell when one hand is below the other or your finger is extended or not, or even that you've made a fist, simply no longer exist for IW.

IW's self-descriptions of his motion and motion control are lucid and clearly articulated. I take these descriptions as important clues in the discussion that follows. He considers that he has discovered new ways to access, activate, and monitor old motor schemas that he (as anyone) had developed over the first years of life. These schemas received feedback from the proprioception and spatial position senses and then suddenly were cut off from these sources, but the schemas were still embedded in motor memory and over time were accessed in new ways. In his description, he distinguishes two kinds of gestures—in his words, 'constructed' gestures versus 'throw-away' gestures. To IW the constructeds are the most important: he makes them to add naturalness to his speech, as part of a deliberate communicative strategy in which information is divided into gestured and spoken streams. For us, the gesture-observers, the throw-aways are the more interesting. They appear to be natural gestures, unintended, unwitting, unmonitored, and occurring spontaneously with speech. They show all the hallmarks of naturally occurring, spontaneous gestures by speakers lacking IW's injuries—synchronous with co-expressive speech, out of awareness and not monitored visually, and with no gaze even when vision is available.

What's Interesting?

We can investigate IW's movements in terms of two different categories: (a) instrumental actions and (b) speech-accompanying gestures, and do this under two conditions—with and without vision. Without vision, IW has no idea of where his hands are located in space. If he is unable to control instrumental movements when vision is denied, but can continue to perform gestures with full accuracy and synchronization with speech, we have demonstrated that gesture can be dissociated from action. Such a dissociation suggests the existence of a specific thought-language-hand link in the brain, distinct at some point from the pathways for controlling actions. This pathway could be disconnected from proprioception and vision as sources of control, if it is organized by other processes still accessible to IW.

THE EXPERIMENTS

The BBC brought IW, Shaun Gallagher, and Jonathan Cole to the University of Chicago for filming in July 1997.[2] Our aim was to record IW under a variety of conditions, both with and without vision. IW cannot be simply blindfolded, since he would be unable to orient himself and at would be risk of falling over. We devised a traylike blind (Figure 8.1) that could be pulled down in front of him, blocking vision of his hands, while allowing him room to move and preserving visual contact with his surroundings.[3] IW was videotaped retelling the standard animated cartoon stimulus. He also was recorded under the blind in casual conversation with Cole.[4] In 1997, we did not appreciate

2. The film was broadcast as part of the BBC Horizon Series, with the catchy title *The Man Who Lost His Body* (1998).

3. Nobuhiro Furuyama suggested the blind experiment. David Klein built the blind itself.

4. We also had IW wear an eye-tracking device as he described the routes he had followed that morning from his hotel to the psychology building and within the psychology building itself, while looking at maps and floor plans. I do not describe these results here but have presented them in various talks.

Fig. 8.1. IW seated at the blind designed for gesture experiments.

the importance of testing IW's instrumental actions without vision, but we had an opportunity to test his performance on this kind of task in April 2002, when IW, Shaun Gallagher, and Jonathan Cole came back for a second visit to the University of Chicago.[5]

An Example (2002)

Figure 8.2 shows a gesture with vision during a conversation, videotaped in 2002. The panels are the successive phases of a single gesture. The co-expressive speech was "gesture for me falls into a number of areas," and the gesture (about a half second long) displays a metaphoric image of a sorting process. The size of the gesture is characteristically small—IW avoids large movements for safety. The full gesture included three repetitions of the circling motion. His gaze, as we can observe, was directed downward at his hands.

Fig. 8.2. IW metaphoric gesture of sorting with vision.

5. The second round of experiments was supported by a grant from the Wellcome Trust to Jonathan Cole and by funds from Ian Waterman.

Significant Variables in Assessing IW's Gesture Performance

To have a systematic approach to IW's gestures, we pay specific attention to the following variables (all but the second and third have figured in earlier chapters):

Timing: synchronization with co-expressive speech.
Morphokinesis: the shape of the gesture in terms of hand forms and use of space.
Topokinesis: the location of hands relative to each other in space, including but not limited to the approach of one hand by the other.
Character viewpoint (CVPT): the perspective of the character being described; a gesture from the CVPT is close to mimicry.
Observer viewpoint (OVPT): the perspective of the narrator or an observer.

With vision, IW's gestures display all the above features (over a sample of gestures). Without vision, they show some but not all features: exact timing with speech, morphokinetic accuracy, and OVPT. Topokinetic accuracy and CVPT, however, become rare. The loss or reduction of these two particular features implies that his gestures without vision depart from the pathway of action control (regarding CVPT as mimicry or an action simulation). The preservation of speech-gesture synchrony implies that the system that remains is integrated with speech. It is this ensemble of preserved and lost features that suggests a dedicated thought-language-hand link.

IW's Gestures with and without Vision (1997)

IW's gestures with vision are similar to those produced by normal speakers, although they are fewer in number and tend to be isolated, performed one by one, in keeping with his self-conscious constructed-gestures strategy. Figure 8.3 shows a narrative gesture made with vision. IW was describing Sylvester after he had swallowed the bowling ball, inside the pipe. Both morphokinesis and topokinesis are indistinguishable from normal. His hand appears to bracket a small figure in the central gesture space and move it downward, wobbling right and left. The motion is co-expressive with the synchronous speech: [//**he** // **wiggles his way down**]. The only clue that control is other than normal is that IW looks at his hand during the stroke phase. The viewpoint in this case

Fig. 8.3. IW iconic gesture with vision.

is that of an observer; elsewhere, in his full description of the bowling ball episode, the character viewpoint also occurs:

OVPT: "tiny little bird"
CVPT: "bowling ball"
OVPT: "wiggles his way down"
CVPT: "places it"
OVPT: "gets a strike."

Figure 8.4 illustrates a narrative gesture without vision, a coordinated two-handed tableau, in which the left hand is Sylvester and the right hand is a trolley pursuing him. IW was saying, "[and the ₁tram ₂**caught** him up]" (numbers referring to the first and second panels of the illustration). His right hand moved to the left in exact synchrony with the co-expressive "caught him

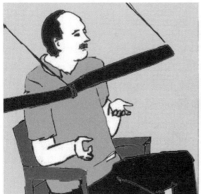

Fig. 8.4. IW coordinated two-handed iconic gesture without vision.

up." Moreover, a poststroke hold extended the stroke image through "him" and "up" and maintained full synchrony of the stroke with the co-expressive speech. It is important to recall that this synchrony and co-expressivity were achieved without proprioceptive or spatial feedback. Meaning alone drove this coordinated use of his hands.

Topokinetic versus Morphokinetic Accuracy

The gesture in Figure 8.4, while clearly accurate morphokinetically, was not accurate topokinetically; as the right hand approached the left, the right and left hands did not line up.

Figure 8.5 illustrates another case of topokinetic approximation. IW was describing "a square plank of wood" and sketched a square in the gesture space. The illustration captures the misalignment of his hands as he completed the top of the square and was about to move both hands downward for its sides.

Fig. 8.5. IW's lack of topokinetic accuracy without vision.

We also asked IW to sketch simple geometric shapes in the air without vision. Morphokinetically, a triangle and a circle were readily created but topokinetically there was always some disparity (Figures 8.6.1–2, respectively). For comparison, we also asked undergraduate students at the University of Chicago to sketch geometric figures without vision. In Figure 8.7 a student sketches a triangle, shown at the moment of bringing his right and left hands together to complete the flat bottom. Having both morphokinetic and topokinetic control, his positioning is exact to the millimeter.

Similarly, instrumental actions are impossible for IW when vision is denied. Such actions require topokinetic accuracy. Figure 8.8 from the 2002 session, shows two steps in IW's attempt to remove the cap of a thermos bottle. The

Fig. 8.6.1–2. IW's misalignment as he outlines a triangle and circle without vision.

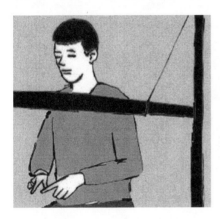

Fig. 8.7. Accurate completion of triangle by subject with intact proprioception and spatial sense without vision.

first is immediately after Jonathan Cole has placed the thermos in IW's right hand and placed his left hand on the cap; the second is one second later, when IW has begun to twist the cap off. As can be seen, his left hand has fallen off and is turning in midair (IW is strongly left-handed). Similar disconnects without vision occurred during other instrumental actions (threading a cloth through a ring, hitting a toy xylophone, etc.—this last being of interest since IW could have made use of acoustic feedback or its absence to know when his hand had drifted off target, but still he could not perform the action).

Significance of the IW Results So Far

An important implication is that, without vision, gestures continue to occur with complete accuracy up to the morphokinetic level. They are apparently carried by circuits available to IW and seem to bypass the links required

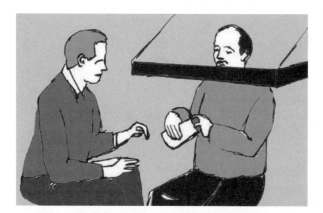

Fig. 8.8.1–2. IW attempts to perform an instrumental action (removing cap from a thermos).

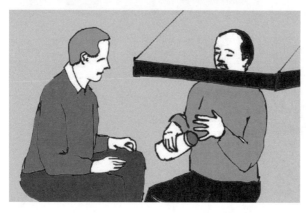

for instrumental actions. Morphokinetic shaping demands guidance by the meaning of the action but does not demand topokinetic control. The use of space in IW's gestures under the blind is especially informative. Although he has no exact sense of where his hands are, he can align them morphokinetically to create a 'triangle', because triangularity is a direct mapping of a concept into motion. This mapping implies that a meaning-action link is possible in the brain.

The morphokinetic/topokinetic distinction also explains the near disappearance of CVPT without vision. Gestures like 'holding it' and 'places it', with CVPT, resemble Tweety's instrumental actions of holding the bowling ball and placing it. These CVPT gestures have meanings as simulated actions of a kind that may require action control, which for IW requires visual guidance. It is not surprising that CVPT gestures tend to disappear when vision is denied.

IW Can Control Speech and Gesture in Tandem (1997)

Perhaps the single most impressive indication of a thought-language-hand link is that IW, without vision, can modulate the speed at which he presents meanings in speech and gesture, and do this *in tandem*. As his speech slows down, his gesture slows down, and to the same extent. During a conversation with Jonathan Cole, while still under the blind, IW reduced his speech rate at one point by about half (paralinguistic slowing), and speech and gesture remained in synchrony (all gestures were metaphoric with metapragmatic content, and presumably were unplanned throw-aways):

> *Normal:* "and [I'm start]ing to use..."
> *Slow:* "[I'm start]ing to get into... trying to explain things."

Comparing just the sections within the brackets, IW's speech covered about a half second at the normal speed and three-quarters of a second at the slow speed. Figure 8.9 shows the hand motions linked to speech at the two rates. This linkage takes place in the same way for both. As he said "I'm," his hands moved forward to start a rotation; as he said "startn'" they moved back, completing it; as he said "to use" or "to get" they rotated out again (IW rotates his hands in phase at normal speed and out of phase at the slow speed, but his inward and

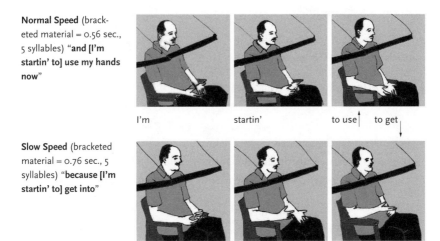

Normal Speed (bracketed material = 0.56 sec., 5 syllables) **"and [I'm startin' to] use my hands now"**

I'm   startin'   to use   to get

Slow Speed (bracketed material = 0.76 sec., 5 syllables) "because **[I'm startin' to] get into**"

Fig. 8.9. IW changes rate of speech and gesture in tandem, maintaining synchrony. Note that motion of hands outward and inward occurs at same speech points.

outward motions occurred at the same points of speech at both speeds; the right hand is the hand to track at slow speed; the left disengages from the gesture in the middle).

This impressive agreement across speeds shows that whatever controlled the slowdown, it was exactly the same for speech and gesture. Bennett Bertenthal (personal communication) points out a possible mechanism for this tandem reduction. Speech and gesture, slowing together, could reflect the operation of a pacesetter in the brain that survived IW's deafferentation; for example, the hand moves outward with a breath pulse accent, an association that could be maintained over a range of speeds. The rotating hands were apparently metaphors for the idea of a process. The pacesetter accordingly could be activated by the thought-language-hand link and co-opted by a significance other than the action of rotation itself. This metaphoric significance is consistent with the timing, since the hands rotated only while IW was saying "I'm starting to" and there was actually a pause between the first (normal speed) and second (reduced speed) rotations as he said "and that's because," indicating that the rotation and any phonetic linkages with it were specifically organized around presenting the idea of a process. Again, it is necessary to remind ourselves that IW had no idea where his hands were other than by the flow of information in speech and gesture. An explanation for this performance is that his gestures and speech were combined online and controlled by meaning. In terms of a dialectic, IW senses the length of time a GP is active, and any change of this duration affects the linguistic and gestured components in tandem.

Summary of IW's Gestures without Vision

The following points summarize what we have seen of IW's gestures in the absence of visual, proprioceptive or spatial position feedback:

- Gestures have diminished use of CVPT.
- Gestures preserve morphokinetic accuracy and lose topokinetic accuracy.
- Gestures are co-expressive and synchronized with speech.

Phantom Limb Gestures

V. S. Ramachandran and S. Blakeslee's *Phantoms in the Brain* (1998) describes Mirabelle, a young woman born without arms. Yet she experiences phantom arms and performs 'gestures' with them—nonmoving gestures, but imagery in actional-visual form.

> Dr: "How do you know that you have phantom limbs?" M: "Well, because as I'm talking to you, they are gesticulating. They point to objects when I point to things."

> "When I walk, doctor, my phantom arms don't swing like normal arms, like your arms. They stay frozen on the side like this" (her stumps hanging straight down). "But when I talk, my phantoms gesticulate. In fact, they're moving now as I speak." Ramachandran & Blakeslee (1998, 41)

Mirabelle's case points to a conclusion similar to IW's—a dissociation of gesture from practical actions. In Mirabelle's case, moreover, intentions create the sensation of gestures when no motion is possible. Presumably, again, the same thought-language-hand link is responsible for this sensation.

Overall Significance of the IW Case

The IW case suggests that control of the hands and the relevant motorneurons is possible directly from the thought-linguistic system. Without vision, IW's dissociation of gesture, which remains intact, and instrumental action, which is impaired, implies that the know-how of gesture is not the same as the know-how of instrumental movement (as Shaun Gallagher has said). In terms of brain function, it implies that producing a gesture cannot be accounted for entirely with the circuits that perform instrumental actions; at some point, the gesture enters a circuit of its own and is tied there to speech. The brain model locates this dedicated thought-language-hand link in areas 44 and 45. These conclusions have implications for the evolution of language, the final topic of this book.

EVOLUTIONARY PRECURSORS

I conclude with my 'ultimate answer' to the question with which we began: why does language have the double character of imagery and language, joined into a single process? The answer I shall offer is that evolution selected the ability to *combine* speech and gesture. Speech would not have evolved without gesture, nor would gesture have evolved without speech. It was the *joint action* of speech and gesture that proved the critical adaptation and was selected as the core of language.

The Nineteenth-Century Ban on the Evolution Topic

However, we should first defend our choice of such a topic, one that was once famously banned. Part of the folklore of the topic of language origins is that the Linguistic Society of Paris in 1865 banned all mention of it. This in fact occurred:

> Article 11: The Society will accept no communication dealing with either the origin of language or the creation of a universal language.

Eight years later in 1873, the Philological Society of London similarly took a dim view of discussion of the topic:

> We shall do more by tracing the historical growth of one single work-a-day tongue, than by filling wastepaper baskets with reams of paper covered with speculations of the origin of all tongues.

Both of these historic prohibitions are quoted by Adam Kendon in his own contribution to the origins topic (Kendon 1991b, p. 199). As Kendon points out, justifying his own effort, we can go much farther now than was possible a century and a half ago. We have a more detailed understanding of language, human evolution, biology, the brain, linguistic performance, and—above all— gesture performance and how it relates to speech than existed in the mid-nineteenth-century. Of course, we can never observe the origin of language, but we are able to constrain the possible scenarios far more tightly than was possible when the bans went into effect. I submit the following limited evolution model, which takes into account the brain model described in Chapter 7, the IW case just outlined, and the discussion presented in this book as a whole of the dynamic dimension of language and an imagery-language dialectic, to explain how speech and gesture evolved together to embody meanings.

What Evolved

The brain model in Chapter 7 converges with a 'gestural' model of speech articulation proposed by Browman and Goldstein (1990). Without going into details, I will emphasize that, in the brain model, language is an orchestration of *actions* by the hands and vocal tract articulators; this converges with Browman and Goldstein, who analyze the flow of speech as oral-'gestural' movements. The acoustic results, i.e., speech itself, which we usually think of as the primary linguistic medium, are in fact not the only medium. Saussurian langage, in this view, is also *patterns for organizing actions.* This concept has great importance for the following theory of language origins. In part, what evolved was a new way of *acting.* The evolutionary model focuses on the selection of brain mechanisms to orchestrate such motor actions in the vocal and manual spheres.

The Proposed Evolution Model

The model is meant to explain how the brain became able to combine hand movements and vocal action sequences under some significance other than that of the action itself. Two things (among undoubtedly others) had to occur:

- *Area 44* (one part of Broca's area) was, preadaptively, the area of the brain where action sequences of all kinds are organized. For language to evolve, it had to be co-opted to accept language-thought inputs.
- *Area 45* (mirror neurons, the other part of Broca's area) became *self-*responding; it began responding one's own actions that were imbued with meaning. This new step implies that area 45 was part of the language-thought system during the evolution of language.[6]

6. See Chapter 7 for references documenting the orchestration functions of Broca's area. In addition, Hamzei et al (2003), using fMRI, find that the peaks of action recognition and production of verbs naming displayed actions share a common functional architecture. Ferrari et al (2003) discovered, in the monkey, populations of neurons in F5—considered the homolog of Broca's area—that fire when significant mouth gestures are displayed, some of which also fire when the monkey makes communicative gestures. Specifically addressing mirror neuron circuits, Wohlschläger et al. (2003) found that the speed with which human subjects detect action onsets in others (presumably engaging mirror neuron circuits) is not different from the speed of detecting the onset of their own similar actions (engaging a lever), and both differ from the speed of detecting the equivalent action onset by a mechanism, implying linked brain mechanisms for self and other's actions. And Grèzes et al. (2003) observed in humans activation of area 44 when subjects imitated gestures and also executed movements in response to objects. All of these recent studies support the claim that Broca's area has the potential to orchestrate

Both steps were critical for bringing gesture and vocalization together and would have been steps not shared by creatures closely related to humans otherwise, specifically other primates with their own mirror neuron systems. In other primates this system responds to actions (both by the self and others) but apparently not to meanings other than the meanings of actions themselves. The reconfiguring of mirror neurons to respond to significances other than actions themselves was a step toward co-opting Broca's area by thought and meaning.

Broca's is not only a so-called speech area but also controls other kinds of orchestrated actions, manual as well as vocal (see Chapter 7). Some evidence of the importance of area 44 for the joint orchestration of speech and gesture is that Broca's aphasia *eliminates both speech and gesture sequences while sparing psychological predicates* (observation due to Susan Duncan, personal communication; data from Pedelty 1987).

Fig. 8.10. Broca's aphasic iconic gesture synchronized with co-expressive speech, occurring at point where normal speakers also perform a semantically equivalent gesture.

For example, this patient from Pedelty's data files (Figure 8.10; patient discussed in Chapter 7 as well) displays classic agrammatism but is able to differentiate newsworthy content in both speech and gesture. She is saying "[**down** d-] [d- **down**]" and as she does, her right hand plunges downward (the figure shows the second gesture). Such a synchrony of co-expressive speech and gesture suggests a GP at this point. Thus, differentiation of a psychological predicate is possible, but the patient has difficulty in orchestrating action sequences of either a spoken or manually gestured kind.

The other component of this evolutionary model, the mirror neuron circuit, has become the subject of much interest and speculation since the discovery of these neurons, much of it focusing on their potential for undergirding a theory of mind. This latter connection is worth emphasizing, because it

---

actions and, in humans, has also been configured to accept inputs that have a significance outside the action itself. I am grateful to Ana Solodkin of the Department of Neurology, University of Chicago, for drawing my attention to these valuable references.

links the emergence of a sense of self, at age three or four, which I described in Chapter 6, to the brain processes underlying a dialectic of imagery and language that is the focus of the current evolution model. Mirror neurons provide a basis for recognizing the actions of others. They are a special class of neurons—identified in monkeys (Rizzolatti & Arbib 1998) and assumed to exist in humans—that fire when specific actions are observed in others. In monkeys, mirror neurons fire when the monkey performs an action and also when it sees the action performed by another. In humans, area 45 is active when a subject observes an action (Decety et al. 1994, Grafton 1996, Rizzolatti et al. 1996), and areas 44 and 45 are active when the person performs this action (Goldenberg 1999, Rizzolatti et al. 1996). On the other hand, this system is not engaged when the subject just observes objects used in actions or looks at passive hands (Nishitani & Hari 2000). In other words, this system seems to be part of a circuit for recognizing intentional goal-directed actions of one's own or of others.

My argument in applying the mirror neuron discovery draws on Rizzolatti & Arbib (1998), which states that the development of the human speech circuit (Broca's and Wernicke's areas) was a consequence of the fact that the precursor of Broca's area was endowed, before speech appearance, with a mechanism for recognizing the actions made by others; these are the mirror neurons. This precursor relationship explains why language and gesture are centered in the same brain areas and why these areas are in the anterior left hemisphere. In the monkey, mirror neurons are found in the prefrontal region known as area F5. F5 is generally agreed to be the homolog of Broca's area, and specifically of area 44 in the human brain. Rizzolatti and Arbib cite PET studies that show that subjects have activation in area 45 while observing grasping. So the evolution of speech and manual action sensitivity could be linked in Rizzolatti and Arbib's view.

However, I do not follow them in their further attempt to link these precursors directly to grammatico-semantic categories (e.g., case grammar). It appears to me that this step bypasses more immediate steps that might have taken place in the origin of language. What would such a more immediate effect have been? My proposal is that a new way to organize sequences of movements in areas 44 and 45 evolved out of the mirror neuron circuit. The crucial new step was the co-opting of these areas by language and meaning. The actions that mirror neurons must react to in this co-opting by language are movements with significances other than as actions, namely, *gestures*. The key to how this might have occurred is from an unexpected source.

MEAD'S LOOP: GESTURE AND
THE SOCIAL DIMENSION

The evolutionary step is co-opting the action orchestration areas by things other than actions themselves. An action of upward motion is not just a movement upward, but is the material carrier of a concept of 'upness'—ascent of the drainpipe, a metaphor of a force, etc. How was this ability to co-op action orchestration by meanings other than the action itself, seemingly unique to human brains, selected and what in the brain is engaged in producing it?

In *Mind, Self, and Society* G. H. Mead (1974), although not writing in evolutionary terms, articulated the logic of this evolutionary step in a way that brings in the social basis of human language and ties it to gesture. He wrote in what he termed 'the philosophy of the gesture', "Gestures become significant symbols when they implicitly arouse in an individual making them the same response which they explicitly arouse in other individuals" (p. 47).

In other words, meaningfulness depends on simulating a social response—the social response of another in yourself, a kind of auto-socialization.

Mirror Neurons Complete Mead's Loop

Mirror neurons could be the mechanism of this gestural self-response. We can posit a self-response via one's own mirror neurons and hypothesize that part of human evolution was to have mirror neurons participate in one's own gesture imagery; this was the selected adaptation (to what it might have been adapting is considered later). It would have been a capacity, according to this hypothesis, selected in the course of human evolution that hooked evolution onto Mead's loop—one's own gestures activating the part of the brain that responds to intentional actions, including gestures, by someone else, *and thus treats one's own gesture as a social stimulus.*

A critical evolutionary event then—unique to *H. sapiens* if it occurred—was this new self-response by mirror neurons.[7] Mirror neurons complete Mead's

---

7. Arbib (in press) emphasizes that changes in the mirror neuron circuit also would have made possible pantomime. He proposes that pantomime, not speech, was the 'proto-language', and that speech, evolving later and separately, became tied to pantomime through an 'expanding spiral' of pantomime preparing the way for speech, then speech helping the cause of pantomime, and so forth. While elegant, this argument does

loop in the part of the brain where action sequences are organized—the two kinds of sequential actions, speech and gesture, converging, with significances other than motor actions themselves as the integrating component. Such an evolution brought meanings into areas 44 and 45, enabling significances other than instrumental actions themselves to orchestrate complex, sequential movements. These movements were both manual and oral/pharyngeal/respiratory, and were organized in the too narrowly labeled 'language area'.

This hypothesis is meant to explain:

- the synchronization of gesture with vocalization on the basis of shared meaning other than actions themselves (this is the way they synchronize); and
- the co-opting of the brain circuits that orchestrate sequential actions by meanings (the circuits exposed in the IW case).

A further implication is that Mead's loop treats gestural imagery as a social stimulus. It thus explains why gestures occur preferentially in social contexts of some kind (face-to-face, on the phone, but not when talking to a tape recorder) (cf. Cohen 1977, Ping 2003). Finally, given the Mead's loop hypothesis, gestures are important because they activate one's own mirror neuron circuit; this could have been the mechanism whereby the 'overhead wires' catchment in Fig. 7.3 enabled an agrammatic speaker to resuscitate a two-clause embedded construction.

Co-opting sequential actions by a socially referenced stimulus (imagery) makes a new kind of action possible, practical actions and speech and gesture,

---

not show how pantomime could have led to the double essence of an imagery-language dialectic of the kind we see now. Pantomime is not gesticulation, and differs from gesticulation on Kendon's continuum in multiple ways elucidated in Chapter 1. Crucially, *pantomime exists without speech*; if anything, pantomime and speech are incompatible within the same time slice. IW's first-person gestures, moreover, which are his gestures closest to pantomime, tended to disappear without vision. It is conceivable that there *was* a pantomime proto-language, but it was a blind alley. It was accompanied or followed by a new, separate evolution of *speech plus gesture* that used Mead's loop, and this led to the thought-language-hand links that we observe today. This hypothesis has the interesting implication that different evolutionary trajectories landed at different points along Kendon's continuum. One path led to pantomime, another to the double essence of co-expressive speech-synchronized gesticulation. These different evolutions are reflected today in distinct ways of combining hand/body movements with speech.

an idea first enunciated by Condillac in the eighteenth century and developed imaginatively by Vygotsky in the 1930s (Vygotsky 1986).

Vygotsky also provided the insight that the source of internal mental life is the social fabric of the individual's ongoing participation in the world. Everything, he famously said in his critique of Piaget (1955), appears in development twice, first on the social plane, later on the mental. Mead's loop addresses this debate since its effect is to treat gesture as a social stimulus. Gesture is a bridge of this two-step development.

Mead's loop would also have produced viewpoints in gesture and beyond, and played a role in the ability (tapped in theory of mind experiments) to take the perspective of others. Perspective is a core component of grounding in Herbert Clark's sense (Clark 1992) and is crucial in general to the ability to tailor messages to recipients. Crucially, Mead's loop generates inhabitance by meaning in the Merleau-Ponty sense. Finally, Mead's loop creates a connection of gestures to discourse, via its implicit dialogic structure (cf. Bakhtin 1981). Such a connection could be the cause, in part, of the inseparability of speech and gesture: because of the loop, gesture naturally links speech to the overarching meta-level structure of discourse. All of these qualities set human linguistic cognition apart from the other primate modes of thought, as far as is currently known.

THE SCENARIO

To complete this model, I propose a sketch of what conditions of life and biological evolution—as they might have existed—selected the role played by Mead's loop described above: mediating and co-opting areas 44 and 45 to create the possibility of an orchestration of motion by language, hence creating the thought-language-hand link. I suggest that, of such contexts, family life, specifically, mother-child interactions, was this setting par excellence. The scenario would had to have been a rich social context in order for Mead's loop to be of adaptive value. Human-style scaffolding, in which adults deliberately and closely monitor a child's activity to help him/her acquire and develop activities in an efficient and adaptive way, is this kind of context, and is phylogenetically unique and present in all human societies (see Tomasello 1999; Rafael Núñez personal communication); in contrast, infant chimpanzees have to figure out activities like nut cracking by themselves through observation, and this acquisition can take years.

Before presenting the scenario, however, I will consider a preliminary step, which is the possibility that the neurogestural joining of manual and vocal movements itself was not part of this evolution, that such a linkage was inherited as part of the general primate line of descent.[8]

Vocalizations and Hand Movements Preadapted?

Research by primatologist William Hopkins (presented at the Evolution, Cognition and Development conference, 2002) reveals that chimpanzees co-produce some vocalizations and gestures. The evidence for this is that hand preference (the right hand) is markedly stronger when gestures co-occur with vocalizations than not. The gestures in question are impromptu creations with seemingly an indexical function. Stereotypic begging, in contrast, is performed with no particular hand preference. Thus, the linkage of spontaneous gesture movements and vocal tract activity (including breathing)[9] may have been a preadaptation available to the early hominid creatures in which the selection of Mead's loop occurred.

Hopkins's chimp, Beleka, hoping to induce one of the researchers to hand her a banana that was placed in view but frustratingly out of reach in front of her cage, extends her right hand on its side with a hoarse panting sound (Figure 8.11). She performs this combination of gesture-plus-vocalization several times. It seems pragmatically geared to get the researcher to notice and retrieve the banana. This was not the classic palm-up begging gesture, the stereotypic signal that appears in much the same form across many primate species, including our own. Figure 8.12 is a begging gesture that Beleka also happened to make, and it took place without vocalization.

8. Such a preadaptation, tying gesture to vocalization before the appearance of language, would seem to be a larger nail than most in the coffin of the Condillacan gesture-first theory. To get gesture-first, the already established vocalization-gesture link would have to have been suppressed. The gesture-first theory has returned to vogue since Condillac's day (e.g., Hewes 1973, Armstrong et al. 1995, Corballis 2002, Arbib in press). My doubts about the theory, apart from the incompatibility with the preadaptation just mentioned, have to do with the seeming impossibility of pantomime, which is essentially what gesture-first posits as the original language, ever leading to an imagery-language dialectic, the form of gesture that has evolved (see also note 7).

9. Emphasized by Nobuhiro Furuyama.

Fig. 8.11. Chimp deixis with vocalization.

Fig. 8.12. Chimp begging without vocalization.

If a preadaptation for language was this kind of a gesture + vocalization combination, it would appear that language could have been, from the start, on a different track from gestures like begging. Also, this combination would have been a natural foundation for evolution to build upon. Gesture + vocalization would have been available for selection if the combination came to have adaptive value.

Family Life

Based on standard timelines for the emergence of *H. sapiens*, we can 'narrow' the dates for Mead's loop and its selection to the interval from 2 MYA to approximately 100–200 KYA.

Gesture used habitually presupposes bipedalism—this commenced about 5 MYA (after the separation of the hominid line from the great apes line). The process leading eventually to the co-opting of action orchestration by language in areas 44 and 45 could not have started until this development, but the step itself presumably did not occur until much later.

The origin of symbolism is linked by Wrangham (2001) to the invention of cooking and by Deacon (1997) to the formation of a gender-based division of labor and 'marriage contracts', both dated to about 2 MYA. Jolly (1999) objects to this description as patriarchal, but even conceding her criticism, some major changes occurred in family life for the creatures living at this time.

This form of living was itself the product of many other changes in reproduction patterns, female fertility cycles, child rearing, neoteny, and other factors—all of which might have been emerging long before the changes posited in areas 44 and 45.

Such a social-cultural development was accompanied by expansion of the prefrontal cortex (Deacon 1997)[10] as well as (per current proposal) the

10. However, recent scanning data suggests that the human frontal cortex is no larger than would be expected of an ape brain with its overall size (Semendeferi 2001).

reconfiguring of areas 44 and 45. To judge from the time course of the prefrontal expansion, the process was completed only 100,000–200,000 years—or 5,000–10,000 generations—ago.

All of this suggests a scenario of organized family life by bipedal creatures inducing changes in brain configuration and function. The selection pressure for Mead's loop would be the family circle (more than 'man the hunter' or 'man the tool maker')—this setting offering a role for Mead's loop where one's own meaningful movements are treated as a social stimulus, especially as an engine of childrearing and infant care (adjusting one's signals to fit the viewpoint of the one cared for would be a powerful selection pressure). Recent opinion of the differences between chimpanzee and human evolution focuses on the unique-to-humans mode of reproduction, including, especially, the family. The selection of vocalizations plus gestures with which to create growth points co-opts the vocalization-gesture preadaptation of the kind shown by current-day chimpanzees and pushes vocalization and gesture into areas 44 and 45 where they fuse into meaning-orchestrated movements. This evolution cannot be tied to a single step ('mutation'). It took place, in this theory, through many converging steps, over a long period, resulting in the creation of family life.

A proposed time line follows.

Timeline

The evolution of a thought-language-hand link could not have started before 5 MYA and the emergence of habitual bipedalism in *Australopithicus*, but this would have been only the beginning. And even earlier there were presumably such preadaptations as an ability to combine vocal and manual gestures, but not yet an ability to orchestrate these movements by meanings other than the meanings of actions themselves.

The period from 5 to 2 MYA—Lucy et al. and the long reign of *Australopithicus*—would have seen the emergence of precursors of language, something an apelike brain would be capable of, such as the kind of protolanguage Bickerton attributes to apes, very young children, and aphasics (Bickerton 1990); also, ritualized incipient actions can become signs at this stage, as described by Kendon (1991).

Starting about 2 MYA with the advent of *H. habilis* and later *H. erectus*, there commenced the crucial selection of self-responsive mirror neurons and the reconfiguring of areas 44 and 45, with a growing co-opting of action by language, this emergence being tied to the appearance of a humanlike family life with the host of other factors shaping this major change (including cultural innovations like the domestication of fire and cooking). Recent archaeological findings strongly suggest that hominids had control of fire, had hearths, and cooked 800 KYA (Goren-Inbar et al. 2004). Thus, the family as the locus for evolving the thought-language-hand link seems plausible.

Along with this sociocultural revolution was the expansion (if it occurred) of the forebrain from 2 MYA, described by Deacon (1997), and a complete reconfiguring of areas 44 and 45, including Mead's loop, into what we now call Broca's area. This development was an exclusively hominid phenomenon and was completed with *H. sapiens* about 200–100 KYA (if it is not continuing; cf. Donald 1991).

Considering these lines of evidence, protolanguage and then language itself seems to have emerged over five million years (far therefore from the big bang mutation that Bickerton 1990 romantically envisioned). Meaning-controlled manual and vocal gestures, synthesized, as we currently know them, under meaning as GP dialectics emerged over the last two million years. The entire process may have been completed not more than 100 KYA.

CONCLUSIONS: EVOLUTION

It is not an accident that the gesture and language centers of the brain are side by side. Mirror neurons in area 45 mimic the categorized imagery of the GP, which some evidence suggests is relayed from the right hemisphere (McNeill & Pedelty 1995), and link it to area 44 for precise coordination in a movement plan.

The result is control of action sequences in Broca's area by meanings other than the meaning of the action itself—the result of Mead's loop, which is possibly a unique circuit in the human brain, and linked in its function and development to the appearance of the self as an independent agent.

The growth point would have been a product of this evolution by making images into the organizational unit of speech; that is, gestures fuel speech, in this reconstruction, and the growth point is the mechanism for doing so.

The evolution of language could accordingly have included a step whereby the action orchestration in areas 44 and 45 was co-opted by the systems in charge of meaning formulation. A panoply of events seems to have been required. Without any one of them it is doubtful that language could have appeared—bipedalism, vocal-manual linkage in the brain, gesture, expansion of the frontal cortex, neoteny, family life, and, the favorite of this discussion, mirror neurons capable of responding to gestures, as a component of movement orchestration in Broca's area.[11]

CONCLUSIONS: OVERALL

Language *is* inseparable from imagery and this is because of how it evolved.

It *does* have the dual reality described by Wundt and Saussure, consisting of both an instantaneous (imagery) and a successive (linguistic-social) component.

According to the Mead's loop scenario, the dual cognitive mode of language was a product of how the capacity for language evolved, and how meaning came to control motor movements and their orchestration in the brain.

11. Of course, this list is not exhaustive either.

Methods of Gesture Recording and Transcription, Including New Semi-Automated Methods, Plus 'The Growth Point'—a Poem

RECORDING, TRANSCRIPTION, CODING

Setting

With Elena Levy, I adopted the method we have used in many investigations some two decades ago (see McNeill and Levy 1982). Our idea simply was to show a film or animated cartoon to subjects and have them immediately retell the story to a listener, from memory (the listener was a genuine listener, not a confederate, and in the early experiments was told that she have to would retell the cartoon story to a third person). Behavior was spontaneous; a discourse was constructed by the subject, and gestures occurred spontaneously. The subjects did not know that gestures were of interest (the experiment was presented as about storytelling). The gestures, together with the narration itself, comprise the raw data, recorded on videotape.

The Circularity Problem

The storytelling method solves a problem that is not always recognized. Because gestures of the kind we record are not culturally encoded objects, like words or emblems, it is not always clear, from the gesture itself, what its significance is. Determining significance is a matter of interpretation that draws on the gesture and its form, its synchronous speech, past and upcoming discourse, and—the point now—our information about the cartoon story and layout. If we were to equate the gesture with the accompanying speech, there is the risk of circularity:

the gesture would mean whatever it coincides with in speech, which is to say, nothing at all. However, the narrative stimulus provides a way out of the circle. Knowing the source (the animated stimulus), we can interpret the gestures we see in relation to *it*, not in relation to the verbal expression. Only in this way can we observe co-expressiveness beyond redundancy.

In the case study of Chapter 4.2, the co-expressive linguistic segments were "it down," with a gesture of Tweety dropping a bowling ball into a pipe. This is a good illustration of what can be observed when the source is known. The lexical affiliate—the word most closely corresponding in meaning to the gesture—would have been "drops," and the speaker in fact did in fact say "and drops it down," but the growth point specifically excluded "drops." This was a major point of the case study. Speech has its own role in avoiding the circularity problem; speech content enables us to identify the event to which the gesture is related, but it is not the content against which the gesture is interpreted.

Other genres besides stimulus-based storytelling also offer a kind of third point of reference. This is available with route and living space descriptions, where we can ask the speaker to draw a map or floor plan.

Still other genres, however, such as conversations, lectures, gossip, etc., do not have such a third point of reference and are therefore vulnerable to the circularity problem. By now, after much experience with gesture performance, we have a far clearer idea of how gestures present meanings and we are no longer so tethered to having a known referent.

We continue to use the storytelling method because it has proven valuable for other reasons. Knowing the stimulus, we can compare speakers as they recount the same event. We have been able in this way to compare adults to children, speakers of different languages, and patients with neurological deficits to unimpaired speakers—all describing, say, the bowling ball episode; these targeted comparisons exploit the known narrative stimulus.

The Stimuli

We have employed two narrative stimuli. Most frequent has been a seven-minute animated color cartoon of the Tweety and Sylvester series (*Canary Row*, ca. 1950). We picked this cartoon partly because we wanted to have a stimulus usable with children. Nonetheless, it has proven valuable with many kinds of subjects— children as young as two and a half, university students, speakers of other languages, speakers with neurological abnormalities, even deaf and blind subjects.

The first results with this technique were presented in the aforementioned paper (McNeill & Levy 1982). The choice of the specific cartoon was based on several factors we thought important—little speech, linear and repetitive plot line, yet varying on the surface from episode to episode, a high concentration of motion events, and brevity. Our initial intuitions have been validated in that we have obtained excellent retellings from the full range of participants, including non-native participants who were very new to the culture of the cartoon at the time of taping. We have also used a full-length film, an early Hitchcock (*Blackmail*), which is suitable obviously only with adults who possess sufficient English language competence to follow the spoken dialogue (*Blackmail* was Hitchcock's first talkie). In contrast to cartoon retellings, the film evokes a high proportion of metaphoric gestures (see the descriptions in *Hand and Mind*).

Other stimuli such as the Frog Story (cf. papers in Berman & Slobin 1994) or the celery-tomato clips (Kita et al. 2001, Allen et al. 2003) differ from film and cartoon stimuli in ways that affect the gestures and speech they make available for observation. The Frog Story provides narrations that, for reasons not completely clear but possibly connected to its static picture-book format, dampens gesture output (this has been our experience). The celery-tomato clips (named after the colors and shapes of its moving geometric figures) are animated but lack a story line and hence a basis for discourse and catchment development. Nonnarrative methods include the mismatches described in Chapter 4.3, which were observed while children or adults solved mathematics problems and explained their solutions. Less constrained are the mathematics discussions in *Hand and Mind* and Smith (2003). McCullough (in preparation) is analyzing an academic lecture (summarized in Chapter 5). The circularity problem is reduced here, since the topic of the lecture is well-understood (a linguistic theory that has been widely discussed).

The Procedure

We show the cartoon either as a whole (with unimpaired adults) or in 2 or 3 segments (with children or adults with neurological impairments), and ask the subject, from memory, to immediately recount the story to a listener who has not seen the cartoon. (*Blackmail* is usually shown straight through.) The living space description in Chapter 5 and later in this Appendix was evoked by asking participants to describe their homes and how to get to them from the testing room on campus.

Transcription

The tape must be transcribed to bring out the data. For details, see the coding manual later in this appendix. The following is a capsule summary.

The first step is to transcribe the speech; this must be done with accuracy, including all hesitations, pauses both filled and unfilled, speech irregularities (repetitions, errors, interruptions, and so forth), and breath pauses where audible. Prosody is registered with changes in font size (usually two levels).

After speech is transcribed, gestures are located, identified, and coded. Gesture coding seeks: (a) the type of gesture (e.g., iconic and deictic); (b) the gesture phrase, the interval from rest to rest or from one gesture to the next (as below), and shown with square brackets; and (c) the gesture phases (preparation, stroke, retraction, plus holds), all located with within-syllable precision with respect to the speech transcript.

Notation: Square brackets show the gesture phrase relative to speech—'['is the onset of the phrase, ']' is its end. Boldface shows the stroke phase—the phase with semantic content and the quality of 'effort'. Unbolded speech after the first bracket up to the stroke is the preparation phase; after the stroke and up to the second square bracket is the retraction phase. Pre- and poststroke holds are shown with underlining. An asterisk is self-interruption of speech. One or more slashes shows silent pauses of increasing duration (bolded when the stroke starts and/or continues during the pause), and # is an audible breath pause. The notation <some sound> represents a filled pause (um, for example). Though not in the example to follow, double letters show vowel elongation and || is a stroke-hold.

The following transcription of a gesture from Chapter 5 illustrates many of these features (transcription by S. Duncan; Figure A.1 shows two phases of the gesture):

09516   <um> /tryi[ng to <u>swi**n**g</u> **acrOss** <u>by</u> a rOpe #]
                  prep   stroke   retract
                        hold   hold

Iconic; 2 similar hands; A-shape; palms toward body; fingers turned down; starts at right and arcs to other side with slight wrist pivot. Hands = S's hands, character vpt = S; arc = trajectory, observer vpt. <S swings on rope>. Larger font sizes reflect intonation peaks as perceived by the coder.

Fig. A.1. Stroke phase of transcribed gesture.

Prestroke hold   Stroke (end)
<um> / tryi[ng to swing **acrOss** by a rOpe #]

The stroke coincided with "across." It was made with the two hands configured in a closed-hand posture (approximating the A-shape in ASL finger spelling). One hand was above the other, as if holding a rope, and the hands holding this position moved together across the gesture space, right to left, in a downward-upward arc. The hands themselves had the inside viewpoint of the character gripping the rope. The right-left movement had that of an observer looking at the event from the outside. Thus the gesture embodied a dual viewpoint.

Referring to the stimulus event, we see that speech and gesture conveyed different aspects of the underlying event and thus were co-expressive. The word "across" conveys the information that the trajectory moved transversely over a landmark (the street); the gesture showed the means of doing it (by holding onto a rope), and the shape of the trajectory (curved). The image depicted how the crossing was effected, as well as the discourse theme of inaccessibility. As described in Chapter 5, this example comprised a narrative-level description embedded within a larger metanarrative comment and was one of several such descriptions offered as a kind of summary of how the cat attempted to cope with the bird's inaccessibility.

Prosody, the most gesture-like aspect of speech (Bolinger 1986), highlighted all the elements that had a referential function ("swing," "across," and "rope"). Then, within this group, the gesture stroke aimed at the path.

In all these ways, speech and gesture worked together in a choreographed flow. It is the information in this flow that coding aims to recover.

GESTURE CODING MANUAL

The following methods have been written by Susan Duncan as a guide for novice gesture/discourse analysts. The attempt is to sketch current best practice, based on decades of analytic experience by coder-analysts working in our lab. As a careful reading of the instructions will show, the procedure is very much one of hypothesis formulation, testing, revision, further testing, and finally (provisional) acceptance: such is the process required for accurate gesture coding and analysis. The procedures are presented in eight successive 'passes' through the speech-video record.

One goal of the descriptive-analytic method is to assess speech-gesture synchrony to a degree of accuracy that permits assessment of how gestural movements co-occur with speech, syllable by syllable. Such analysis requires the ability to play the audio-video data at varying slow-motion speeds—crucially, with access to the concurrent audio track at all playback speeds, including frame-by-frame. Consumer grade VCRs do not provide the requisite playback capabilities. With tape media we have used Sony EVO 9650 Hi-8 VCRs (which, unfortunately, are no longer manufactured), because they have excellent jog/shuttle tape control and the required audio playback functionality. As this goes to press we are, as well, exploring use of digitized audio-video with various software implementations that support playback at all slow-motion speeds, with audio.

A further goal is to annotate speech-co-occurring gesturing with sufficient clarity, depth, detail, and consistency such that:

A. other analysts who make use of the annotated transcript, or add to it later, will be able to accurately infer previous analysts' decision-making process, in regard to parsing gesture phrases and phases, and inferring gesture meanings; and
B. the annotated transcript will serve as a 'visualization tool' for multi-modal analyses of language that focus on how speech and gesture mesh, both at moment-to-moment and extended discourse levels of analysis.

Start of Duncan Coding Manual

Pass 1

Watch the complete product of the elicitation (for example, a cartoon or movie narration, a lecture, or conversation) once, all the way through. This pass permits the analyst to develop an initial sense of speaker 'style'. This facilitates interpretations of gesture productions on later passes.

Pass 2

Transcribe all the words (including partials and unintelligibles) spoken in the discourse, from beginning to end, making little attempt to annotate sentence grammatical structuring or production characteristics (pauses, intakes of breaths, and so on). The 'end' of a discourse, for example in the case of one elicited with a movie or cartoon stimulus, is when the speaker or listener speaks his/her final utterances pertaining to the content of the stimulus, or pertaining to whatever elaborated, stimulus-related discussion of it speaker and listener may have developed between them. That is, a complete transcription also includes any responses either interlocutor may make to an investigator's prompts for further information about the stimulus, but need not include added-on conversation about other topics that may have been captured on the tape by accident.

Pass 3

Organize the speech into short utterances, reflecting the (sentence-approximating) grammatical structuring of the speech sequences (and/or larger intonational contouring of intervals of speech; a matter of analyst preference); that is, break up the stream of speech onto separate lines in units such as 'sentences', 'clauses', or intonation units. Use the typographic speech-annotation conventions given in the *Gesture notations conventions* section of this appendix, or some other system that captures dimensions of speaking of interest to the analyst. In all instances, typographic conventions are a matter of analyst preference and different schemes have different virtues.

Annotate:

A. The passage of time by periodically inserting, on the left hand side of the typewritten transcript, the time stamp that appears on the video image.
B. Pauses ('unfilled' and 'filled'), breaths (intakes and exhalations), nonspeech sounds (marked with a '%') such as laughter and audible mouth noises, and so on
C. 'Listener' (in the case of a quasi-monologic speaker narration) contributions ("mm-hm," %laugh, [nod], and so on).

Save this non-gesture-annotated speech transcript separately for use in analyses where only the speech is of interest, taking care to keep it updated, when repeated listenings during subsequent passes (for gesture annotation) reveal errors of speech transcription.

The remaining passes—passes 4 through 8—are executed recursively on multiline chunks rather than on the discourse as a whole.

Pass 4

On a copy of the speech transcript developed in passes 2 and 3, annotate points of primary peak prosodic emphasis (and secondary emphasis if the opportunity arises), assessed by ear (preferably, native-speaker ear). Use enlarged font (not capitals) for these annotations. Limit the enlargement to the syllable(s) that your ear tells you is/are prosodically emphasized. (N.B.: lexical stress can complicate these judgments.)

Pass 5

Square-bracket the gesture phrases. Do this exhaustively across the discourse; that is, leave unannotated no intervals of speech that co-occur with hand gestures or gestural movements of other body parts. Use the gesture-annotation conventions described earlier, or another system that captures dimensions of gesture that are of interest to the analyst.

Pass 6

Annotate the within-phrase phase-structure of gestures.

A. Locate gesture stroke phases through a process of comparing meanings the hands (or other body parts) appear to express, with meanings conveyed in co-occurring speech (considering individual words and phrases, but also more comprehensive discourse units). Take into account also the gesture movement dynamics, as the stroke phase of a gesture will typically (but not always!) be the interval of apparent greatest gestural effort; determination of 'effort' made with reference to parameters such as relative forcefulness of movement or apparent tenseness of handshapes, and so on. Annotate the extent of a stroke phase in relation to speech using boldface font.
   1. Assess the location of the stroke first at full and one-fifth tape speeds
   2. Fine-tune at one-tenth and frame-by-frame tape speeds (N.B: always while listening to the co-occurring speech).
   N.B. Step (6.A.2) is important not only if the analyses planned for the data are to take precise speech-gesture synchrony into account, but also generally, in that fine-grained observation often spurs reassignment of phases. Furthermore, fine-grained analysis, dependent upon multiple viewings at slow-motion speeds, tends

to make additional, distinct gesture phases visible that are too small to be observable at faster speeds.

A weird empirical fact: Gestures' apparent locations in relation to the speech stream can migrate very slightly right-to-left (in relation to the typewritten sequence of spoken syllables), or backward in 'speech time' when viewed at progressively slower and slower tape speeds; e.g., a gesture stroke that, viewed at full speed, appears to synchronize with "down" in the phrase "rolls down" may appear at frame-by-frame speed to synchronize instead with "rolls".

B. With annotation of gesture phrases ([...] demarcating the co-occurring speech) and stroke phases (**bold** font for the speech with which the stroke co-occurs), preparation and retraction phases of gesture are de facto also annotated. That is, the interval of speech between a left bracket and onset of bold font is what co-occurs with the gesture preparation phase and the interval between offset of bold font and the right bracket is the interval of gesture retraction. Bear in mind that there is nothing to prevent a speaker from launching a new stroke phase immediately upon termination of the preceding stroke phase. That is, a gesture phrase may lack preparation and retraction phases.

N.B. The question often arises: Where does one gesture phrase end and another begin? That is, in regard to a movement phase between gesture strokes, there is often a question of whether to interpret the movement as a retraction phase of the preceding gesture or the preparation phase of the following gesture. Recommendation:absent (gesture featural) evidence to the contrary, decide most times in favor of preparation phase of the following gesture. This recommendation reflects the working assumption that gesturing is a largely forward-directed activity, reflective of idea units yet to come in speech.

C. It seems to be at this point of dividing phrases into phases (preparation, stroke, holds, retraction), that the 'nested' nature of some gesture productions becomes apparent. Phrase-within-phrase nesting may be annotated using outer and inner brackets, like this: [[...][...]]. Two or more gesture phrases may be considered to function as part of a more encompassing gesture phrase when there is some maintained imagistic feature (realized, for instance, as a handshape, a body orientation, a marked spatial location, or similar) that they share and are unified by (on some level).

D. Annotate hold phases with underlines, distinguishing full holds (solid underline: no detectable movement) from 'feature' or 'virtual' holds (dotted underline: some movement, but maintenance of handshape and/or general location in gesture space, for instance).

E. Below the line of gesture-annotated speech, enter information concerning assessment of and interpretation of the gesture, including:

1. The gesture's 'type'/function, e.g., iconic, metaphoric, deictic, beat, interactive, emblem, pragmatic, and so on.

N.B. Bear in mind that such type designations are meant solely to be 'convenient handles', designed to further one target analysis or another. We do not consider these semiotic dimensions (iconicity, metaphoricity, and so on) to function as mutually exclusive categories. Indeed, any observation of natural gesturing reveals that they do not function this way. An essential descriptive-analytic concept that governs this aspect of our work is that these semiotic dimensions 'layer' in gestures. For example, any gesture (whether labeled iconic, deictic, or metaphoric) whose stroke coincides with a point of speech prosodic emphasis is analyzed as being also, underlyingly, a beat (Tuite 1993; see also Loehr 2004). Also, gestures are typically placed at particular locations in gesture space. They therefore manifest deixis, or, we say, all gesturing is 'deictically framed'. Consider, too, that the type categories that constitute coding schemes for much gesture research cannot really be understood independently of one another; for example, a metaphoric gesture is an iconic gesture, in that its form is a depiction of the base of some conceptual metaphor. In summary, though it may be true that some gestural productions may be accurately construed to be 'loaded' more on one semiotic dimension than another, virtually every gesture production is assumed to manifest multiple dimensions.

2. Indication of whether the gesture is, in overall form or in some feature, a repeat of, or related in form, location, motion, or some other feature, to another gesture in the preceding discourse.

3. A description of the physical form of the gesture, including handshape, location, and movement characteristics. Use the coding conventions described earlier, or some other scheme that captures dimensions relevant to the target of the particular analysis.

4. The inferable meaning of the gesture.

5. If necessary, for difficult-to-analyze cases, notes about the process of inference that resulted in the descriptive hypothesis (see Cautions, D.2, below), recorded in the transcript, about a gesture's phrase and phase structure, and/or meaning.

6. Notes to support various specific analytic purposes; for example, the gesture's use of space, specifics of speech-gesture synchrony, character of speech prosodic patterning, connections between this speech-plus-gesture production and the larger discourse frame, and so on.

F. The exercise of analyzing and annotating speech-co-occurring gesture, since it is dependent on repeated, slow-motion viewing, causes previously overlooked aspects of speech production to become evident. Therefore, on pass 6, one adds in or modifies all the many:

1. speech pauses missed on pass 3;
2. intervals of dysfluent speech missed on pass 3;
3. words and phrases that are now heard differently;
4. listener productions overlooked or misheard on pass 3; and so on.

N.B. Be sure to make all such modifications as well to the separate, speech-only transcript, saved earlier.

Pass 7

Reorganize the manner in which the transcript was earlier broken up into short utterances (pass 2) in accord with what the gesture phraseology reveals about the organization of speech/gesture 'production pulses'. (A 'pulse' is a unit of speaker effort, encompassing prosodic highlighting, discourse highlighting, a gesture phrase; also, gaze, posture, and other dynamic factors—clearly, then, a judgment reflecting the analyst's final hypothesis concerning the organization of the example under analysis.)

N.B. There are analytic purposes for which the ideal, final, typewritten speech-gesture transcript is organized—as far as is possible—as one pulse per line, even when some of the pulses are quite short in terms of utterance length (a phrase or even a word). Often, these short utterances will not correspond to grammatical units (such as a clause or phrase).

Pass 8

The exercise of gesture analysis and annotation is necessarily backward-adjusting. As the analyst moves forward through the narration from segment to segment, insights accumulate about how the particular speaker typically executes certain types of gestures, the speaker's handshapes, what is typical of the speaker's gestures during intervals of dysfluency (for instance, holding versus repeating gestures across such intervals); on and on. Multitudes of tiny insights accumulate. An interval of gesturing at discourse segment no. 47 may require annotation that calls into question how an interval at segment no. 33 was annotated (at any level: gesture 'type', gesture meaning, any aspect). The analyst is obliged to return to segment no. 33 and redo the annotations or add a note of some kind.

A. When an analysis is to be based on a sample size of $n > 1$, if the insights gained from annotating speaker no. 25 call into question annotations for speakers nos. 3, 4, and 15, the annotator is obliged to go back and adjust those speakers' transcripts.

B. Item 8.A may be especially important when $n > 1$ analyses incorporate a subject-grouping variable; for example, language (e.g., English/Spanish/Chinese) or brain-language pathological condition (e.g., non-brain-damaged versus left hemisphere stroke). Insights gained from annotating transcripts of speakers in group 1 may be relevant to some dimension that crucially distinguishes group 1 speakers from groups 2 and 3. Annotations on transcripts for multiple speakers within all three groups may need to be adjusted to reflect the new insights.

Cautions

A. The majority of speech-gesture co-productions display relatively transparent semantic coexpressivity.

B. However, some proportion of all gestures are vague or ambiguous; either:

   1. At the level of the totality of data we have to muster in support of competing hypotheses concerning phrase structure or meaning, within the universe defined by the audio-video data we collect on an individual discourse, or,

   2. At the level of speaker speech-thinking. That is, at some moments in a narration a speaker's speech-thinking representations may simply be a bit indeterminate or confused. One has the impression that a speaker may have two conflicting notions in mind simultaneously and these facts of speaker mental state will manifest in gesture.

C. Gestures pattern in multiple levels simultaneously. They are multifunctional. Therefore, various hypotheses about them may all be supportable. Some hypotheses, though, are truly in competition with one another, at a given level of analysis. For such, the hope is that evidence available from the discourse as a whole will aggregate in support of one hypothesis over any other.

D. It is important to retain access to all reasonable hypotheses (those not disconfirmed by all available evidence) about each gesture production. Currently, this is how we attempt to meet this requirement:

1. Type all hypotheses concerning a production into the transcript, with, if necessary, the reasoning underlying each.

2. Procedure for dealing with difficult-to-interpret gestures:

   a. Enter a note about the difficulty, take a stab at formulating a hypothesis about the phrasing, function, and/or meaning of the gesture, and move on with annotating the transcript, promising to return.

   b. Return, either:

      i. after annotating some more of the discourse yields insight about the problem case, or

      ii. after just annotating some more.

   c. Upon returning:

      i. Ponder the problem case, considering the speaker's discourse locally and narrowly as well as broadly. Include consideration of what is known, as well, from having analyzed other speakers.

      ii. Fine-tune parsing and annotations, if necessary. Also, if the decision about how to parse a gesture and interpret it crucially hangs on small details of changes in motion or handshape, insert time stamp(s) from the videotape above the line of speech-gesture, indicating where these articulations occur, and/or elaborate the descriptive text associated with the production to make clear the reasoning underlying the decision.

      iii. Refine, change, or eliminate individual hypotheses of D.1 and add a note to the transcript stating the evidence for the changes, or for retaining any hypothesis. The latter is necessary because subsequent analysts may have the same difficulties with the same production. They will find assistance in such notes; also, because without such notes, an analyst wanting to incorporate the production in an analysis may do so without noticing that there is something problematic about it.

   d. Know that it is not possible to interpret the meanings and functions of every individual gesture (see Cautions, B.2, immediately above).

E. Underspecified in the above is the foundational issue of how a stroke's meaning is inferred. Many of the steps in the procedure outlined above interact with this issue. The approach to gesture phraseology and phaseology is **in its essence** meaning-driven. Locating the beginnings and ends of gesture phrases, or locating the gesture stroke among a movement's several phases of execution, is a matter of how the phases (movement or hold phases) coordinate, in terms of meaning, with units of the co-occurring speech and/or with larger-scale discourse meanings currently in play. One goal of the descriptive-analytic exercise is to try to observe where, in a sequence of movement-speech or hold-speech pairings, the two modalities seem linked in meaning, at one or more levels of discourse analysis. Inferring the meaning of a gesture stroke is an act heavily influenced by considerations outside the particular speech-gesture production pulse the analyst is working on. To be adequate, the process must draw on the larger discourse frame(s) that the pulse is embedded in, what meanings are emerging sequentially in the speaker's utterances, what viewpoint the speaker is embodying, what this speaker typically does with his hands in gesture, and so on; also, in the case of a cartoon (or similar stimulus) narration, what stimulus-derived image the speaker likely has in mind at the moment of speaking. An assessment based solely on physical features of the gestures in a single production (e.g., movement dynamics, handshape features) **will be inadequate.**

The experienced analyst expects and does not avoid dealing with whatever phenomena may emerge to complicate an interpretation or analysis. The essence of this approach to analysis is analytic and annotative flexibility. Our analyses are conceived of as basic linguistic descriptive work rather than as 'coding' exercises.

Risks Inherent in Deviating from the Above Procedure

1. Time wastage
2. Bogging down
3. Commission of avoidable errors
4. Production of transcripts that are sketchy and/or internally inconsistent at the level of their annotated representations.

Final Caution

A speech transcription can approach a state of completion. Gesture annotations to it (likely) never do.

End of Duncan Coding Manual

SINGLE EXAMPLES

Examining individual gestures, in context and with speech, has long been our mainstay, and throughout this book it has been my method of data presentation.

I have not combined individual cases into statistical samples for the most part. I would like to take a few words in this appendix to explain and justify this approach. A single-case analysis runs the obvious risk of capitalizing on chance, but four facts justify the method and tip the balance from the risk side to the benefit side. In any event, the chance issue is minimized when the same conclusions—the inseparability of speech from imagery, the incorporation of context into gestures, and others—are reached, as has occurred, over and over from numerous single examples.

The method has these advantages:

First, context is an essential part of interpreting gesture, and since each context is uniquely the background for a given gesture, there is no way to summate gestures, without losing this essential thread.

Second, experience teaches us that very little in gesture is 'error', in the sense that very little is due to random processes and beyond explanation or is irrelevant to the speech-gesture system that is our target.

Third, and a corollary to the lack of error, is the realization that the more we look at single gestures, in their context, the more we find of significance—summating gestures would hide these discoveries. The 'final caution' in the coding manual above refers to this phenomenon.

Fourth, as the coding manual above makes clear, each individual gesture, with its meaning, its synchrony with speech, and its context, is the test phase of a hypothesis-test-revision procedure, and this status would be obscured if cases were combined.

Theoretically, and this is perhaps the fifth justification, summating gestures makes little sense if we regard gestures as components of momentary states of a dialectic and cognitive being.

For all these reasons, we do not summate gestures but focus instead on single occurrences. This position we take in preference to the Platonic ideal of statistical abstraction.

GESTURE NOTATION CONVENTIONS

The following annotation conventions are used for gesture form, space, and trajectory and are based on the practices of Nobuhiro Furuyama.

Handedness

BH	both hands	LH	left hand
RH	right hand		

Hand Orientation

PTC   palm facing toward center
PAC   palm away from center
PUP   palm facing upwards
PDN   palm facing downwards
PTB   palm facing towards body
PAB   palm facing away from body

FTC   finger facing center
FAC   finger facing away from center
FUP   finger facing upwards
FDN   finger facing downwards
FTB   finger facing towards body
FAB   finger facing away from body

Hand Position

CC   center center (@chest)
C-UP center-upper (@neck)
C-UR center-upper-right
      (@R-shldr)
C-UL center-upper-left (@L-shldr)
C-RT center-right (@R-arm)
C-LT center-left (@L-arm)
C-LW center-lower (@stomach)
C-LR center-lower-right
C-LL center-lower-left

P-UP periphery upper (@face)
P-UR periphery upper right
      (@abv R-shldr)
P-UL periphery upper left
      (@abv L-shldr)
P-RT periphery right
P-LT periphery left
P-LW periphery lower (@lap)
P-LR periphery lower right
P-LL periphery lower left

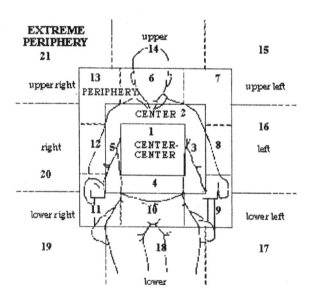

Fig. A.2. Space manikin.

EP-UP	extreme periphery upper	EP-RT	extreme periphery right
EP-UR	extreme periphery upper right	EP-LT	extreme periphery left
		EP-LW	extreme periphery lower
EP-UL	extreme periphery upper left	EP-LR	extreme periphery right
		EP-LL	extreme periphery left

Phases

PREP	preparation	HLD	hold
STRK	stroke	SADPTR	self adaptor
RTRCT	retraction		

Coding Gesture Re speech: Typographic Conventions

[...]	Bracket the extent of speech with which a gesture times.
[[...]]	Use nested brackets when there are gestures within gestures.
[mmRH]	Use subscripts when actions of the left and right hand are not in synch. with each other in some way that is significant to understanding the gesture.
bold	Boldface stroke phases.
<u>hold</u>	Underline hold phases.
‖	Use two enlarged, boldface vertical lines to indicate the location of a stroke-hold.
^	A beat. The caret is placed before the speech segment with the beat.

Common Handshapes (ASL Finger Spelling Approximations)

While spontaneous gestures rarely if ever exactly match ASL finger spelling shapes, the letter and number names are convenient for notating handshape. The ASL shapes are only approximations, and it is often necessary to annotate them ("loose S," etc.). *Hand and Mind* (McNeill 1992, Table 3.5) gives the ASL shapes and tallies of how frequently the different shapes appear in a sample of spontaneous speech-synchronized gesture occurrences. There is no ASL shape without at least one gesture occurrence approximating it in this table.

Notes on speech transcription from Duncan Coding Manual

/ *UNFILLED SPEECH PAUSE*

Indicate any soundless break in the speech stream with the slash mark, whether the speaker pauses in the middle or at the end of some kind of standard grammatical unit. It is important not to confuse the slash mark with the period (.) punctuation mark. The slash isn't for indicating the end of sentences, but only for when speakers pause in speaking momentarily—including when they do so at the end of sentences.

<...> FILLED SPEECH PAUSE

For example, "<um>" or "<ehhh>"; in Spanish sometimes, "<este>." Use this convention also when speakers noticeably lengthen syllables; for example,

ya segunda / se ve que va<aaa> subiendo por un* por un tubo de
drena* de desague* / un bajante

BREATH PAUSE

It is often difficult to hear when a person breathes in, but if you do hear it, or you can see them do an intake of breath, indicate the place in the transcript with the pound sign (#).

* SPEAKER SELF-INTERRUPT, SELF-CORRECTION OR RESTART

A bit of a challenge to use correctly, the asterisk is for when the transcriber's native-speaker-sense says that the speaker's speech plan *has gotten into trouble*. This can be stuttering, incompletely uttered words, phrases, or sentences, repeated words or phrases (when 'trouble' underlies the repetition; i.e., as opposed to a repetition 'for effect' or something like that), or restarts, as when a speaker says something, breaks it off, and then backs up to say it again, usually with some word change. Examples:

y entonces toma una<a>* una pel* <oh> otro caso mas un *bowling ball* /
y <este> lo arroja por el* por la cañeria /
y entra a un* a un centro de bowling /

Note: no asterisk after the first "va rodando" in the following example:

y cuando llega a la calle / va rodando / va rodando y entra a una* a un <deste>

When trying to decide whether or not to insert an asterisk, think Trouble (*pauses*, however—filled or unfilled—do not get an asterisk; in other words, don't do this:

"<um>*" or " /* ").

{...} UNCERTAIN SPEECH TRANSCRIPTION

If a piece of what the speaker says is completely uninterpretable, transcribe that piece using three dots surrounded by curly brackets. If you have an idea of what the speaker has said, but it's not clear enough to be completely certain, enclose your best guess in curly brackets. In general, if you are able to make out anything at all, even if it's just the number of syllables, it's a good idea to type that into the curly brackets. This will benefit the next person who listens to the same sequence. Use combinations of dots and words, if necessary; for example:

y entonces {toma ... pel (+ 3 syllables)} caso mas un *bowling ball* /

% NONSPEECH SOUND
For example, laughter, lip smacking, throat clearing, etc. Transcribe such non-speech sounds like this: "%laugh," "%smack," "%throat."

onom ONOMATOPOETIC SPOKEN FORMS
Use capital letters to show the nonnative speaker that, in your judgment, the utterance is a spontaneously created, nonstandard form. Spell onomatopoeia as close as possible to the way they actually sound (be creative); for example, "BONG," "HWAH," "DRZDRZDRZ."
Italics Italicize words from other languages.
Punctuation Do not use commas or periods in the speech transcription line of a marked transcript. Save them for the English translation line. If a speaker pauses, use a slash mark (/).

End of Duncan notes on speech transcription

Purpose Hierarchies

Barbara Grosz and colleagues (see summary in Nakatani et al. 1995) have devised a procedure for recovering discourse purposes from a transcribed text. The method consists of questions with which to guide the analysis and uncover the speaker's goals in producing each successive line of text. Following this procedure with the living space text in Chapter 5, we produced a four-level discourse structure, repeated below. Not all discourse samples follow such a systematic hierarchical design (Park-Doob 2001).

For the same discourse sample, purposes can be compared to catchments. The gesture-based and text-based pieces are independently derived but the resulting correlation is remarkably strong, as described in Chapter 5.

In the Chapter 5 hierarchy, the uppermost level was labeled "locating the back staircase." It is at this level that the discourse as a whole had significance. The middle level concerned the first staircase and its location (introducing the second floor), and the lowest level was the front of the house and the restarting of the house tour. The text is broken up so that each line is an intonation unit (e.g., Chafe 1994). The parenthetical numbers refer to the level of the purpose; the 'C' numbers are the catchments (cf. Chapter 5).

WHY? To locate the back staircase (1.1) C1
[so <oo> you're in the kitchen]
WHY? Ways of getting to the second floor (1) C4
['n' then there's a s<sss>*]
[the back stairc*]

WHY? To note the existence of the first staircase (1.1.1)
[I forgot to say]

WHY? To restart the tour (1.1.1.1) C2
[when you come through the*]
[when you enter the house from the front]
[annd you <ou> openn the doors with t][he*]
[<uumm> %smack /]
[/ the glas][s inn them #]

WHY? To explain first staircase (1.1.1) C3
[there's a*
the front staircase] [runs
right up there
o][n* on your left]
[so you can go straight up][stair]
[s to the se][econd floo][r from there]
[if you wannt]

WHY? To locate the back staircase (1.1) C1
[but if you come around through the ki]
[tchen into the bac][k

WHY? Ways of getting to the second floor (1) C4
there's a back s sta]
[ircase that winds around like this]

WHY? To connect to the second floor (1.2) C4 + C3
[and putss you up on the second floor]

Mischa Park-Doob (2001), however, has argued strongly that such a hierarchical structuring of purposes appears only in a certain discourses—others of the kinds he collected were more 'ludic' in character, and seemed to be motivated by forces (Park-Doob likens them to momentum rather than purposes) that can propel the discourse forward but are remote from anything that can be called 'purposeful'.

Semi-Automated Catchment Recovery

I describe here a new approach toward the measurement of gesture and gestural catchments. This work has been conducted in close collaboration with computer engineers, Francis Quek and his students, and makes crucial use of algorithms and interface designs that Quek has pioneered to mesh with our gesture coding and to target certain of the theoretical entities described in this current book, the catchment in particular (see McNeill et al. 2001 and McNeill et al. 2002 for early results, the latter providing somewhat more technical detail). We apply Quek's parallelizable fuzzy image processing approach known as *vector coherence mapping* (VCM) (Quek et al. 1999, Quek & Bryll 1998) and use this to track hand motion in ordinary video. VCM is able to apply spatial coherence, momentum (temporal coherence), motion, and skin color constraints in a vector field computation by using a fuzzy-combination strategy and produces good results for hand gesture tracking. See Quek et al. (1999) and Quek & Bryll (1998) for detailed descriptions of the approach.

Figures A.3, A.4, and A.5 are based on outputs of VCM. Figure A.3 traces the hand movements of the living-space speaker at two critical points in C4 (the back staircase)—first, her aborted start of the back staircase; second, her completion of the back staircase after more than thirty seconds of intervening front door and front staircase description. The gesture feature recurrences in the right hand spiraling upward are clearly present (the first record is truncated, of course). Figures A.4 and A.5 cover the entire discourse with annotations. All automatic entries are time locked so that hand movements and speech signals are in synchrony (to one video frame, 1/30 second accuracy).

The top two plots of each figure describe the horizontal (x) and vertical (y) hand positions respectively. In the second and third charts the horizontal bars under the y direction plot is an analysis of gesture features—LH hold, RH hold, two-handed anti-symmetry, two-handed symmetry (mirror symmetry), two-handed asymmetry (no detected symmetry), single LH, and single RH respectively. Beneath this is the fundamental frequency Fo plot of the audio signal. The voiced utterances in the Fo plot are numbered sequentially to correlate with the speech transcript presented in Chapter 5 (corresponding to the numbers above each line

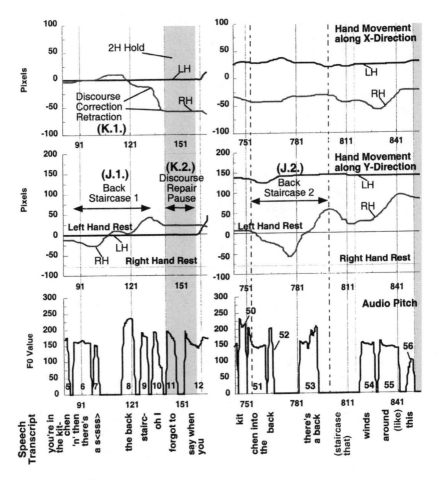

Fig. A.3. Traces of the 'back staircase' at two points.

of text there). We have reproduced the synchronized speech transcript at the bottom of each chart, as it correlates with the *F*o units. The vertical shaded bars that run across the charts mark durations in which both hands are determined to be stationary (holding).

Francis Quek's Analysis

A number of interesting details of the discourse are revealed in these charts. The following analyses were conducted by Quek, utilizing only the VCM outputs, and demonstrate the kind of interpretive analyses that automatic motion detection

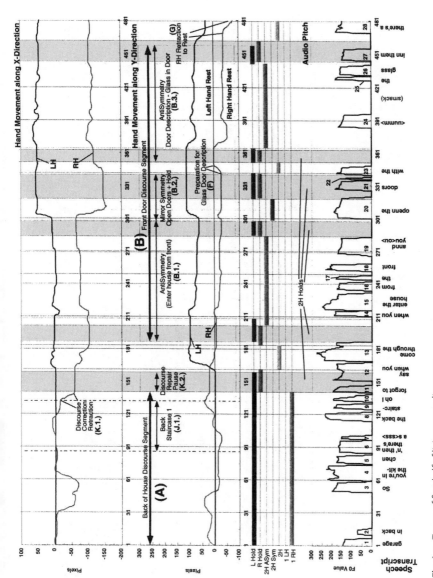

Fig. A.4. Traces of first half of living space discourse.

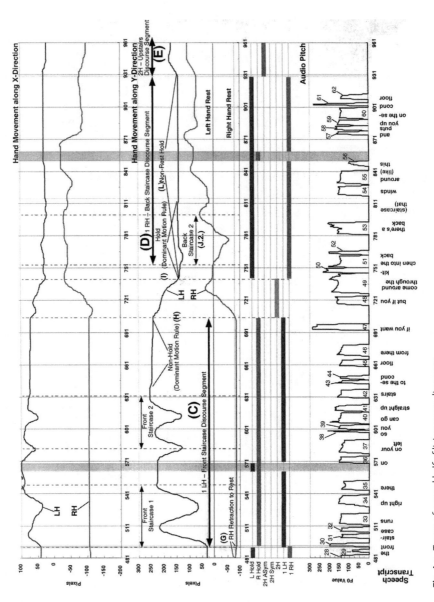

Fig. A.5: Traces of second half of living space discourse.

techniques are able to support. This analysis was included in our joint paper (McNeill et al. 2002, pp. 19–25) and is reprinted in the following paragraphs.

Labels (A) through (E) mark the distinctive motion segments accessible from the gestural traces independently from the speech data. These segments are determined solely from the hold and motion patterns of the speaker's hands. The question is: do they capture the catchment structures described above? The catchment numbers are indicated at the start of each line. As can be seen, every catchment corresponds to a motion segment. In addition, three motion segments subdivide one catchment (**C2**). On examination, we find that the subdivisions correspond to discourse themes in their own right.

(A) **C1** *Back-of-house discourse segment, 1 RH (Frames 1–140):* These gestures accompany the references to the back of the house that launch the discourse. This 1 H catchment is replaced by a series of two-handed gestures in (B), marking the shift to a different discourse purpose, that of describing the front of the house. Notice this catchment feature of 1 H-RH gestures (i.e. the LH is holding) reprises itself in segment (D) when the subject returns to describing the back of the house.

(B) **C2** *Front door discourse segment, 2 Synchronized Hands (Frames 188–455):* Two-handed gestures occur when the discourse theme is the front of the house, but there are variants that mark sub-parts of the theme—the existence of the front door, opening it, and then describing it. These subdivisions have thematic unity. Each sub-theme is initiated by a gesture hold, marking off in gesture the internal divisions of the discourse hierarchy. The sub-divisions are not evident in the text and thus were not picked up by the text-only analysis.

(**B.1.**) **C2** *'Enter house from front' discourse segment Two-Handed Anti-symmetric (Frames 188–298):* Anti-symmetric two-handed movements iconically embody the image of the two front doors; the anti-symmetric movements themselves contrast with the following mirror-image movements, and convey, not motion as such, but the surface and orientation of the doors.

(**B.2.**) **C2** *'Open doors' discourse segment Two-Handed Mirror Symmetry (Frames 299–338):* In contrast with the preceding two-handed segment, this gesture shows opening the doors and the hands moving apart. The segment terminates in a non-rest two-handed hold of sizeable duration of (more than 0.75 secs.: all other pre-stroke and post-stroke holds are less than 0.5 secs. in duration). This suggests that it is actually a 'stroke hold' (i.e. an information-laden component). This interpretation corresponds well with the text transcription.

The thrusting open of the hands indicating the action of opening the doors (coinciding with the words: 'open the'), and the two-handed stroke hold indicating the object of interest (coinciding with the word: 'doors'). The division of gestures agrees with the discourse analysis that carries the thread of the 'front door' as the element of focus. Furthermore, the two-handed mirror-symmetric motion for opening the doors carries the added information that these are double doors (information unavailable from the text transcription alone).

(**B.3.**) **C2** *Door description discourse segment Two-Handed Anti-symmetric (Frames 351–458):* The form of the doors returns as a sub-theme in their own right, and again the movement is anti-symmetric, in the plane of the closed doors.

(**C**) **C3** *Front staircase discourse segment, 1 LH (Frames 491–704):* The LH becomes active in a series of distinctive up-down movements coinciding exactly with the discourse goal of introducing the front staircase. These are clearly one-handed gestures in the chart with the RH at the rest position.

(**D**) **C4** *Back staircase discourse segment 1 RH (Frames 754–929):* The gestures for the back staircase are again made with the RH, but now, in contrast to the (A) catchment, the LH is at a non-rest hold, and still in play from (C). This changes in the final segment of the discourse.

(**E**) **C3 + C4** *'Upstairs' discourse segment Two-Handed Synchronized (Frames 930–):* The LH and RH join forces in a final gesture depicting ascent to the second floor via the back staircase. This is another place where gesture reveals a discourse element not recoverable from the text (no text accompanied the gesture).

Other gestural features:

Beside the overall gesture hold analysis, this 32 seconds of discourse contains several other gestural features and cues. We have labeled these (F) through (L).

(**F**) *Preparation for glass door description (Frames 340–359):* In the middle of the discourse segment on the front door (B), we have the interval marked (F) that appears to break the symmetry. This break is actually the preparation phase of the RH to the non-rest hold (for both hands) section that continues into the strongly anti-symmetric (B.3.) 'glass door' segment. The break clarifies the interpretation of the two-handed holds preceding and following (F). The former is the post-stroke hold for the 'open doors' segment (B.2.), and latter is the pre-stroke hold for segment (B.3.), which implies that we can then extend segment (B.3.) backward to the beginning of (F). Doing so groups *F*o unit 23 ('with the') with (B.3.) and matches the discourse segmentation 'with the . . . <uumm> glass in them'. The speaker had interrupted her speech stream and is 'searching' for the next words to describe what she wants to say. The cohesion of the phrase would be lost in a pure speech pause analysis.

(G) *RH retraction to rest (Frames 468–490 straddles both charts):* The RH movement labeled (G) spanning both plots terminate in the resting position for the hand. We can therefore extend the starting point of the target rest backward to the start of this retraction for discourse segmentation. Hence, we might actually begin the (C) front staircase discourse segment marked by the 1 LH feature backward from frame 491 to frame 340. This matches the discourse analysis from *Fo* units 28–30: ". . . there's the front- . . . "

(H) & (I) *Non-Hold for (H) in (C) (Frames 643–704) and Hold for (I) in (D) (Frames 740–811):* The LH was transcribed to be not holding in (H) while it was judged to be holding in (I). An examination of the video shows that in (H) the speaker was making a series of small oscillatory motions (patting motion with her wrist to signify the floor of the 'second floor') with a general downward trend. In segment (I), the LH was holding, but the entire body was moving slightly because of the rapid and large movements of the RH. This distinction cannot be made from the motion traces of the LH alone. To account for it, Quek introduces a *dominant motion rule* for rest determination. He uses the motion energy differential of the movements of both hands to determine if small move-ments in one hand are interpreted as holds. In segment (H), the RH is at rest, hence any movement in the alternate LH becomes significant. In segment (I), the RH exhibits strong motion, and the effects of the LH motion are attenuated.

(J.1.) & (J.2.) *Backstaircase Catchment 1 (Frames 86–132), and Backstaircase Catchment 2 (Frames 753–799):* These catchments were shown in the first chart.

(K.1.) & (K.2.) *Discourse repair retraction (Frames 133–142), and discourse repair pause (Frames 143–159):* Segments (K.1.) and (K.2.) correspond with the speech 'Oh I forgot to say' and flags a repair in the discourse structure. The sub-ject actually pulls her RH back toward herself rapidly and holds an emblematic gesture with an index finger point (corresponding to "wait a minute!"). It is likely that such an abrupt gestural trajectory change, where the hand is retracted from the gestural space, suggests a discourse repair in other cases as well.

(L) *Non-rest hold (Frames 740–929):* An interesting phenomenon is seen in the (L) non-rest hold. This is a lengthy hold spanning 190 frames or 6.33 seconds. Such an extended hold means that it cannot be a pre-stroke or post-stroke hold. It could be a hold gesture or a stationary reference hand in a two-handed gesture sequence. In the discourse example at hand, it actually serves as an 'idea hold', prolonging the idea of the second floor. The subject had just ended her description of the front staircase with a mention of the second floor. While her LH is holding, she proceeds to describe the back staircase that takes her to the same location. At the end of this non-rest hold, she proceeds to a two-handed gesture sequence (E) describing the second floor. This means that her 'discourse plan' to proceed to the second floor was already in place at the end of the (C) discourse segment. The LH suspended above her shoulder could be interpreted as holding the upstairs discourse segment in abeyance while she describes the back staircase (segment D). Such holds may thus be thought of as super-segmental cues for the overall discourse structure. The non-rest hold (L), in essence, allows us to connect the end of (C) with the (E) discourse segment.

'THE GROWTH POINT'—A POEM

In June 2003, my students, former students, and colleagues put on a Fest for me, the charm and affection of which I continue to relish. One of the high points was a poem read at the banquet by Adam Kendon, attributed by him to a remarkable author-cat and wit, which I reproduce here with Kendon's permission (as literary executor). The cat is not shy about his skepticism over one of the major concepts of this book, the growth point. Nonetheless, since the book begins with continuum/continua named after Kendon, it is only fitting that it should end with a poem (to be sure, only administered) by him, and conclude it all with the phrase, "the growth point."

The Growth Point
Attributed to William Warambungle, Cat, Esq.
(with apologies to Edward Lear)

Who or why or which or what
Is the Growth Point?
Is it round and smooth or square and rough?
Can you eat one, and if you did, would you find it tough?
Or can you swallow it down like pill,
That you take when you're feeling rather ill,
The Growth Point?

Is it made of gold or copper or zinc,
Can you grind it up and use it for ink?
Or is its substance, rather, not easily stated
Being something that can only be *triangulated*?
The Growth Point?

Can you pick one up and keep it warm,
And let it expand and acquire a new form
Or colour or smell or feel or weight?
Or does it constantly change its state,
Becoming at once a mere reflection
Of someone's abstract theoretical conception,
The Growth Point?

Does it float about on a summer's breeze,
Ready at any moment to seize
Some hapless speaker with nothing to say
Who then finds himself compelled to stay
And formulate something not said before?
Or does it, rather, insert itself
In some crevice of the brain, and then by stealth
Unfold itself in germination
To bring some utterance to termination,
The Growth Point?

Does it suffer much from its inner dialectic
Between images rich and categories analytic?
Or does it smoothly resolve this tension
By managing a clever semiotic extension,
The Growth Point?

And when Tweety seizes that bowling ball
And drops it down the drain pipe, and all
Does it then step in smartly to make quite sure
That it is 'it down' only and nothing more,
The Growth Point?

And when Sylvester swallows that awful ball,
And rolls directly from street to hall

Giving the pins a fearful swipe
Having squirted out from that terrible pipe,
Does it choose manner or does it choose path,
As it follows the action, and does it laugh,
The Growth Point?

If someone is doing thinking for speaking,
Does it make itself heard with a terrible squeaking?
Or does it move hither and yon quite discretely
Lining up images and words very neatly,
In rows,
The Growth Point?

If cohesives and catchments collide in the air,
If Butterworths are flying here and there,
If metaphorix are struggling to give expression
And iconix are trying to make an impression,
Does it put all in order, make everything right?
Or does it just yell loudly, giving all a big fright,
The Growth Point?

There's someone indeed who knows I wot,
Who or why or which or what
Is the Growth Point!

He's sitting here among us now,
He will certainly be able to tell us how,
Thought imagistic and analytic,
Engage together in a manner balletic,
Wrapped up together in that one small moment,
The Growth Point!

So let us all raise our glasses high,
And cheer till our voices reach the sky,
And celebrate as best we can
This very unusual sort of a man
Who has plunged to the depths of deepest time
And retrieved for us
The Growth Point!

REFERENCES

Alibali, Martha. W., Heath, Dana C., & Meyers, Heather J. 2001. Effects of visibility between speaker and listener on gesture production: Some gestures are meant to be seen. *Journal of Memory and Language* 44: 169–188.

Allen, Shanley, Özyürek, Asli, Kita, Sotaro, Brown, Amanda, Turanli, Reyhan, & Ishizuka, Tomoko. 2003. Early speech about manner and path in Turkish and English: Universal or language-specific? In B. Beachley et al. (eds.), *Proceedings of the Boston University Conference on Language Development*, pp. 63–72. Somerville, MA: Cascadilla Press.

Anscombe, G. E. M. 1979. *Intention*. London: Basil Blackwell.

Arbib, Michael A. In press. From monkey-like action recognition to human language: An evolutionary framework for neurolinguistics. *Behavioral and Brain Sciences*.

Armstrong, David F., Stokoe, William C., & Wilcox, Sherman E. 1995. *Gesture and the Nature of Language*. Cambridge: Cambridge University Press.

Aske, Jon 1989. Path predicates in English and Spanish: A closer look. In Kira Hall, Michael Meacham, & Richard Shapiro (eds.), *Proceedings of the 20th Meeting of the Berkeley Linguistic Society*, pp. 1–14. Berkeley: Berkeley Linguistics Society.

Austin, Gilbert. 1806. *Chironomia: Or, A treatise on rhetorical delivery: comprehending many precepts, both ancient and modern, for the proper regulation of the voice, the countenance, and gesture*. Illustrated by many figures. London: Bulmer.

Baker, Mark C. 2001. *The Atoms of Language: The Mind's Hidden Rules of Grammar*. New York: Basic Books.

Bakhtin, Mikhail M. 1981. *The Dialogic Imagination* (M. Holquist, ed.). Austin: University of Texas Press.

Bates, Elizabeth, Benigni, Laura, Bretherton, Inge, Camaioni, Luigia, & Volterra, Virginia. 1979. *The Emergence of Symbols: Cognition and Communication in Infancy*. New York: Academic Press.

Bates, Elizabeth, & Dick, Frederic. 2002. Language, gesture, and the developing brain. In B. J. Casey & Y. Munakata (eds.) Special issue: Converging method approach to the study of developmental science. *Developmental Psychobiology* 40: 293–310.

Bavelas, Janet B., Chovil, Nicole, Lawrie, Douglas A., & Wade, Allan. 1992. Interactive gestures. *Discourse Processes* 15: 469–489.

Beattie, Geoffrey. 2003. *Visible Thought: The New Psychology of Body Language*. Hove: Routledge.

Beattie, Geoffrey, & Shovelton, Heather. 2000. Iconic hand gestures and the predictability of words in context in spontaneous speech. *British Journal of Psychology* 91: 473–491.

Beckman, Mary E., & Hirschberg, Julia. 1994. *The ToBI Annotation Conventions*. http://www.ling.ohio-state.edu/Phonetics/ToBI/ToBI.6.html.

Bekkering, Harold, Wohlschläger, Andreas, & Merideth, Gattis. 2000. Imitation of gestures in children is goal-directed. *Quarterly Journal of Experimental Psychology*. 53A: 153–164.

Ben-Shachar, Michal, Hendler, Talma, Kahn, Itamar, Ben-Bashat, Dafna, & Grodzinsky, Yosef. 2003. The neural reality of syntactic transformations: Evidence from functional magnetic resonance imaging. *Psychological Science* 14: 433–440.

Berman, Ruth A., & Slobin, Dan I. 1994. *Relating Events in Narrative: A Crosslinguistic Developmental Study*. Hillsdale, NJ: Erlbaum.

Bickerton, Derek. 1990. *Language and Species*. Chicago: University of Chicago Press.

Binkofski, Ferdinand, Amunts, Katrin, Stephan, Klaus Martin, Posse, Stefan, Schormann, Thorsten, Freund, Hans-Joachim, Zilles, Karl, & Seitz, Rüdiger J. 2000. Broca's region subserves imagery of motion: A combined cytoarchitectonic and fMRI study. *Human Brain Mapping* 11: 273–285.

Blumenthal, Arthur (ed. and trans.). 1970. *Language and Psychology: Historical Aspects of Psycholinguistics*. New York: John Wiley & Sons.

Bock, J. Kathryn. 1986. Syntactic persistence in language production. *Cognitive Psychology* 18: 355–387.

Boegehold, Alan L. 1999. *When a Gesture Was Expected*. Princeton: Princeton University Press.

Bolinger, Dwight. 1986. *Intonation and Its Parts: Melody in Spoken English*. Stanford: Stanford University Press.

Bonda, Eva, Petrides, Michael, & Evans, Alan C. 1994. Frontal cortex involvement in organized sequence of hand movements: Evidence from positron emission tomography study. *Society for Neuroscience Abstracts* 20: 353.

Bowerman, Melissa. 1982. Starting to talk worse: Clues to language acquisition from children's late speech errors. In S. Strauss (ed.), *U-Shaped Behavioral Growth*, pp. 101–145. New York: Academic Press.

Bremmer, Jan, & Roodenburg, Herman 1991. *A Cultural History of Gesture*. Ithaca: Cornell University Press.

Browman, Catherine P., & Goldstein, Louis. 1990. Tiers in articulatory phonology, with some implications for casual speech. In J. Kingston & M. E. Beckman (eds.), *Papers in Laboratory Phonology I: Between the Grammar and Physics of Speech*, pp. 341–376. Cambridge: Cambridge University Press.

Brown, Penelope, & Levinson, Stephen C. 1987. *Politeness: Some Universals in Language Usage*. Cambridge: Cambridge University Press.

Bühler, Karl. 1982a [1934]. *Sprachtheorie: Die Darstellungsfunktion der Sprache*. Stuttgart: Fischer.

———. 1982b. The deictic field of language and deictic words. In R. J. Jarvella & W. Klein (eds.), *Speech, Place, and Action*, pp. 9–30. Chichester, Eng: John Wiley & Sons.

Bulwer, John. 1974 [1644]. *Chirologia: Or the natural language of the hand, and Chironomia: Or the art of manual rhetoric* (J. W. Cleary. ed.). Carbondale: Southern Illinois University Press.

Butcher, Cynthia, & Goldin-Meadow, Susan. 2000. Gesture and the transition from one- to two-word speech: When hand and mouth come together. In D. McNeill (ed.), *Language and Gesture*, pp. 235–257. Cambridge: Cambridge University Press.

Butterworth, Brian, & Beattie, Geoffrey. 1978. Gesture and silence as indicators of planning in speech. In R. N. Campbell & P. Smith (eds.), *Recent Advances in the Psychology of Language: Formal and Experimental Approaches*, pp. 347–360. New York: Plenum Press.

Butterworth, Brian, & Hadar, Uri. 1989. Gesture, speech, and computational stages: A reply to McNeill. *Psychological Review* 96: 168–174.

Calbris, Geneviève. 1990. *The Semiotics of French Gestures*. Bloomington: Indiana University Press.

Cantalupo, Claudio, & Hopkins, William D. 2001. Asymmetric Broca's area in great apes. *Nature* 414: 505.

Capirici, Olga, Iverson, Jana M., Pizzuto, Elena, & Volterra, Virginia. 1996. Gestures and words during the transition to two-word speech. *Journal of Child Language* 23: 645–673.

Cassell, Justine, & McNeill, David. 1990. Gesture and ground. In Kira Hall, Jean-Pierre Koenig, Michael Meacham, Sondra Reinman, & Laurel A. Sutton (eds.), *Proceedings of the Sixteenth Annual Meeting of the Berkeley Linguistics Society*, pp. 57–68. Berkeley: Berkeley Linguistics Society.

———. 1991. Gesture and the poetics of prose. *Poetics Today* 12: 375–404.

Cassell, Justine, McNeill, David, & McCullough, Karl-Erik. 1999. Speech-gesture mismatches: Evidence for one underlying representation of linguistic and nonlinguistic information. *Pragmatics and Cognition* 7: 1–34.

Cassell, Justine, & Prevost, Scott. 1996. Distribution of semantic features across speech and gestures by humans and machines. In Lynne S. Messing (ed.), *Proceedings of WIGLS*, pp. 253–269. Wilmington, DE: Applied Science and Engineering Laboratories.

Chafe, Wallace. 1976. Givenness, contrastiveness, definiteness, subjects, topics, and point of view. In C. N. Li (ed.), *Subject and Topic*, pp. 25–55. New York: Academic Press.

———. 1994. *Discourse, consciousness, and time: The flow and displacement of conscious experience in speaking and writing*. Chicago: University of Chicago Press.

Chase, W. G., & Eriksson, K. A. 1981. Skilled memory. In J. R. Anderson (ed.), *Cognitive Skills and Their Acquisition*, pp. 227–249. Hillsdale, NJ: Erlbaum.

Choi, Soonja, & Bowerman, Melissa. 1991. Learning to express motion events in English and Korean: The influence of language-specific lexicalization patterns. *Cognition* 41: 83–121.

Chomsky, Noam. 1957. *Syntactic Structures*. The Hague: Mouton.

———. 1965. *Aspects of the Theory of Syntax*. Cambridge: MIT Press.

———. 1981a. Principles and parameters in syntactic theory. In N. Hornstein & D. Lightfoot (eds.), *Explanation in Linguistics: The Logical Problem of Language Acquisition*, pp. 32–75. London: Longman.

———. 1981b. *Lectures on Government and Binding*. Dordrecht: Foris.

———. 1995. *The Minimalist Program*. Cambridge: MIT Press.

Church, R. Breckinridge, & Goldin-Meadow, Susan. 1986. The mismatch between gesture and speech as an index of transitional knowledge. *Cognition* 23: 43–71.

Cienki, Alan 1998. Metaphoric gestures and some of their relations to verbal metaphoric expressions. In J.-P. Koening (ed.), *Discourse and Cognition: Bridging the Gap*, pp. 189–204. Stanford: CSLI Publications.

Clark, Herbert H. 1992. *Arenas of Language Use*. Chicago: University of Chicago Press.

Cogill, Dorothea. 2003. *Signed Language Classifier Predicates as Templated Visual Representation*. Ph.D. thesis, University of New England, Armidale, NSW, Australia.

Cohen, Akiba A. 1977. The communicative function of hand illustrators. *Journal of Communication* 27: 54–63.

Cohen, Akiba A., & Harrison, Randall P. 1973. Intentionality in the use of hand illustrators in face-to-face communication situations. *Journal of Personality and Social Psychology* 28: 276–279.

Cohen, Einya, Namir, Lila, & Schlesinger, Izchak M. (eds). 1977. *A New Dictionary of Sign Language: Employing the Eshkol-Wachmann Movement Notation System*. The Hague: Mouton.

Cole, Jonathan. 1995. *Pride and a Daily Marathon*. Cambridge: MIT Press.

Corballis, Michael C. 2002. *From Hand to Mouth: The Origins of Language*. Princeton: Princeton University Press.

Crawford, L. Elizabeth, Regier, Terry, & Huttenlocher, Janellen. 2000. Linguistic and non-linguistic spatial categorization. *Cognition* 75: 209–235.

Croft, William. 1999. *Event Structure and the Grammar of Verbs*. Colloquium at the University of Chicago, May.

Culler, Jonathan D. 1976. *Ferdinand de Saussure*. New York: Penguin Books.

Damasio, Antonio R. 1994. *Descartes' Error: Emotion, Reason, and the Human Brain*. New York: Putnam.

———. 1999. *The Feeling of What Happens: Body and Emotion in the Making of Consciousness*. New York: Harcourt Brace.

De Ruiter, Jan-Peter. 2000. The production of gesture and speech. In D. McNeill (ed.), *Language and Gesture*, pp. 285–311. Cambridge: Cambridge University Press.

De Ruiter, Jan-Peter, & Wilkins, David P. (eds.). 1998. *Max Planck Institute for Psycholinguistics Annual Report 17*. Nijmegen: Max Planck Institute.

Deacon, Terrence W. 1997. *The Symbolic Species: The Co-evolution of Language and the Brain*. New York: Norton.

Decety, Jean, Perani, Daniela, Jeannerod, Marc, Bettinardi, Valentino, Tadary, B., Woods, Roger, Mazziotta, John C., & Fazio, Feruccio. 1994. Mapping motor representations with positron emission tomography. *Nature* 371: 600–602.

Decety, J., & Sommerville, J. A. 2003. Shared representations between self and others: A social cognitive neuroscience view. *Trends in Cognitive Science* 7: 527–533.

Dell, Cecily. 1970. *A Primer for Movement Description Using Effort Shape and Supplementary Concepts*. New York: Dance Notation Bureau.

Dennett, Daniel. 1986. The logical geography of computational approaches: A view from the east pole. In M. Brand & R. M. Harnish (eds.), *The Representation of Knowledge and Belief*, pp. 59–79. Tucson: University of Arizona Press.

———. 1991. *Consciousness Explained*. Boston: Little, Brown.

Donald, Merlin. 1991. *Origins of the Modern Mind: Three Stages in the Evolution of Culture and Cognition*. Cambridge: Harvard University Press.

Dray, Nancy L., & McNeill, David. 1990. Gestures during discourse: The contextual structuring of thought. In S. L. Tsohatzidis (ed.), *Meaning and Prototypes: Studies in Linguistic Categorization*, pp. 466–488. London: Routledge.

Dreyfus, H. 1994. *Being-in-the-World: A Commentary on Heidegger's Being and Time, Division I*. Cambridge: MIT Press.

Duncan, Starkey Jr., & Fiske, Donald W. 1977. *Face-to-Face Interaction: Research, Methods, and Theory*. Hillsdale, NJ: Erlbaum.

Duncan, Susan. 1996. *Grammatical Form and 'Thinking for Speaking' in Chinese and English: An Analysis Based on Speech-Accompanying Gestures*. Ph.D. dissertation, University of Chicago.

———. 2002. Left- and right-brain hemisphere contributions to speech-gesture production. Paper given at Conference on Multimodality of Human Communication: Theories, Problems, and Applications, University of Toronto, May 3–5.

———. In press. Gesture and discourse prosody in signing: A case study from Taiwan Sign Language. *Languages and Linguistics*.

Duncan, Susan, McNeill, David, & McCullough, Karl-Erik. 1995. How to transcribe the invisible—and what we see. In D. O'Connell, S. Kowal, & R. Posner (eds.), *Zeichen für Zeit: Zur Notation und Transkription von Bewegungsabläufen* (special issue of KODIKAS/CODE) 18: 75–94. Tübingen: Gunter Narr Verlag.

Duranti, Alessandro, & Goodwin, Charles. 1992. Rethinking context: An introduction. In A. Duranti & C. Goodwin (eds.), *Rethinking Context: Language as an Interactive Phenomenon*, pp. 1–42. Cambridge: Cambridge University Press.

Efron, David. 1941. *Gesture and Environment.* Morningside Heights, NY: King's Crown Press.

Ekman, Paul, & Friesen, Wallace. 1969. The repertoire of non-verbal behavior: Categories, origins, usage, and coding. *Semiotica* 1: 49–98.

Emmorey, Karen, & Herzig, Melissa. 2003. Categorical versus gradient properties of classifier constructions in ASL. In K. Emmorey (ed), *Perspectives on Classifier Constructions in Signed Languages,* pp. 222–246. Mahwah, NJ: Erlbaum.

Emmorey, Karen, & Reilly, Judith. 1995. *Language, Gesture, and Space.* Hillsdale, NJ: Erlbaum.

Enfield, Nick J. 2001. 'Lip-pointing': A discussion of form and function with reference to data from Laos. *Gesture* 1: 185–211.

———. 2004. On linear segmentation and combinatorics in co-speech gesture: A symmetry-dominance construction in Lao fish trap descriptions. *Semiotica* 149-1/4:57–123.

Engle, Randi A. 2000. *Toward a Theory of Multimodal Communication: Combining Speech, Gestures, Diagrams, and Demonstrations in Instructional Explanations.* Ph.D. dissertation, Stanford University.

Fadiga, Luciano, Fogassi, Leonardo, Pavesi, Giovanni, & Rizzolatti, Giacomo. 1995. Motor facilitation during action observation: A magnetic stimulation study. *Journal of Neurophysiology* 73: 2608–2611.

Fauconnier, Gilles. 1994 [1985]. *Mental Spaces.* Cambridge: Cambridge University Press.

Fauconnier, Gilles, & Turner, Mark. 2002. *The Way We Think: Conceptual Blending and the Mind's Hidden Complexities.* New York: Basic Books.

Federmeier, Kara D., & Kutas, Marta. 1999. Right words and left words: electrophysiological evidence for hemispheric differences in meaning processing. *Cognitive Brain Research* 8: 373–392.

Ferrari, Pier Francesco, Gallese, Vittorio, Rizzolatti, Giacomo, & Fogassi, Leonardo. 2003. Mirror neurons responding to the observation of ingestive and communicative mouth actions in the monkey ventral premotor cortex. *European Journal of Neuroscience* 17: 1703–1714.

Feyereisen, Pierre. 1997. The competition between gesture and speech production in dual-task paradigms. *Journal of Memory and Language* 36:13–33.

Fillmore, Charles J. 1985. Frames and the semantics of understanding. *Quaderni de Semantica* 6: 222–254.

Firbas, Jan. 1971. On the concept of communicative dynamism in the theory of functional sentence perspective. *Philologica Pragensia* 8: 135–144.

Fischer-Lichte, Erika. 1992. *The Semiotics of Theater* (J. Gaines & D. L. Jones, trans.). Bloomington: Indiana University Press.

Fox, Barbara. 1995. On the embodied nature of grammar: Embodied being-in-the-world. Plenary talk at the International Conference on Functional Grammar, University of New Mexico, July.

Frick-Horbury, Donna, & Guttentag, Robert. 1998. The effects of restricting hand gesture production on lexical retrieval and free recall. *American Journal of Psychology* 111: 43–62.

Freyd, Jennifer J. 1983. Shareability: The social psychology of epistemology. *Cognitive Science* 7: 191–210.

Furuyama, Nobuhiro. 2000. Gestural interaction between the instructor and the learner in origami instruction. In D. McNeill (ed.), *Language and Gesture*, pp. 99–117. Cambridge: Cambridge University Press.

———. 2001. *De-syntacticizing the Theories of Reference Maintenance from the Viewpoint of Poetic Function of Language and Gesture: A Case of Japanese Discourse*. Ph.D. dissertation, University of Chicago.

Furuyama, Nobuhiro, McNeill, David, & Park-Doob, Mischa. 2002. Is speech-gesture production ballistic or interactive? Paper presented at the Congress of the International Society for Gesture Studies, Austin.

Gardner, Howard. 1974. *The Shattered Mind*. New York: Vintage Books.

Gardner, Howard, Brownell, Hiram H., Wapner, Wendy, & Michelow, Diane. 1983. Missing the point: The role of the right hemisphere in the processing of complex linguistic material. In Ellen Perecman (ed.), *Cognitive Processing in the Right Hemisphere*, pp. 169–191. New York: Academic Press.

Gazzaniga, Michael S. 1970. *The Bisected Brain*. New York: Appleton-Century-Crofts.

———. 1995. Consciousness and the cerebral hemispheres. In M. S. Gazzaniga (ed.), *The Cognitive Neurosciences*, pp. 1391–1400. Cambridge: MIT Press.

Gelb, A., & Goldstein, K. 1925. Über Farbennamenamnesie. *Psychologische Forschung* 6: 127–186.

Givón, Talmy. 1985. Iconicity, isomorphism, and non-arbitrary coding in syntax. In J. Haiman (ed.), *Iconicity in Syntax*, pp. 187–219. Amsterdam: John Benjamins.

Goldberg, Adele. 1995. *Constructions: A Construction Approach to Argument Structure*. Chicago: University of Chicago Press.

———. 1997. Making One's Way through the Data. In A. Alsina, J. Bresnan, & P. Sells (eds.), *Complex Predicates*, pp. 151–173. Stanford: CSLI Publications.

Goldenberg, Georg. 1999. Matching and imitation of hand and finger postures in patients with damage in the left or right hemispheres. *Neuropsychologia* 37: 559–566.

Goldin-Meadow, Susan. 1997. When gestures and words speak differently. *Current Directions in Psychological Science* 6: 138–143.

———. 2003a. *Hearing Gesture: How Our Hands Help Us Think*. Cambridge: Harvard University Press.

———. 2003b. *The Resilience of Language: What Gesture Creation in Deaf Children Can Tell Us about How All Children Learn Language*. New York: Psychology Press.

Goldin-Meadow, Susan, & Butcher, Cynthia. 2003. Pointing toward two-word speech in young children. In S. Kita (ed.), *Pointing: Where Language, Culture, and Cognition Meet*, pp. 85–107. Mahwah, NJ: Erlbaum.

Goldin-Meadow, Susan, McNeill, David, & Singleton, Jenny. 1996. Silence is liberating: Removing the handcuffs on grammatical expression in the manual modality. *Psychological Review 103*: 34–55.

Goldin-Meadow, Susan, & Mylander, Carolyn. 1984. *Gestural Communication in Deaf Children: The Effects and Non-effects of Parental Input on Early Language Development.* Chicago: University of Chicago Press.

Goldin-Meadow, Susan, Nusbaum, Howard, Garber, Philip, & Church, R. Breckinridge. 1993. Transitions in learning: Evidence for simultaneously activated hypotheses. *Journal of Experimental Psychology: Human Perception and Performance* 19: 1–16.

Goldin-Meadow, Susan, Nusbaum, Howard, Kelly, Spencer D., & Wagner, Susan. 2001. Explaining math: Gesturing lightens the load. *Psychological Science* 12: 516–522.

Goldin-Meadow, Susan, & Singer, Melissa A. 2003. From children's hands to adults' ears: Gesture's role in teaching and learning. *Developmental Psychology* 39: 509–520.

Goldin-Meadow, Susan, Wein, Debra, & Chang, Cecilia. 1992. Assessing knowledge through gesture: Using children's hands to read their minds. *Cognition and Instruction* 9: 201–219.

Goldman Eisler, Frieda. 1968. *Psycholinguistics: Experiments in Spontaneous Speech.* London: Academic Press.

Goodman, Nelson. 1968. *Languages of Art: An Approach to a Theory of Symbols.* Indianapolis: Bobbs-Merrill.

Goren-Inbar, Naama, Alperson, Nira, Kislev, Mordechai E., Simchoni, Orit, Melamed, Yoel, Ben-Nun, Adi, & Werker, Ella. 2004. Evidence of hominid control of fire at Gesher Benot Ya'aqov, Israel. *Science* 304: 725–727.

Grafton, Scott T., Arbib, Michael A., Fadiga, Luciano, & Rizzolatti, Giacomo. 1996. Location of grasp representations in humans by PET: 1. Observation versus execution. *Experimental Brain Research* 112: 103–111.

Greenfield, Patricia Marks, & Smith, Joshua. 1976. *The Structure of Communication in Early Language Development.* New York: Academic Press.

Greeno, Catherine. 1981. *Fundamental Axioms of Language Study.* A.B. paper, University of Chicago.

Gregory, Richard L. (ed.). 1987. *The Oxford Companion to the Mind.* Oxford: Oxford University Press.

Grèzes, Julie, Armony, Jorge L., Rowe, James B., & Passingham, Richard E. 2003. Activations related to "mirror" and "canonical" neurons in the human brain: an fMRI study. *NeuroImage* 18: 928–937.

Hadar, Uri, & Butterworth, Brian. 1997. Iconic gestures, imagery, and word retrieval in speech. *Semiotica* 115: 147–172.

Halliday, Michael. 1985. *An Introduction to Functional Grammar.* London: Edward Arnold.

Hamzei, Farsin, Rijntjes, Michel, Dettmers, Christian, Glauche, Volkmann, Weiller, Cornelius, & Büchel, Christian. 2003. The human action recognition system and its relationship to Broca's area: an fMRI study. *NeuroImage* 19: 637–644.

Hanks, William F. 1996. Language form and communicative practices. In J. J. Gumperz & S. Levinson (eds.), *Rethinking Linguistic Relativity*, pp. 232–270. Cambridge: Cambridge University Press.

Harris, Roy. 2002. Why words really do not stay still. *Times Literary Supplement*, 26 July, 30.

———. 2003. *Saussure and His Interpreters*. 2nd ed. Edinburgh: Edinburgh University Press.

Harris, Roy, & Taylor, Talbot J. 1989. *Landmarks in Linguistic Thought: The Western Tradition from Socrates to Saussure*. New York: Routledge.

Haviland, John. 2000. Pointing, gesture spaces, and mental maps. In D. McNeill (ed.), *Language and Gesture*, pp. 13–46. Cambridge: Cambridge University Press.

Hewes, Gordon W. 1973. Primate communication and the gestural origins of language. *Current Anthropology* 14: 5–24.

Hopper, Paul J. 1979. Aspect and foregrounding in discourse. In T. Givón (ed.), *Discourse and Syntax*, pp. 213–241. New York: Academic Press.

———. 1998. Emergent Grammar. In Michael Tomasello (ed.), *The New Psychology of Language: Cognitive and Functional Approaches to Linguistic Structure*, pp. 155–175. Englewood Cliffs, NJ: Erlbaum.

———. In press. The openness of grammatical constructions. In N. Adams, A. Cooper, F. Parrill, & T. Wier (eds.), *Proceedings of the 40th Annual Meeting of the Chicago Linguistic Society*. Chicago: Chicago Linguistic Society.

Hopper, Paul J., & Thompson, Sandra A. 1980. Transitivity in Grammar and Discourse. *Language* 56: 251–299.

Horwitz, Barry, Amunts, Katrin, Bhattacharyya, Rajan, Patkin, Debra, Jeffries, Keith, Zilles, Karl, & Braun, Allen R. 2003. Activation of Broca's area during the production of spoken and signed language: A combined cytoarchitectonic mapping and PET analysis. *Neuropsychologia* 41: 1868–1876.

Hurley, Susan. 1998. *Consciousness in Action*. Cambridge: Harvard University Press.

Iacoboni, Marco, Woods, Roger P., Brass, Marcel, Bekkering, Harold, Mazziotta, John C., & Rizzolatti, Giacomo. 1999. Cortical mechanisms of human imitation. *Science* 286: 2526–2528.

Inhelder, Bärbel, & Piaget, Jean. 1958. *The Growth of Logical Thinking from Childhood to Adolescence: An Essay on the Construction of Formal Operational Structures* (A. Parsons & S. Milgram, trans.). New York: Basic Books.

Ishino, Mika. 2001a. Conceptual metaphors and metonymies of metaphoric gestures of anger in discourse of native speakers of Japanese. In M. Andronis, C. Ball, H. Elston, & S. Neuvel (eds.), *CLS 37: The Main Session*, pp. 259–273. Chicago: Chicago Linguistic Society.

———. 2001b. Gesture handedness: The use of the right hand as "evidential markers." In C. Cavé, I. Guaïtella, & S. Santi (eds.), *Oralité et Gestualité: Interactions et Comportments Multimodaux dans la Communication*, pp. 236–239. Paris: L'Harmattan.

Iverson, Jana M., & Goldin-Meadow, Susan. 1997. What's communication got to do with it? Gesture in congenitally blind children. *Developmental Psychology* 33: 453–467.

Iverson, Jana M., & Goldin-Meadow, Susan. 1998. Why people gesture when they speak. *Nature* 396: 228.

Jackendoff, Ray. 1990. *Semantic Structures*. Cambridge: MIT Press.

Jakobson, Roman. 1960. Closing statement: Linguistics and poetics. In T. A. Sebeok (ed.), *Style in Language*, pp. 350–377. Cambridge: MIT Press.

Johnson, Mark. 1987. *The Body in the Mind: The Bodily Basis of Meaning, Imagination, and Reason*. Chicago: University of Chicago Press.

Jolly, Alison. 1999. *Lucy's Legacy: Sex and Intelligence in Human Evolution*. Cambridge: Harvard University Press.

Karmiloff-Smith, Annette. 1979. Micro- and macrodevelopmental changes in language acquisition and other representational systems. *Cognitive Science* 3: 91–118.

Kant, Immanuel. 1973 [1787]. *Immanuel Kant's Critique of Pure Reason* (N. K. Smith, trans.). London: Macmillan Press.

Kelly, Barbara Frances. 2003. *The Emergence of Argument Structure from Gesture to Speech*. Ph.D. dissertation, University of California, Santa Barbara.

Kelly, Spencer D., Barr, Dale J., Church, R. Breckinridge, & Lynch, Katheryn. 1999. Offering a hand to pragmatic understanding: The role of speech and gesture in comprehension and memory. *Journal of Memory and Language* 40: 577–592.

Kelly, Spencer D., Kravitz, Corinne, & Hopkins, Michael. 2004. Neural correlates of bimodal speech and gesture comprehension. *Brain and Language* 89: 253–260.

Kelso, J. A. Scott. 1995. *Dynamic Patterns: The Self-Organization of Brain and Behavior*. Cambridge: MIT Press.

Kendon, Adam. 1972. Some relationships between body motion and speech. In A. Siegman & B. Pope (eds.), *Studies in Dyadic Communication*, pp. 177–210. New York: Pergamon Press.

———. 1980. Gesticulation and speech: Two aspects of the process of utterance. In M. R. Key (ed), *The Relationship of Verbal and Nonverbal Communication*, pp. 207–227. The Hague: Mouton and Co.

———. 1981. Geography of gesture. *Semiotica* 37: 129–163.

———. 1988a. How gestures can become like words. In F. Poyatos (ed.), *Cross-Cultural Perspectives in Nonverbal Communication*, pp. 131–141. Toronto: Hogrefe.

———. 1988b. *Sign Languages of aboriginal Australia: Cultural, Semiotic, and Communicative Perspectives*. Cambridge: Cambridge University Press.

———. 1991. Some considerations for a theory of language origins. *Man* 26: 199–221.

———. 1994. Do gestures communicate? A review. *Research on Language & Social Interaction* 27: 175–200.

———. 1995. Gestures as illocutionary and discourse structure markers in southern Italian conversation. *Journal of Pragmatics* 23: 247–279.

————, intro. and trans. 2000. *Gesture in Naples and Gesture in Classical Antiquity: A Translation of Andrea de Jorio's La mimica degli antichi investigata nel gestire napoletano*. Bloomington: Indiana University Press.

Kimbara, Irene. 2002. *On Gestural Mimicry*. Unpublished ms., University of Chicago, Department of Linguistics.

Kita, Sotaro. 1990. *The Temporal Relationship between Gesture and Speech: A Study of Japanese-English Bilinguals*. MA thesis, University of Chicago.

————. 2000. How representational gestures help speaking. In D. McNeill (ed.), *Language and Gesture*, pp. 162–185. Cambridge: Cambridge University Press.

Kita, Sotaro, Gijn, Ingeborg van, & Hulst, Harry van der. 1998. Movement phases in signs and co-speech gestures, and their transcription by human coders. In I. Wachsmuth & M. Fröhlich (eds.), *Gesture and Sign Language in Human-Computer Interaction*, pp. 23–35. Berlin: Springer-Verlag.

Kita, Sotaro, & Özyürek, Asli. 2003. What does cross-linguistic variation in semantic coordination of speech and gesture reveal? Evidence for an interface representation of spatial thinking and speaking. *Journal of Memory and Language* 48: 16–32.

Kita, Sotaro, Özyürek, Asli, & Allen, Shanley. 2001. *Animated Motion Event Stimuli Prepared for Analysis of Speech and Gesture Motion Event Descriptions*. Nijmegen: Max Planck Institute for Psycholinguistics.

Kosslyn, Stephen Michael 1980. *Image and Mind*. Cambridge: Harvard University Press.

Krauss, Robert M., Chen, Yihsiu, & Gottesman, Rebecca F. 2000. Lexical gestures and lexical access: A process model. In D. McNeill (ed.), *Language and Gesture*, pp. 261–283. Cambridge: Cambridge University Press.

Labov, William, & Waletsky, Joshua. 1967. Narrative analysis: oral versions of personal experience. In J. Helm (ed.), *Essays on the Verbal and Visual Arts*, pp. 12–44. Seattle: University of Washington Press.

Lakoff, George. 2003. The brain's concepts. Paper presented at the 8th International Cognitive Linguistics Conference, Logroño, Spain.

Lakoff, George, & Johnson, Mark. 1980. *Metaphors We Live By*. Chicago: University of Chicago Press.

————. 1999. *Philosophy in the Flesh: The Embodied Mind and Its Challenge to Western Thought*. New York: Basic Books.

Langacker, Ronald W. 1987. *Foundations of Cognitive Grammar*. Vol. 1: *Theoretical Prerequisites*; vol. 2: *Descriptive Application*. Stanford: Stanford University Press.

————. 2000. *Grammar and Conceptualization*. Berlin: Mouton.

Lausberg, Hedda, Kita, Sotaro, Zaidel, Eran, & Ptito, Alain. 2003. Split-brain patients neglect left personal space during right-handed gestures. *Neuropsychologia* 41: 1317–1329.

LeBaron, Curtis, & Streeck, Jürgen. 2000. Gestures, knowledge, and the world. In D. McNeill (ed.), *Language and Gesture*, pp. 118–138. Cambridge: Cambridge University Press.

Levelt, Willem J. M. 1989. *Speaking: From Intention to Articulation*. Cambridge: MIT Press/Bradford Books.

Levelt, Willem J. M., Richardson, Graham, and La Heij, Wido. 1985. Pointing and voicing in deictic expressions. *Journal of Memory and Language* 24: 133–164.

Levy, Elena, & McNeill, David. 1992. Speech, gesture, and discourse. *Discourse Processes* 15: 277–301.

Li, Charles N., & Thompson, Sandra A. 1976. Subject and topic: A new typology of language. In C. N. Li (ed.), *Subject and Topic*, pp. 457–489. New York: Academic Press.

Li, Charles N., & Thompson, Sandra A. 1981. *Mandarin Chinese: A Functional Reference Grammar*. Berkeley: University of California Press.

Liddell, Scott. 2000. Blended spaces and deixis in sign language discourse. In D. McNeill (ed.), *Language and Gesture*, pp. 331–357. Cambridge: Cambridge University Press.

———. 2003a. *Grammar, Gesture, and Meaning in American Sign Language*. Cambridge: Cambridge University Press.

———. 2003b. Sources of meaning in ASL classifier predicates. In K. Emmorey (ed.), *Perspectives on Classifier Constructions in Sign Languages* pp. 199–219. Mahway, NJ: Erlbaum.

Lieberman, Philip. 2002. On the nature and evolution of the neural bases of human language. *Yearbook of Physical Anthropology* 45: 36–63.

Loehr, Daniel 2004. *Gesture and Intonation*. Doctoral dissertation, Georgetown University.

Lucy, John A. 1992a. *Language Diversity and Thought: A Reformulation of the Linguistic Relativity Hypothesis*. Cambridge: Cambridge University Press.

———. 1992b. *Grammatical Categories and Cognition: A Case Study of the Linguistic Relativity Hypothesis*. Cambridge: Cambridge University Press.

MacDougall, Judith, & MacDougall, David. 1977. *Lorang's Way* [film]. Berkeley: University of California Extension Media Center.

MacNeilage, Peter F. 1998. The frame/content theory of evolution of speech production. *Behavioral and Brain Sciences* 21: 499–546.

Mandel, Mark. 1977. Iconic devices in American Sign Language. In L. A. Friedman (ed.), *On the Other Hand*, pp. 57–107. London: Academic Press.

Marslen-Wilson, William, Levy, Elena, & Tyler, Lorraine Komisarjevsky. 1982. Producing interpretable discourse: The establishment and maintenance of reference. In R. J. Jarvella & W. Klein (eds.), *Speech, Place, and Action*, pp. 339–378. London: John Wiley & Sons.

Mayberry, Rachel, & Jaques, Joselynne. 2000. Gesture production during stuttered speech: Insights into the nature of gesture-speech integration. In D. McNeill (ed.). *Language and Gesture*, pp. 199–214. Cambridge: Cambridge University Press.

Max-Planck-Institute for Psycholinguistics. Annual Reports. Nijmegen, The Netherlands: Max-Planck-Institute for Psycholinguistics.

McClave, Evelyn Z. 2000. Linguistic functions of head movements in the context of speech. *Journal of Pragmatics* 32: 855–878.

McCullough, Karl-Erik. In preparation. *Using Gestures in Speaking: Self-Generating Indexical Fields*. Ph.D. dissertation, University of Chicago.

McFarland, David H. 2001. Respiratory markers of conversational interaction. *Journal of Speech, Language, and Hearing Research* 44: 128–143.

McNeill, David. 1992. *Hand and Mind: What Gestures Reveal about Thought*. Chicago: University of Chicago Press.

———. 2000a. Introduction. In D. McNeill (ed.), *Language and Gesture*, pp. 1–10. Cambridge: Cambridge University Press.

———. 2000b. Growth points, catchments, and contexts. *Cognitive Studies: Bulletin of the Japanese Cognitive Science Society* 7: 22–36.

———. 2002. Gesture and language dialectic. *Acta Linguistica Hafniensia* 34: 7–37.

———. 2003. Pointing and morality in Chicago. In S. Kita (ed.), *Pointing: Where Language, Culture, and Cognition Meet*, pp. 293–306. Mahwah, NJ: Erlbaum.

McNeill, David, Cassell, Justine, & McCullough, Karl-Erik. 1994. Communicative effective effects of speech-mismatched gestures. *Research on Language and Social Interaction* 27: 223–237.

McNeill, David, & Duncan, Susan D. 2000. Growth points in thinking for speaking. In D. McNeill (ed.), *Language and Gesture*, pp. 141–161. Cambridge: Cambridge University Press.

McNeill, David, & Levy, Elena. 1982. Conceptual Representations in Language Activity and Gesture. In R. J. Jarvella & W. Klein (eds.), *Speech, Place, and Action*, pp 271–296. Chichester, Eng: John Wiley & Sons.

McNeill, David, McCullough, Karl-Erik, & Duncan, Susan D. 2004. An ontogenetic universal and how to explain it. In C. Müller & R. Posner (eds.), *The Semantics and Pragmatics of Everyday Gestures*, pp. 157–171. Berlin: Weidler Verlag.

McNeill, David, & Pedelty, Laura. 1995. Right brain and gesture. In K. Emmorey & J. Reilly (eds.), *Sign, Gesture, and Space*, pp. 63–85. Hillsdale, NJ: Erlbaum.

McNeill, David, Quek, Francis, McCullough, Karl-Erik, Duncan, Susan D., Furuyama, Nobuhiro, Bryll, Robert, Ma, Xin-Feng, & Ansari, Rashid. 2001. Catchments, prosody, and discourse. *Gesture* 1: 9–33.

———. 2002. Dynamic imagery in speech and gesture. In B. Granström, D. House, & I. Karlsson (eds.), *Multimodality in Language and Speech Systems*, pp. 27–44. Dordrecht, the Netherlands: Kluwer Academic Publishers.

Mead, George Herbert. 1974. *Mind, Self, and Society from the Standpoint of a Social Behaviorist* (C. W. Morris, ed. and introduction). Chicago: University of Chicago Press.

Merleau-Ponty, Maurice. 1962. *Phenomenology of Perception* (C. Smith, trans.). London: Routledge.

Montaigne, Michel de. 1958. *The Complete Essays of Montaigne* (D. Frame, trans.). Stanford: Stanford University Press.

Morris, Desmond, Collett, Peter, Marsh, Peter, & O'Shaughnessy, Marie. 1979. *Gestures: Their Origins and Distribution*. New York: Stein & Day.

Morton, John, Marcus, Steve, & Frankis, Clive. 1976. Perceptual centers. *Psychological Review* 83: 105–108.

Müller, Cornelia. 1998. *Redebegleitende Gesten: Kulturgeschicht-Theorie-Sprachvergleich*. Berlin: Berlin Verlag.

———. 2000. *Lectures on Gesture*. University of Chicago.

———. 2002. A brief history of the origins of the International Society for Gesture Studies (ISGS). *Gesture* 2: 127–132.

———. 2004a. *Metaphors, Dead and Alive, Sleeping and Waking: A Cognitive Approach to Metaphors in Language Use*. Habilitationsschrift, Free University Berlin.

———. 2004b. The palm-up-open-hand: A case of a gesture family? In C. Müller & R. Posner (eds.), *The Semantics and Pragmatics of Everyday Gestures*, pp. 233–256. Berlin: Weidler Verlag.

———. In preparation. *Metaphors: Consciousness in Discourse*.

Nakatani, Christine H., Grosz, Barbara J., Ahn, David D., & Hirschberg, Julia. 1995. *Instructions for Annotating Discourse*. Technical Report TR-21–95, Center for Research in Computational Technology. Cambridge: Harvard University.

Nelson, Keith, Loncke, Filip, & Camarata, Stephen. 1993. Implications of research on deaf and hearing children's language learning. In M. Marschark & M. D. Clark (eds.), *Psychological Perspectives on Deafness*, pp. 123–151. Hillsdale, NJ: Erlbaum.

Newmeyer, Frederick J. 2003. Grammar is grammar and usage is usage. *Language* 79: 682–707.

Newport, Elizabeth L. O. 1981. Constraints on structure: Evidence from American Sign Language and language learning. In W. A. Collins (ed.), *Aspects of the Development of Competence*, pp. 93–124. Hillsdale, NJ: Erlbaum.

Nishitani, Nobuyuki, & Hari, Riitta. 2000. Temporal dynamics of cortical representation for action. *Proceedings of the National Academy of Sciences* 97: 913–918.

Nobe, Shuichi. 1996. *Representational Gestures, Cognitive Rhythms, and Acoustic Aspects of Speech: A Network/Threshold Model of Gesture Production*. Ph.D. dissertation, University of Chicago.

———. 2000. Where do *most* spontaneous representational gestures actually occur with respect to speech? In D. McNeill (ed.), *Language and Gesture*, pp. 186–198. Cambridge: Cambridge University Press.

Núñez, Rafael E., & Sweetser, Eve. In press. In Aymara, next week is behind you: Convergent evidence from language and gesture in the crosslinguistic comparison of spatial construals of time. *Cognitive Science*.

Okrent, A. 2002. A modality-free notion of gesture and how it can help us with the morpheme vs. gesture question in sign language linguistics. In R. P. Meier, K. Cormier, and D. Quinto-Pozos (eds.), *Modality and Structure in Signed and Spoken Language*, pp. 175–198. Cambridge: Cambridge University Press.

Özçalıskan, Seyda, & Goldin-Meadow, Susan. 2004. Gesture is at the cutting edge of early language development. Paper presented at the Boston University Conference on Language Development, Boston.

Özyürek, Asli. 2000. The influence of addressee location on spatial language and representational gestures of direction. In D. McNeill (ed.), *Language and Gesture*, pp. 64–83. Cambridge: Cambridge University Press.

———. 2001a. What do speech-gesture mismatches reveal about language specific processing? A comparison of Turkish and English. In C. Cavé, I. Guaïtella, & S. Santi (eds.), *Oralité et Gestualité: Interactions et Comportments Multimodaux dans la Communication*, pp. 577–581. Paris: L'Harmattan.

———. 2001b. What do speech-gesture mismatches reveal about speech and gesture integration? A comparison of Turkish and English. Proceedings of the 27th Meeting of the Berkeley Linguistics Society. Berkeley: Berkeley Linguistics Society.

———. 2002. Do speakers design their co-speech gestures for their addressees? The effect of addressee location on representational gestures. *Journal of Memory and Language* 46: 688–704.

Palmer, Stephen E., & Kimchi, Ruth. 1986. The information processing approach to cognition. In T. J. Knapp & L. C. Robertson (eds.), *Approaches to Cognition: Contrasts and Controversies*, pp. 37–77. Hillsdale, NJ: Erlbaum.

Park-Doob, Mischa. 2001. Deconstructing 'topic': Relevance, consciousness, and the momentum of ideas. MA thesis, University of Chicago.

Parrill, Fey. 2003. Intuitions and violations of good form in metaphoric conduit gestures. Paper presented at the theme session, Metaphor and Gesture, at the 8th International Cognitive Linguistics Conference, Logroño, Spain, July 23.

———. 2003. *Growth Points and Argument Structure Constructions: Manipulating Speech and Gesture via Structural Priming*. MA thesis, University of Chicago.

Parrill, Fey, & Sweetser, Eve. 2004. What we mean by meaning: Conceptual integration in gesture analysis and transcription. *Gesture* 4: 197–219.

Payrató, Lluís. 2002. Non-verbal communication. In J. Vershueren, J.-O. Östman, J. Blommaert, & C. Bulcaen (eds.), *Handbook of Pragmatics: 2002 Installment*, pp. 1–35. Amsterdam: Benjamins.

Pedelty, Laura L. 1987. *Gesture in Aphasia*. Ph.D. dissertation, University of Chicago.

Peirce, Charles S. 1960 [1931]. Division of signs. In C. Hartshorne & P. Weiss (eds.), *Collected Papers of Charles Sanders Peirce*, vol. 1: *Principles of Philosophy, Elements of Logic*. Cambridge: Harvard University Press.

Peña, Marcela, Bonatti, Luca L., Nespor, Marina, & Mehler, Jacques. 2002. Signal-driven computations in speech processing. *Science* 298: 604–607.

Piaget, Jean. 1955. *The Language and Thought of the Child* (Marjorie Gabain, trans.). Cleveland: Meridian.

Ping, Raedy M. 2003. *The Effects of Observation and Listener's Level of Knowledge on Gesture Use*. BA thesis, Indiana University.

Pinker, Steven. 1994. *The Language Instinct*. New York: Harper Perennial.

Poggi, Isabella. 2003. Symbolic gestures: The case of the Italian gestionary. *Gesture* 2: 71–98.

Postal, Paul M. 2004. *Skeptical Linguistic Essays*. Oxford: Oxford University Press.

Quek, Francis, & Bryll, Robert. 1998. Vector coherence mapping: A parallelizable approach to image flow computation. *Proceedings of the Asian Conference on Computer Vision*, Vol. 2, pp. 591–598. Hong Kong: Asian Conference on Computer Vision.

Quek, Francis, Ma, Xin-Feng, and Bryll, Robert. 1999. A parallel algorithm for dynamic gesture tracking. *ICCV99 International Workshop on Recognition, Analysis, and Tracking of Faces and Gestures in Real-Time Systems (RATFG-RTS'99)*. Corfu, Greece, September 26–27.

Quintilian, Marcus Fabius. 1977. *Institutio Oratoria Classici della Nuova Italia*. Firenze: La Nuova Italia.

Ramachandran, Vilayanur S., & Blakeslee, Sandra. 1998. *Phantoms in the Brain: Probing the Mysteries of the Human Mind*. New York: William Morrow.

Reddy, Michael J. 1979. The conduit metaphor: a case of frame conflict in our language about language. In A. Ortony (ed.), *Metaphor and thought*, pp. 284–297. Cambridge: Cambridge University Press.

Richards, Ivor A. 1936. *The Philosophy of Rhetoric*. New York: Oxford University Press.

Rimé, Bernard. 1982. The elimination of visible behaviour from social interactions: Effects on verbal, nonverbal, and interpersonal variables. *European Journal of Social Psychology* 12: 113–129.

Rizzolatti, Giacomo, & Arbib, Michael. 1998. Language within our grasp. *Trends in Neurosciences* 21: 188–194.

Rizzolatti, Giacomo, Fadiga, Luciano, Matelli, Massimo, Bettinardi, Valentino, Paulesu, Eraldo, Perani, Daniela, & Fazio, Fogassi. 1996. Location of grasp representations in humans by positron emission tomography: 2. Observation compared with imagination. *Experimental Brain Research* 111: 246–252.

Roeloff, Ardi. 2002. Spoken language planning and the initiation of articulation. *Quarterly Journal of Experimental Psychology* 55: 465–483.

Ross, Háj. In press. Rotorooters: Watching appositives of focus-first pseudos punch through anaphoric islands. In J. Cihlar, A. Franklin, D. Kaiser, & I. Kimbara (eds.), *Proceedings of the 39th Annual Meeting of the Chicago Linguistic Society*. Chicago: Chicago Linguistic Society.

Rummelhart, David E., & McClelland, John L. 1986. On learning the past tense of English verbs. In J. L. McClelland & D. E. Rummelhart (eds.), *Parallel Distributed Processing: Explorations in the Microstructure of Cognition*, pp. 216–271. Cambridge, MA: The MIT Press.

Saussure, Ferdinand de. 1966 [1959]. *Course in General Linguistics* (C. Bally & A. Sechehaye, eds., in collaboration with A. Riedlinger; W. Baskin, trans.). New York: McGraw-Hill.

———. 2002. *Ecrits de linguistique general* (compiled and edited by S. Bouquet and R. Engler). Paris: Gallimard.

Schegloff, Emanuel A. 1984. On some gestures' relation to talk. In J. M. Atkinson & J. Heritage (eds.), *Structures of Social Action*, pp. 266–298. Cambridge: Cambridge University Press.

Schlaug, Gottfried, Knorr, Uwe, & Seitz, Rüdiger J. 1994. Inter-subject variability of cerebral activations in acquiring a motor skill: a study with positron emission tomography. *Experimental Brain Research* 98: 523–534.

Schütze, Carson T. 1996. *The empirical base of linguistics: Grammaticality judgments and linguistic methodology*. Chicago: University of Chicago Press.

Semendeferi, Katerina. 2001. Advances in the study of hominoid brain evolution: magnetic resonance imaging (MRI) and 3-D reconstruction. In D. Falk & K. R. Gibson (eds.), *Evolutionary Anatomy of the Primate Cerebral Cortex*, pp. 257–289. Cambridge: Cambridge University Press.

Senghas, Ann, Özyürek, Asli, & Kita, Sotaro. 2003. Encoding motion events in an emerging sign language: From Nicaraguan gestures to Nicaraguan signs. In A. Baker, B. van den Bogaerde, & O. Crasborn (eds.), *Cross-Linguistic Perspectives in Sign Language Research*, pp. 119–131. Hamburg: Signum Press.

Severance, Elizabeth, & Washburn, Margaret F. 1907. The loss of associative power in words after long fixation. *American Journal of Psychology* 18: 182–186.

Silverstein, Michael. 1985. On the pragmatic "poetry" of prose: Parallelism, repetition, and cohesive structure in the time course of dyadic conversation. In D. Schiffrin (ed.), *Meaning, Form, and Use in Context: Linguistic Applications*, pp. 181–199. Washington: Georgetown University Press.

———. 1997. The improvisational performance of culture in realtime discursive practice. In R. K. Sawyer (ed.), *Creativity in Performance*, pp. 265–312. Greenwich, CT: Ablex.

Slobin, Dan I. 1987. Thinking for speaking. In J. Aske, N. Beery, L. Michaelis, & H. Filip (eds.), *Proceedings of the Thirteenth Annual Meeting of the Berkeley Linguistic Society*, pp. 435–445. Berkeley: Berkeley Linguistic Society.

———. 1996. From "thought and language" to "thinking for speaking." In J. J. Gumperz & S. C. Levinson (eds.), *Rethinking Linguistic Relativity*, pp. 70–96. Cambridge: Cambridge University Press.

———. 2004. The many ways to search for a frog: Linguistic typology and the expression of motion events. In S. Strömqvist & L. Verhoeven (eds.), *Relating Events in Narrative*, vol. 2: *Typological and contextual perspectives*, pp. 219–257. Mahwah, NJ: Lawrence Erlbaum Associates.

Smith, Nathaniel. 2003. *Gestures and Beyond*. A.B. paper, University of California at Berkeley.

Spencer, Rebecca M. C., Zelaznik, Howard N., Diedrichsen, Jörn, & Ivry, Richard B. 2003. Disrupted timing of discontinuous but not continuous movements by cerebellar lesions. *Science* 300: 1437–1439.

Stokoe, William C. 1991. Semantic phonology. *Sign Language Studies* 71: 107–114.

Strauss, Sidney, & Stavy, Ruth (eds.). 1982. *U-shaped Behavioral Growth*. New York: Academic Press.

Supalla, Ted. 1982. *Structure and Acquisition of Verbs of Motion and Location in American Sign Language*. Ph.D. dissertation, University of California, San Diego.

———. 2003. Revisiting visual analogy in ASL classifier predicates. In Karen Emmorey (ed.), *Perspectives on Classifier Constructions in Sign Languages*, pp. 249–257. Mahwah, NJ: Erlbaum.

Talmy, Leonard. 1975. Syntax and semantics of motion. In J. P. Kimball (ed.), *Syntax and Semantics*, vol. 4, pp. 181–238. New York: Academic Press.

———. 1985. Lexicalization patterns: Semantic structure in lexical forms. In T. Shopen (ed.), *Language Typology and Syntactic Description*, vol. 3: *Grammatical Categories and the Lexicon*, pp. 57–149. Cambridge: Cambridge University Press.

———. 2000. *Toward a Cognitive Semantics*. Cambridge: MIT Press.

Taub, Sarah F. 2001. *Language from the Body: Iconicity and Metaphor in American Sign Language*. Cambridge: Cambridge University Press.

Tomasello, Michael. 1999. *The Cultural Origins of Human Cognition*. Cambridge: Harvard University Press.

Tuite, Kevin. 1993. The production of gesture. *Semiotica* 93: 83–105.

Turner, Mark. 2001. *Cognitive Dimensions of Social Science: The Way We Think about Politics, Economics, Law, and Society*. Oxford: Oxford University Press.

Valbonesi, Lucia, Ansari, Rashid, McNeill, David, Quek, Francis, Duncan, Susan D., McCullough, Karl-Erik, & Bryll, Robert. 2001. Temporal correlation of speech and gesture focal points. Paper presented at the Congress of the International Society for Gesture Studies, Austin.

Vygotsky, Lev S. 1978. *Mind in Society*. M. Cole, V. John-Steiner, S. Scribner, & E. Souberman (eds.). Cambridge: Harvard University Press.

———. 1986. *Thought and Language*. Edited and translated by E. Hanfmann and G. Vakar, revised and edited by A. Kozulin. Cambridge: MIT Press.

Wagner, Susan, & Goldin-Meadow, Susan. 2004. Probing the mental representation of gesture: Is handwaving spatial? *Journal of Memory and Language* 50: 395–407.

Webb, Rebecca. 1996. Linguistic features of metaphoric gestures. In Lynn S. Messing (ed.), *Proceedings of WIGLS*, pp. 79–93. Wilmington, DE: Applied Science and Engineering Laboratories.

Werner, Heinz, & Kaplan, Bernard. 1963. *Symbol Formation*. New York: John Wiley & Sons [reprinted in 1984 by Erlbaum].

Whorf, Benjamin Lee. 1956. *Language, Thought, and Reality: Selected Writings of Benjamin Lee Whorf*. J. B. Carroll (ed.). Cambridge: MIT Press.

Wilkins, David P. 1999. Spatial deixis in Arrernte speech and gesture: On the analysis of a species of composite signal as used by a central Australian Aboriginal group. In E. André, M. Poesio, & H. Rieser (eds.), *Proceedings of the Workshop on Deixis, Demonstration, and Deictic Belief in Multimedia*, pp. 31–45. Utrecht: ESSLII.

Wimmer, Heinz, & Perner, Josef. 1983. Beliefs about beliefs: representation and constraining function of wrong beliefs in young children's understanding of deception. *Cognition* 13: 103–128.

Wohlschläger, Andreas, Haggard, Patrick, Gesierich, Benno, & Prinz, Wolfgang. 2003. The perceived onset time of self- and other-generated actions. *Psychological Science* 14: 586–591.

Wrangham, Richard W. 2001. Out of the pan, into the fire: How our ancestors' evolution depended on what they ate. In F. de Waal (ed.), *Tree of Origin: What Primate Behavior Can Tell Us about Human Social Evolution*, pp. 119–143. Cambridge: Harvard University Press.

Wundt, Wilhelm. 1970. The psychology of the sentence. In Arthur Blumenthal (ed. and trans.), *Language and Psychology: Historical Aspects of Psycholinguistics*, pp. 20–33. New York: John Wiley & Sons.

Yates, Frances Amelia. 1966. *The Art of Memory*. Chicago: University of Chicago Press.

Zaidel, Eran. 1978. Concepts of cerebral dominance in the split brain. In P. A. Buser & A. Rougeul-Buser (eds.), *Cerebral Correlates of Conscious Experience*, pp. 263–284. Amsterdam: Elsevier.

Zinchenko, V. P. 1985. Vygotsky's ideas about units for the analysis of mind. In James V. Wertsch (ed.), *Culture, Communication, and Cognition: Vygotskian Perspectives*, pp. 94–118. Cambridge: Cambridge University Press.